EUROPEAN HANDF

BENELᵁ.
RAILWAYS

LOCOMOTIVES & COACHING STOCK

FIFTH EDITION

The complete guide to all Locomotives and Coaching Stock of
the Railways of Belgium, Netherlands and Luxembourg

David Haydock, Peter Fox and Brian Garvin

Published by Platform 5 Publishing Ltd., Wyvern House, Sark Road, Sheffield S2 4HG, England.
Printed in England by Wyndeham-Gait, Grimsby.
ISBN 978 1 902336 64 0

Above: Vossloh type G1206 locos Veolia 1509 and an unidentified Rail4chem loco run light through Gilze-Rijen on 6 October 2007. Veolia took over Rail4chem early in 2008, but the fleets had not been integrated at the time of going to press. **Robin Ralston**

Front Cover: SNCB/NMBS Class 11 No. 1182 in Benelux livery leaves Den Haag HS with the 12.52 Amsterdam Centraal–Brussels Midi on 19 March 2008. The coaching stock is in the new NS Hispeed colours. **Peter Fox**

Back Cover Top: The CFL Class 4000 are Bombardier "TRAXX" locos, similar to DB Class 185. 4010 is seen at Michelau with the 13.05 Wiltz–luxembourg formed of the new De Dietrich double-deck stock on 7 October 2007. **Robin Ralston**

Back Cover Bottom: NS 4-car IRM unit 9520 stands at Rotterdam Centraal on 27 April 2006, Two IRMs and three "Koploper" EMUs have been painted in this special Olympic games livery. **Peter Fox**

CONTENTS

INTRODUCTION

This book contains full details of all locomotives, multiple units and coaching stock of the railways of the 'Benelux' countries. The word "Benelux" is cobbled together from the first two or three letters of the three countries concerned, Belgium, the Netherlands and Luxembourg. These three countries had a free trade area with no customs inspection at borders before the European Union was formed. Information is updated to July 2008.

In the Netherlands the language spoken is, of course, Dutch or *Nederlands* to give it is proper name. In Belgium two main languages are spoken. The north of the country, Flanders (*Vlaanderen*) is Dutch speaking with the population referred to in English as Flemings whilst the south, Wallonia (*Wallonie*) is French speaking with the population referred to in English as Walloons. The Flemish people refer to their language as *Vlaams* (Flemish), but it is actually the same as Dutch. Indeed, the *Nederlandse Taal Unie* (Dutch language union) is actually based in Belgium. Brussels, the capital of Belgium is officially a dual-language city and is named Brussel in Dutch and Bruxelles in French. In addition there is a part of Belgium around Eupen where the population's first language is German.

In Luxembourg two languages are in common use. These are French and a low dialect of German known as *Letzeburgisch*. Standard German is also spoken.

English is understood by a large proportion of the population of the Netherlands, a fewer proportion of Dutch-speaking Belgians and even less of French-speaking Belgians. Common terms used in French and Dutch are detailed in Appendix IV on page 174.

FOREWORD TO THE FIFTH EDITION

It is now nine years since the last edition of "Benelux Locomotives & Coaching Stock" was published, during which there have been many changes mainly due to EU open access regulations and increased cross-border freight operations. In Belgium little has changed with SNCB/NMBS being the only passenger operator and only two open access freight operators plus Fret SNCF being in action. Nevertheless there have been many changes to stock with many older diesel locomotives being withdrawn and more new operators and cross-border freight operations expected soon.

In Luxembourg there are no open access operationsyet, the main changes being the complete renewal of the electric locomotive fleet and the new double-deck passenger stock.

However the most radical changes have been in the Netherlands. Many local passenger services have been franchised out to private operators, but the main change has been on freight operations with NS Cargo having been acquired by DB (Railion) and numerous open access operators have come into the market. These changes, which include the hiring of new electric locos of the Bombardier TRAXX and Siemens Dispolok types plus diesel locos of Vossloh types G1206 and G2000 and EMD Class 66 have necessitated a change in the layout of the book with the section on private operators now split into three new sections covering private passenger operators, Railion and private freight operators (including leasing companies).

LAYOUT OF INFORMATION

For each class of vehicle general data and dimensions in metric units are provided. Vehicle lengths are lengths over buffers or couplers. The following standard abbreviations are used:

km/h	kilometres per hour	m	metres
kN	kilonewtons	mm	millimetres
kW	kilowatts		

Builder codes see Appendix I on page 170. For explanation of codes used for accommodation in hauled coaching stock and multiple units see Appendix II on page 171.

For each vehicle the number is given in the first column. Where a vehicle has been renumbered the former number is generally shown in parentheses after the current number. Further columns show, respectively, the livery (in bold condensed type), any detail differences, the owning company in serif type (Dutch locos only), the depot allocation and name where appropriate. Depot and livery codes are shown separately for each railway in the appropriate section.

For an explanation of the UIC hauled stock numbering system see Appendix III on pages 172/173.

ACKNOWLEDGEMENTS

We would like to thank all who have helped with the writing of this book, especially Messrs. Marcel Barthel, Michel Van Ussel, Carlo Hertogs, Quintus Vosman and friends at Patrimoine Ferroviaire Touristique (PFT) and the websites www.rail.lu, railfan.nl, somda.nl and nltrein.net.

SNCB Class AM62 EMUs 197 + 177 pass Spriete heading towards Kortrijk at 12.39 on 13 June 2007.
Colin J. Marsden

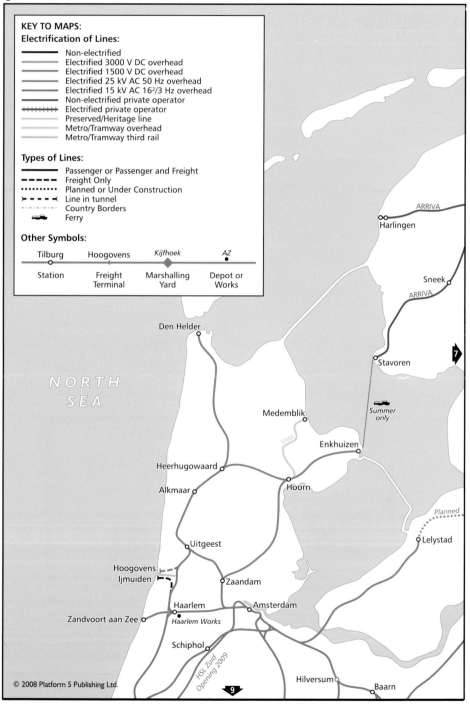

KEY TO MAPS:

Electrification of Lines:

Non-electrified
Electrified 3000 V DC overhead
Electrified 1500 V DC overhead
Electrified 25 kV AC 50 Hz overhead
Electrified 15 kV AC 16²/3 Hz overhead
Non-electrified private operator
++++++ Electrified private operator
Preserved/Heritage line
Metro/Tramway overhead
Metro/Tramway third rail

Types of Lines:

Passenger or Passenger and Freight
- - - - Freight Only
••••••••• Planned or Under Construction
►- - - ◄ Line in tunnel
Country Borders
Ferry

Other Symbols:

Tilburg	Hoogovens	*Kijfhoek*	AZ
Station	Freight Terminal	Marshalling Yard	Depot or Works

NORTH SEA

Harlingen

ARRIVA

Sneek

ARRIVA

Den Helder

Stavoren

7

Medemblik

Summer only

SHM

Enkhuizen

Heerhugowaard

Hoorn

Alkmaar

Planned

Lelystad

Uitgeest

Hoogovens Ijmuiden

Zaandam

Haarlem

Amsterdam

Zandvoort aan Zee

Haarlem Works

Schiphol

HSL Zuid Opening 2009

Hilversum

Baarn

9

© 2008 Platform 5 Publishing Ltd.

© 2008 Platform 5 Publishing Ltd.

Eemshaven

ARRIVA
Roodeschool

ARRIVA
Delfzijl

Sauwerd

ARRIVA

Groningen

Leeuwarden

● ON

Nieuweschans

Leer →

Zuidbroek

ARRIVA

Winschoten

Veendam

Assen

Ter-Apel

N E T H E R L A N D S

6

Emmen

Hoogeveen

Meppel

Coevorden

BE

Bad Bentheim

Kampen

Planned

Mariënberg

G E R M A N Y

Zwolle

ZL

Wierden

Almelo

Bad
Bentheim →

Oldenzaal

Harderwijk

Hengelo

Deventer

Enschede

Münster →

Boekelo

Apeldoorn

MBS

VSM

Zutphen

10

Haaksbergen

Dortmund
↓

8

AMSTERDAM

Koog Bloemwijk
Zaandam-Kogerveld
Zaandam
Buikslotermeerplein
Westhaven
AZ
Sloterdijk
Isolatorweg
Amsterdam Centraal
IJMEER
Lelylaan
50
50/53/54
Muiderpoort
WG
Zuid WTC
50/51
Amstel
Diemen
RAI
1 2
51
53
Weesp
Schiphol
Bijlmer
Gaasperplas
Gein
1 Duivendrecht
2 Diemen Zuid
51 Amstelveen
Westwijk
50/54

NORTH SEA

© 2008 Platform 5 Publishing Ltd.

9

Middelburg
Goes
Vlissingen Sloe Haven
SGB
Oudelande

NETHERLANDS

Terneuzen

Zeebrugge
Knokke
Blankenberge
Tramway
Oostende
FSD
DE LIJN
Maldegem
Brugge
SCM
Eeklo
KANAL
Moerbeke
Lokeren
De Panne
BELGIUM
Gent
Gent Zeehaven
FKR
Lichterfelde
Deinze
De-Pinte
Burst
Poperinge
Ieper
11
Kortrijk
Oudenaarde
Zottegem

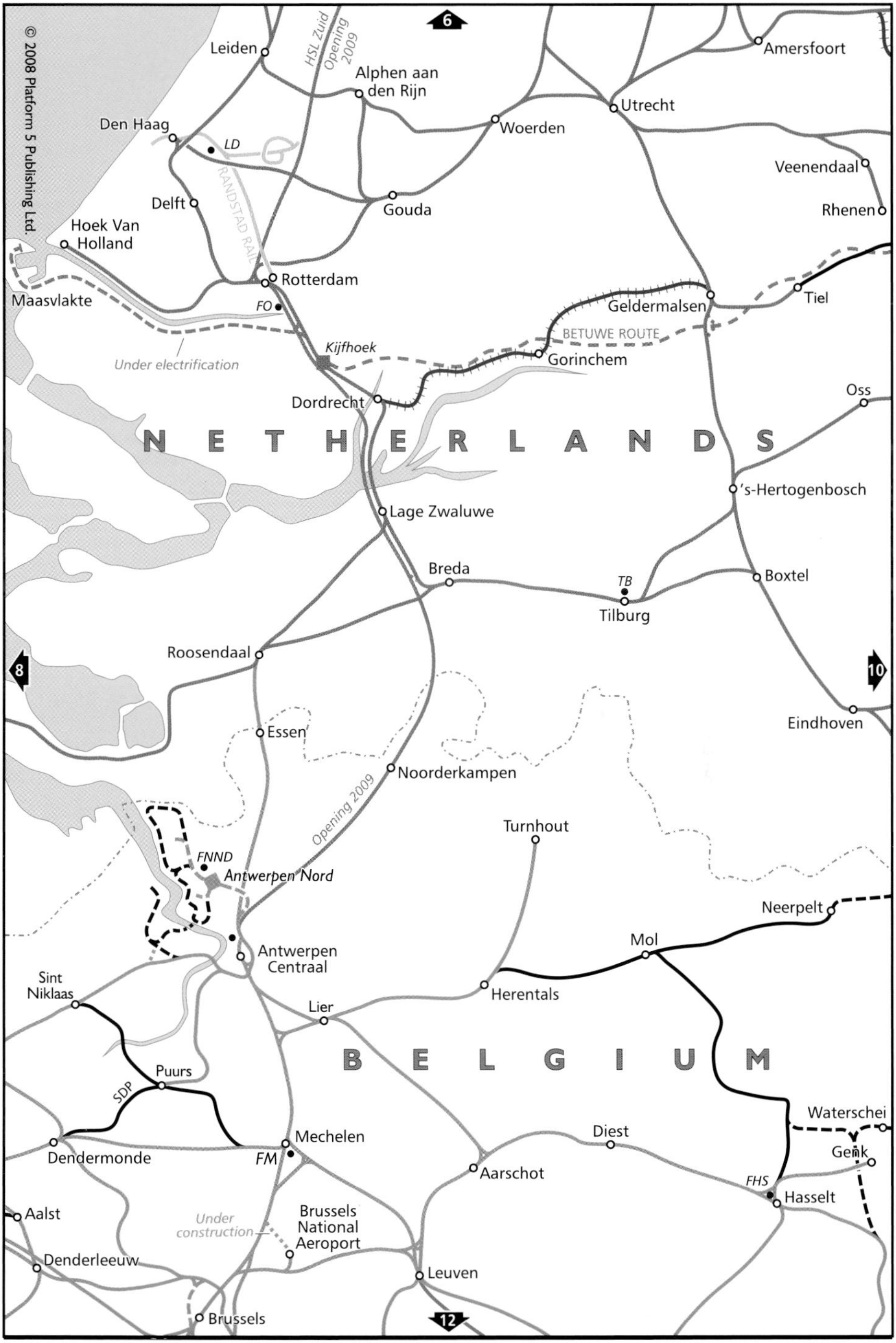

© 2008 Platform 5 Publishing Ltd.

Leiden

HSL Zuid Opening 2009

Alphen aan den Rijn

Amersfoort

Den Haag

LD

Woerden

Utrecht

Veenendaal

Delft

Gouda

Rhenen

Hoek Van Holland

RANDSTAD RAIL

Maasvlakte

Rotterdam

FO

Kijfhoek

Under electrification

BETUWE ROUTE

Geldermalsen

Tiel

Gorinchem

Dordrecht

Oss

N E T H E R L A N D S

's-Hertogenbosch

Lage Zwaluwe

Breda

TB

Boxtel

Tilburg

Roosendaal

Eindhoven

Essen

Opening 2009

Noorderkampen

Turnhout

FNND

Antwerpen Nord

Neerpelt

Mol

Sint Niklaas

Antwerpen Centraal

Lier

Herentals

Puurs

SDP

B E L G I U M

Waterschei

Dendermonde

FM

Mechelen

Diest

Genk

Aarschot

FHS

Hasselt

Aalst

Under construction

Brussels National Aeroport

Denderleeuw

Leuven

Brussels

© 2008 Platform 5 Publishing Ltd.

Komen

8

Mouscron

Ronse

Geraardsbergen

Tourcoing

B E L G I U M

Lille

Lille

Tournai

Leuze

Ath

London
Paris

Jurbise

Mons

St. Ghislain

12

F R A N C E

Quiévrain

Quévy

Paris

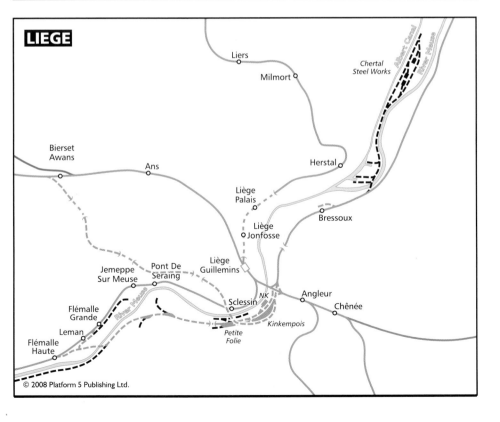

LIEGE

Liers

Milmort

Chertal
Steel Works

Albert Canal

River Meuse

Bierset
Awans

Ans

Herstal

Liège
Palais

Bressoux

Liège
Jonfosse

Liège
Guillemins

Jemeppe
Sur Meuse

Pont De
Seraing

Angleur

Chênée

Flémalle
Grande

Sclessin

NK

Leman

Kinkempois

River Meuse

Flémalle
Haute

Petite
Folie

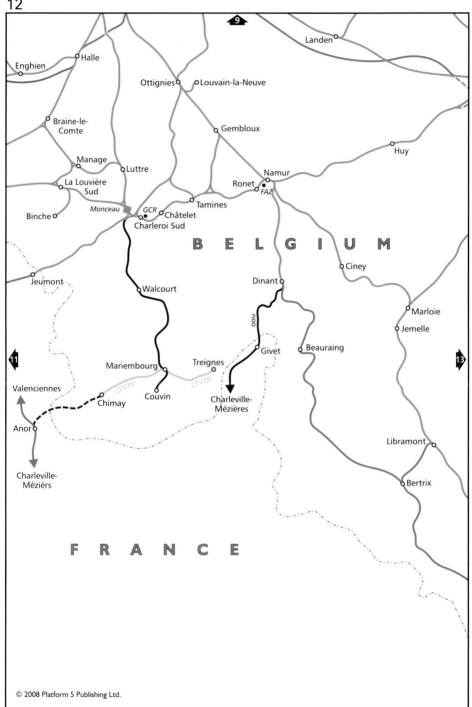

9

Landen

Enghien

Halle

Ottignies   Louvain-la-Neuve

Braine-le-Comte

Gembloux

Huy

Manage   Luttre

Namur

La Louvière Sud

Ronet   FAZ

Binche   Monceau   GCR   Châtelet
Charleroi Sud   Tamines

B E L G I U M

Ciney

Jeumont   Walcourt

Dinant

Marloie
Jemelle

11   13

noo

Givet   Beauraing

Valenciennes

Mariembourg   Treignes

CFV3V   CFV3V

Anor   Chimay   Couvin   Charleville-Mézières

Libramont

Charleville-Mézièrs

Bertrix

F R A N C E

Stolberg

Visé *Montzen*

Walheim

Welkenraedt

Raeren

oou

Liège Eupen

Monschau

Pepinster

Rivage Geronstère

Trois Ponts

B E L G I U M

Gouvy

Trois-Vierges

Clervaux **G E R M A N Y**

Wiltz Kautenbach

Diekirch

Ettelbruck

L U X E M B O U R G

Mersch

Wasserbillig Trier

Marbehan

MKM Airport

Arlon

Stockem

Autelbas Luxembourg Oetrange

Kleinbettingen • *Depot*

Athus

Virton

Rodange Pétange

Longwy Bettembourg

Esch *Bettembourg*

Longuyon Dudelange

Rumelange

F R A N C E Thionville

© 2008 Platform 5 Publishing Ltd.

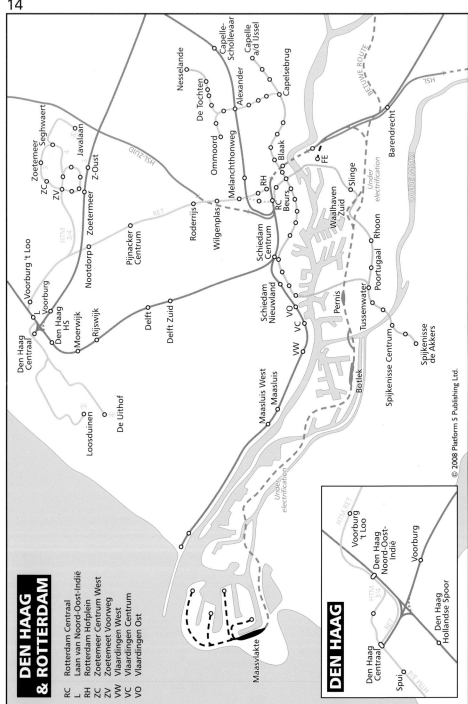

© 2008 Platform 5 Publishing Ltd.

DEN HAAG & ROTTERDAM

RC Rotterdam Centraal
L Laan van Noord-Oost-Indië
RH Rotterdam Hofplein
ZC Zoetemeer Centrum West
ZV Zoetemeer Voorweg
VW Vlaardingen West
VC Vlaardingen Centrum
VO Vlaardingen Ost

DEN HAAG

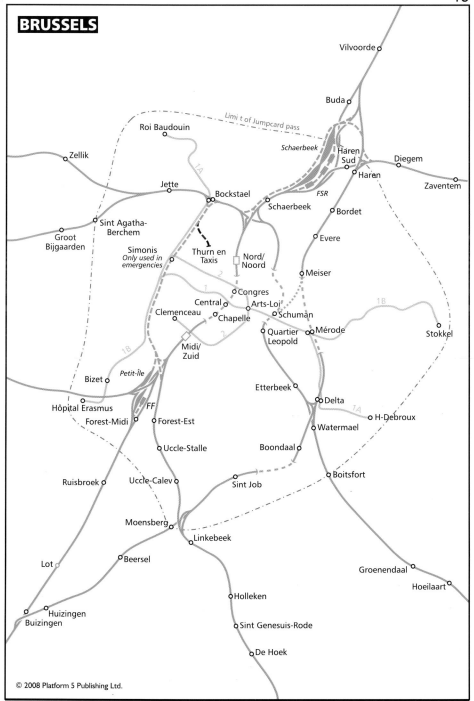

   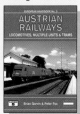 
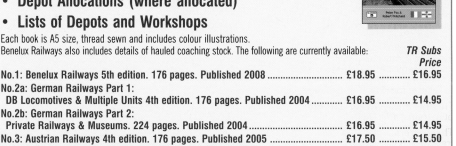

TICKETS & PASSES

Belgium

Singles and day returns are available, but a return costs twice the single. The maximum second class single in Belgium costs €18.40. There is also a weekend return which gives a 50% discount off the ordinary return fare. It is valid from 19.01 on Friday to midnight on Sunday.

For €71 in second and €109 in first class, the Rail Pass gives ten journeys from any station to any other station in Belgium within a year. The holder (the ticket is transferable) fills in the day, date, origin and destination stations for each journey.

A 50% card is available which gives a 50% discount when buying first or second class tickets, regardless of destination in Belgium (excluding frontier points). The 50% card is registered in your name (with identity photo), and consists of a main card and a validation ticket. The main card is valid for 10 years and costs €4.50 when initially made up. It is then necessary to buy a one-year validation ticket, costing €100.

Seniors over 65 pay €4 return in second class anywhere in Belgium after 09.01 (all day on Saturdays, Sundays and Public Holidays), but the facility is not available in first class. This fare is not available at weekends from May to mid September.

Netherlands

There are two types of standard ticket, single and day return (*dagretour*). There is also a weekend return which is the same price as a day return except that it is valid from 19.00 on Friday to 04.00 on Monday. Tickets bought from booking offices are €1 more expensive than those from machines. A fine of €35 is added to the fare if bought on the train!

An off-peak discount pass known as the *Voordeelurenabonnement* is available price €55. This is available to anyone and provides a 40% discount on all tickets after 09.00 (all day on Saturdays, Sundays and Public Holidays) for the holder and up to three companions. In addition, Seniors over 60 (*Zestigplussers*) can pay an extra €14 second class or €42 first class and receive seven days unlimited free travel after 09.00 (not on Mondays or Fridays). This consists of one pass every two months (measured from the first day of validity of the ticket) plus one which can be used in any period. Seniors also receive a "Rail Plus" card free of charge which gives a 25% discount on international journeys. Other people pay €1 for this.To obtain the pass it is necessary to fill in a form obtained from an NS booking office. A passport photo is required.

There is a Day Ticket (*Dagkaart*) for €40.30 (second) or €68.40 (first), and for an additional €5 bus, tram and metro is added (*OV Dagkaart*).

The *Zomertoer* pass is usually issued in the summer which gives unlimited second class rail travel for 3 days out of 10 for one or two persons. The *Zomertoer Plus* pass also includes all trams, buses and metros. Prices are not available at the time of writing.

Luxembourg

There are three types of ticket, all valid for the whole network in second class on all trains and buses:

(1) A short duration ticket (*Kuurzzäitbilljee–Billet courte durée*) costs €1.50 and is valid for two hours after validation. For first class travel there is a €0.80 supplement per journey. A carnet of ten tickets costs €12.

(2) A day ticket (*Dagesbilljee/Billet longue durée*) costs €4 and is valid after validation all day and until 08.00 the next morning. For first class travel there is a €2 supplement per journey. A carnet of five tickets costs €16.

(3) A weekend ticket (*Billet Weekend*) is valid for up to five people on a Saturday, Sunday or Public Holiday until 03.00 the next morning. It costs €6.

Various special day return tickets are issued to nearby stations in Belgium, France and Germany. For details see the CFL website: www.cfl.lu

Passes

The former "Eurodomino" pass has been replaced by an Inter Rail "single country" pass which covers **all three** Benelux countries priced in 2008 between €109 for any three days and €229 for any eight days in one month in second class. First class costs 35% more. For five days in a month, the Benelux Pass, not on sale in the Netherlands, is cheaper at €130 than Inter Rail.

For details of other passes, please see the annual feature in "Today's Railways Europe"

ABBREVIATIONS

Standard abbreviations used in this book are:

CFL	Chemins de Fer Luxembourgois (Luxembourg Railways)
CFR	Compania Nationala de Cai Ferate (Romanian State Railways)
CS	Centraal Station (Central station)
DB	Deutsche Bahn AG (German Railway) or Deutsche Bundesbahn (former West German State Railway)
DR	Deutsche Reichsbahn (former East German State Railway)
EWS	English, Welsh and Scottish Railway (UK). (Now owned by DB).
EU	Eurostar (UK) Ltd
HTM	Haagsche Tram Maatschappi ("The Hague Tram Company" – The Hague's public transport operator)
NS	Nederlandse Spoorwegen (Netherlands Railways)
NMBS	Nationale Maatschappij der Belgische Spoorwegen (Belgian Railways – *Dutch language*)
ÖBB	Österreichische Bundesbahnen (Austrian Federal Railways)
PKP	Polskie Koleje Panstwowe (Polish State Railways)
RET	Rotterdamsche Elektrische Tram ("Rotterdam Electric Tram" – Rotterdam's public transport operator)
SJ	Statens Järnvägar (Swedish State Railways)
SNCB	Société Nationale des Chemins de Fer Belges (Belgian Railways – *French language*)
SNCF	Société Nationale des Chemins de Fer Français (French Railways)
STIB	Société des Transports Intercommunaux de Bruxelles
SZD	Soviet Union Railways

GETTING THERE FROM GREAT BRITAIN

By Rail

Eurostar services run from London St. Pancras International to Brussels Midi taking around two hours. Some of these call at Ebbsfleet. There are onward connections to Amsterdam by the hourly "Benelux push-pull" service which also calls at Mechelen, Antwerpen Centraal, Roosendaal, Dordrecht, Rotterdam Centraal, Den Haag HS and Schiphol, and also by *Thalys* services which call only at Antwerpen Centraal, Rotterdam Centraal, Den Haag HS and Schiphol. When the new *HSL Zuid* high speed line is open there will be fast services betwen Brussels and Amsterdam in addition to the Thalys services which will be diverted over it. These will initially be loco-hauled until the new Italian high speed trains are commissioned.

By Sea

Stena Line offer a Harwich–Hoek van Holland ferry service which takes 6–7 hours. Cabins are compulsory on night sailings. P&O Ferries operate Hull–Zeebrugge/Rotterdam Europoort (12½/14½ hrs). DFDS Seaways run daily from Newcastle International Ferry Terminal at North Shields to IJmuiden taking 15–16 hrs. There is a bus connection to Amsterdam.

By Air

There are flights from all London airports and many regional airports direct to Amsterdam and Brussels. Amsterdam airport (Schiphol) and Brussels airport are both rail-connected, as are the London airports of Gatwick, Heathrow, Luton and Stansted and the British regional airports at Birmingham and Manchester. East Midlands Parkway is due to open in December 2008 and this will serve East Midlands Airport by a shuttle bus. Newcastle Airport is served by the Tyne & Wear Metro. Flights also operate from the UK to Antwerpen, Charleroi, Eindhoven, Groningen, Luxembourg and Rotterdam.

1. BELGIAN NATIONAL RAILWAYS (NMBS/SNCB)

Because of the language situation, Belgian National Railways use their logo rather than initials as these differ according to the language used! In Dutch the railway company is NMBS (Nationale Maatschappij der Belgische Spoorwegen) whilst in French it is SNCB (Société Nationale des Chemins de Fer Belges).

Belgian railways are going through a sustained period of modernisation with high speed lines from the French border to Brussels, Leuven to Liège and in 2008/9 Antwerpen to the Netherlands and Liège–Aachen. Other major upgrades include Brussels–Leuven, lines serving Brussels airport and the future Brussels RER network. A new underground station has been built at Antwerpen and Liège Guillemins is transformed. Modernisation of passenger trains continues apace with new M6 stock still arriving, 305 new EMUs ordered and refurbishment of EMUs and hauled coaches continuing.

For freight, the electrification from Montzen to Aachen and introduction of new multi-voltage locos on this route will see off some very old diesel and electric locos. The arrival of open access operators is also transforming the scene. One wonders how long B-Cargo will remain as a national operator.

PLACE NAMES

Listed below are some of the Belgian towns and cities with their alternative rendering. Lille in France is included since Dutch speaking Belgians refer to it as Rijssel, which can be very confusing! NL. Dutch, F. French.

Local Name	Alternative	Local Name	Alternative
Aalst	Alost (F)	Kortrijk	Courtrai (F)
Arlon	Aarlen (NL)	Leuven	Louvain (F)
Antwerpen	Anvers (F)	Lille	Rijssel (NL)
Ath	Aat (NL)	Liège	Luik (NL)
Brugge	Bruges (F)	Mechelen	Malines (F)
Dendermonde	Termonde (F)	Mons	Bergen (NL)
Gent	Gand (F)	Namur	Namen (NL)
Geraardsbergen	Grammont (F)	Oudenaarde	Audenarde (F)
Ieper	Ypres (F)	Tournai	Doornik (NL)

PASSENGER TRAIN SERVICES

Belgian Railways are mostly electrified and operate regular interval services over most routes. The principal express services are Intercity (IC) and Inter Regio (IR) which call at principal centres. Local trains (L) serve the other routes and stations. Other types of trains are

CR	CityRail – Brussels suburban services
EC	EuroCity – high quality international train
ICE	German high speed train with special fares
INT	International train
P	Peak hour
ICT	Tourist train
Thalys	High speed TGV with special fares

INTER CITY SERVICES (IC)

The network has route letters in upper case. Details of the routes and usual traction:

A	Oostende–Gent–Brussels–Liège–Eupen	Class 13 and I11 push-pull stock
B	Brussels–Antwerpen–Amsterdam	Class 11 and Benelux push-pull stock
C	Oostende–Brugge–Kortrijk–Lille	AM96 dual-voltage
	Antwerpen–Gent–Kortrijk–Lille	AM96 dual-voltage
D	Herstal–Liège–Charleroi–Mons–Tournai–Lille	AM96 dual-voltage
E	Knokke/Blankenberge–Brussels–Hasselt–Tongeren	Class 27 and M6 push-pull stock
F	Quiévrain–Mons–Brussels–Leuven–Liège	Class 21 & M4 stock and AM80
G	Antwerpen–Gent–Brugge–Oostende	AM96

ⒷⒷ

H	Schaarbeek–Brussels–Tournai–Mouscron	Class 21 and M4 push-pull stock
I	Antwerpen–Brussels–Nivelles–Charleroi	Class 27 and M6 push-pull stock
J	Brussels–Namur–Arlon–Luxembourg	AM96, some Class 13 and M6 stock
K	Genk–Landen–Brussels–Aalst–Gent	Class 27 and M6 stock
L	Poperinge–Denderleeuw–Brussels–St. Niklaas	AM80
M	Brussels–Ottignies–Namur–Dinant/Liège–Liers	AM80
N	Antwerpen–Brussels–Nivelles–Charleroi	Class 27 and M6 push-pull stock
O	Brussels–Liège–Maastricht	Class 13 and I11 push-pull stock
P	Antwerpen–St Niklaas–Gent	Class 27 and M6 push-pull stock
Q	Antwerpen–Mechelen–Leuven	
R	Brussels–Mechelen–Turnhout	AM80

INTER REGIO SERVICES (IR)

This network has route letters in lower case. Details of routes and usual traction :

a	Antwerpen/St Niklaas–Mechelen–Leuven	AM86
b		
c	Antwerpen–Hasselt–Liège	AM86
d	Antwerpen–Brussels–Ath–Geraardsbergen	AM66/70 etc.
e	Antwerpen–Mol–Neerpelt/Hasselt	Class 41 DMUs
f	Lier–Mechelen–Gent–Kortrijk	Class 21 and M4 stock
g	Antwerpen–Turnhout	
h	Gent–Aalst–Brussels–Brussels Airport	AM96 and AM80
i	De Panne–Gent–Brussels–Brussels Airport–Landen	AM80
j	Quévy–Mons–Brussels–Brussels Airport	AM96 and AM80
k	Tournai–Mons–Charleroi–Namur–Jambes	AM66
l	Binche–La Louvière–Brussels–Louvain La Neuve	AM75
m	Liers–Liège–Gouvy–Luxembourg	CFL 3000 and I10 stock
n	Brussels–Antwerpen–Essen	AM75
o	Leuven–Brussels Airport–Brussels–Nivelles	AM66
q	Liège–Welkenraedt–Aachen Hbf	AM62

LOCAL SERVICES

These are mainly two-car EMUs but some lines are served by Class 41 DMUs. Routes worked by DMUs are Antwerpen–Mol–Neerpelt/Hasselt; Gent to Eeklo, Ronse and Geraardsbergen; Charleroi–Couvin; Dinant–Bertrix–Libramont and Bertrix–Virton–Rodange–Arlon.

PEAK SERVICES

Examination of the Belgian timetable for the Brussels area will show many peak hour extras. These bring a lot of variety into the scene with all sorts of locos and stock appearing such as Class 22 and 23 as well as Classes 21 and 27 on double-deck sets. Further examination of the timetable will show that "P" trains cover some rare curves and routes!

TOURIST SERVICES

These operate in the summer months to coastal resorts as well as places in the Ardennes. These are indicated in the timetable by a sun symbol.

NUMBERING SYSTEM

The SNCB list is quite straightforward although new multi-voltage Class 28 does not conform to the system! The present scheme dates from 01/01/71 and is as follows:

0001–0999	Electric multiple units. (Leading '0' not carried).
1001–1999	Electric locomotives. Multi-voltage.
2001–2999	Electric locomotives. 3000 V DC only.
3001–3999	Now used for Eurostar sets.
4001–4999	Diesel railcars (43xx series is also used for Thalys and 45xx for TGV Réseau)
5001–5999	Diesel locomotives. Higher power.
6001–6999	Diesel locomotives. Medium power.
7001–7999	Diesel shunting locomotives. Heavy duty.
8001–8999	Diesel shunting locomotives. Medium power.
9001–9999	Diesel shunting locomotives. Low power.

WORKSHOPS

There are only two workshops for the general overhaul of locomotives and multiple units. However, most of the main depots can undertake quite heavy repairs. The main works are:

FMN   Mechelen: All EMUs, DMUs and coaching stock.
FAZ   Salzinnes (near Namur): All locomotives.

DEPOTS

The SNCB has used codes for depots for many years dating back to the days of the telegraphic system. These codes are still in use today as official abbreviations. However on locomotives the allocation is normally stencilled on in full on the main frame somewhere below the cab. EMUs and diesel railcars do not normally carry their allocations but sometimes the code will be found on them against repair data etc. (S) after the allocation denotes the vehicle is stored.

Depot codes will be found on Page 176.

STABLING POINTS

Apart from the depots shown above, trains are stabled at many points on the Belgian network. The list is far from complete and does not include every station where the odd EMU may be stabled.

Aalst, Aarschot, Antwerpen Oost, Antwerpen Schijnpoort, Antwerpen Noorderdokken, Arlon, Ath, Brugge, Brussels Midi/Zuid station, Charleroi Sud, Châtelet, Denderleeuw, Dendermonde, De Panne, Gent St Pieters, Gent Zeehaven, Geraardsbergen, Huy, Jemelle, Kortrijk, Liège Guillemins, Liers, Mechelen, Mol, Mons, Montzen, Namur, Ottignies, Oudenaarde, Ronet, St Ghislain, Tournai, Turnhout, Virton, Welkenraedt.

LIVERIES

Electric Locomotives: The standard electric locomotive livery is blue with a yellow band. Class 11 are painted in the Benelux livery which reflects their international use, as the upper half of the body is painted Bordeaux red, the former SNCB InterCity colour, whilst the lower part is painted yellow, the NS colour. Class 13 is in the new Inter City livery of white to match the I11 IC stock whilst Class 25.5 retains the old Benelux livery of dark blue with a yellow band.

Diesel Locomotives: The main-line diesel locomotive fleet are in yellow with a green band. Exceptions are Class 55 fitted with e.t.h. which are blue with a yellow band.

Diesel Railcars: Class 41 units all carry a white livery.

Electric Multiple Units: Old EMUs and were originally painted plain green. The "Break" and AM86/89 "Snorkel" EMUs were introduced in Bordeaux red, and all remaining old EMUs were repainted in that colour, including Type AM75/76/77 units which were originally grey and orange. "Break" units were then repainted in the silver/red/blue "Memling" livery. AM96 EMUs were delivered in a new standard livery of pale grey with blue bodyside stripes and red doors. EMUs numbered from 601 onwards are being refurbished and were painted in this new livery. The latest refurbished sets are in the slightly altered CityRail livery.

Loco-hauled Coaches. Coaches for internal Belgian services were originally painted plain green. M4 and M5 loco-hauled stock were built in Bordeaux red livery. New Class I11 and M6 coaches have been delivered in a new standard livery of pale grey with blue bodyside stripes and red doors. Most international stock was originally orange, but all is now in the same livery as I11 stock. M4 stock is now all in this livery.

ACTIVITY CODES

The Belgian Railways fleet has not yet been completely divided between passenger, freight and infrastructure activities, but a start has been made with diesel locos. Codes used in this book are as follows:

C   B-Cargo (freight operator)
H   SNCB/NMBS historic fleet.
I   Infrabel (infrastructure manager)
P   Operating department

1.1. ELECTRIC MULTIPLE UNITS

Belgian EMUs operate in fixed formations and therefore only unit numbers are quoted. All classes of EMU may work in multiple with one another except for Types AM80/82/83, AM86 and Type AM96, which may work with other members of the same type only. "Type" refers to the year in which the batch of units were ordered. Seating is 2+2 in first class and 3+2 in second class, except where stated otherwise. Individual car numbers are normally the unit number with a figure 1, 2, 3 or 4 for the position in the set. Hence the B car of unit 153 is 1531 and the ABD is 1532. Exceptions can occur to this – in particular AM80/82/83 "Break" units had the centre cars inserted randomly and therefore these do not conform to the general scheme. All units have electro-pneumatic braking and disc brakes. All EMUs (and domestic hauled stock) were in a maroon livery lined in white until the current decade when a much more pleasant white livery highlighted in red and blue was adopted. Belgian Railways ordered 315 new EMUs for the Brussels RER network and IC/IR services in April 2008. They will be 3-car sets, based on the Desiro ML design.

TYPE AM62/63/65   2-CAR UNITS

These units are in general use on local stopping services throughout Belgium. They are now being withdrawn.

BD + AB (DMBSO–DMCO).

Built: 1962–1965. 151–210 are Type AM62, 211–250 are AM63 and 251–270 are AM65.
Builder–Mechanical Parts: BN, Ragheno, BLC, ABR, Germain, CWFM.
Builder–Electrical Parts: ACEC.
Traction Motors: 4 x 155 kW.   **Weight:** 50 + 52 tonnes.
Wheel Arrangement: A1-1A + A1-1A.   **Length over Couplers:** 23.71 + 23.59 m.
Accommodation: –/104 1T + 28/48 1T.   **Maximum Speed:** 130 km/h.

Originally numbered 228.151–270.
t Equipped to test TBL2 signalling. Owned by Infrabel.

153	MKM	184	FSD	215	FSD	243	MKM
154	MKM	185	FSD	216	FSD	244	MKM
155	MKM	186	FSD	217	FSD	245	MKM
156	MKM	187	FSD	218	FSD	246	MKM
157	MKM	188	FSD	220	FSD	247	MKM
158	MKM	189	FSD	221	FSD	248	MKM
159	NK	190	FSD	222	FSD	249	NK
160	NK	191	FSD	223	FSD	250	NK
161	NK	193	FSD	224	FSD	251	NK
162	NK	195	FSD	225	FSD	252	NK
163	NK	196	FSD	226	FSD	253	NK
164	NK	197	FSD	227	FSD	254	NK
165	NK	198	FSD	228	FSD	255	NK
166	NK	201	FSD	229	FSD	256	NK
168	MKM	202	FSD	230	FSD	257	NK
169	MKM	203	FSD	231	FSD	258	NK
171	MKM	204	FSD	232	FSD	259	NK
174	MKM	205	FSD	233	FSD	260	NK
175	MKM	206	FSD	234	FSD	261	NK
176	MKM	207	FSD	235	FSD	262	NK
177	FSD	208	FSD	236	FSD	263	NK
178	FSD	209	FSD	237	FSD	265	NK
179	FSD	210	FSD	238	FSD	267	NK
180	FSD	212	FSD	239	FSD	268	NK
181	FSD	213	FSD	240	MKM	269	NK
182	FSD	214	FSD	241	MKM	270	NK
183	FSD						

TYPE AM80/82/83   "BREAK"   3-CAR UNITS

These units, known as "Break" sets, are the EMU version of Type M4 coaches and are thyristor controlled. Built as two-car sets they have all been made up to three-car by the insertion of a trailer with 2+2 second class seating. At the same time units were repainted into a new silver livery. The trailer numbers are out of sequence as the new trailers were built in number order but inserted into any set that just happened to be in works at the time. (e.g. set 428 is formed 4281, 3752, 4283). The units are used mostly on IR services. Some sets have been sold to US companies and leased back. Units are expected to be refurbished starting in 2008. 308 is the prototype set for this.

B + B + ABD (DMSO–TSO–PDTBCO).

Built: 1980–1985. 301–335 are Type AM80, 336–370 are AM82 and 371–440 are AM83.
Builder–Mechanical Parts: BN.   **Traction Motors:** 4 x 310 kW.
Builder–Electrical Parts: ACEC.   **Wheel Arrangement:** Bo-Bo + 2-2 + 2-2.
Weight: 61 + 43 + 47 tonnes.   **Maximum Speed:** 160 km/h.
Accommodation: –/99 1T + –/83 1T + 32/40 1T.
Length over Couplers: 25.425 + 24.96 m + 25.425 m.

Regenerative braking.
b Brecknell-Willis pantograph.

301	M	NK	337	M	NK	372	M	FHS	407	M	FHS
302	M	NK	338	M	NK	373	M	FHS	408	M b	FHS
303	M	NK	339	M	NK	374	M	FHS	409	M	FHS
304	M	NK	340	M	NK	375	M	FHS	410	M	FHS
305	M	NK	341	M	NK	376	M	FHS	411	M	FHS
306	M	NK	342	M	NK	377	M	FHS	412	M	FHS
307	M	NK	343	M	NK	378	M	FHS	413	M	FHS
308	M	NK	344	M	NK	379	M	FHS	414	M	FHS
309	M	NK	345	M	NK	380	M	FHS	415	M b	FHS
310	M	NK	346	M	NK	381	M	FHS	416	M	FKR
311	M	NK	347	M	NK	382	M	FHS	417	M	FKR
312	M	NK	348	M	NK	383	M	FHS	418	M	FKR
313	M	NK	349	M	NK	384	M	FHS	419	M	FKR
314	M	NK	350	M	NK	385	M	FHS	420	M b	FKR
315	M	NK	351	M	NK	386	M	FHS	421	M b	FKR
316	M	NK	352	M	NK	387	M	FHS	422	M	FKR
317	M	NK	353	M	NK	388	M	FHS	423	M	FKR
318	M	NK	354	M	NK	389	M	FHS	424	M b	FKR
319	M	NK	355	M	NK	390	M	FHS	425	M b	FKR
320	M	NK	356	M	NK	391	M	FHS	426	M	FKR
322	M	NK	357	M	NK	392	M	FHS	427	M	FKR
323	M	NK	358	M	FHS	393	M	FHS	428	M	FKR
324	M	NK	359	M	FHS	394	M	FHS	429	M	FKR
325	M	NK	360	M	FHS	395	M	FHS	430	M b	FKR
326	M	NK	361	M	FHS	396	M	FHS	431	M	FKR
327	M	NK	362	M	FHS	397	M	FHS	432	M	FKR
328	M	NK	363	M	FHS	398	M	FHS	433	M	FKR
329	M	NK	364	M	FHS	399	M	FHS	434	M	FKR
330	M	NK	365	M	FHS	400	M	FHS	435	M	FKR
331	M	NK	366	M	FHS	401	M	FHS	436	M	FKR
332	M	NK	367	M	FHS	402	M	FHS	437	M	FKR
333	M	NK	368	M	FHS	403	M	FHS	438	M	FKR
334	M	NK	369	M	FHS	404	M	FHS	439	M b	FKR
335	M	NK	370	M	FHS	405	M	FHS	440	M	FKR
336	M	NK	371	M	FHS	406	M	FHS			

TYPE AM96   3-CAR UNITS

These sets are the latest IC units that brought new standards of comfort to Belgian main line services and are the same design as Type I11 carriages. Front end design is based on the successful "rubber nose" of Danish IC3 DMUs. There are two versions with the dual-voltage sets equipped for services into France (Antwerpen–Lille, Oostende–Lille and Herstal–Liège–Lille). The DC sets work IC services from the coast to Hasselt. 501 to 524 are equipped to operate into Luxembourg.

B + B + AD (DMSO–SO–DFSO).

Built: 1996–1999.
Systems (441–490): 3000 V DC, 25 kV AC 50 Hz.
Builder–Mechanical Parts: Bombardier.
Builder–Electrical Parts: Alstom.
Traction Motors: Four 4EXA3046 asynchronous of 350 kW.
Length over Couplers: 26.40 + 26.40 + 26.40 m.
Wheel Arrangement: Bo-Bo + 2-2 +2-2.   **Weight:** 60 + 50 + 50 tonnes.
Accommodation: –/79 1T + –/88 1T + 45/– 1T.   **Maximum Speed:** 160 km/h.

Dual-voltage sets:

441	W	FSD	454	W	FSD	467	W	FSD	479	W	FSD
442	W	FSD	455	W	FSD	468	W	FSD	480	W	FSD
443	W	FSD	456	W	FSD	469	W	FSD	481	W	FSD
444	W	FSD	457	W	FSD	470	W	FSD	482	W	FSD
445	W	FSD	458	W	FSD	471	W	FSD	483	W	FSD
446	W	FSD	459	W	FSD	472	W	FSD	484	W	FSD
447	W	FSD	460	W	FSD	473	W	FSD	485	W	FSD
448	W	FSD	461	W	FSD	474	W	FSD	486	W	FSD
449	W	FSD	462	W	FSD	475	W	FSD	487	W	FSD
450	W	FSD	463	W	FSD	476	W	FSD	488	W	FSD
451	W	FSD	464	W	FSD	477	W	FSD	489	W	FSD
452	W	FSD	465	W	FSD	478	W	FSD	490	W	FSD
453	W	FSD	466	W	FSD						

3000 V DC sets:

501	W	MKM	519	W	MKM	537	W	FHS	554	W	FHS
502	W	MKM	520	W	MKM	538	W	FHS	555	W	FHS
503	W	MKM	521	W	MKM	539	W	FHS	556	W	FHS
504	W	MKM	522	W	MKM	540	W	FHS	557	W	FHS
505	W	MKM	523	W	MKM	541	W	FHS	558	W	FHS
506	W	MKM	524	W	MKM	542	W	FHS	559	W	FHS
507	W	MKM	525	W	FHS	543	W	FHS	560	W	FHS
508	W	MKM	526	W	FHS	544	W	FHS	561	W	FHS
509	W	MKM	527	W	FHS	545	W	FHS	562	W	FHS
510	W	MKM	528	W	FHS	546	W	FHS	563	W	FHS
511	W	MKM	529	W	FHS	547	W	FHS	564	W	FHS
512	W	MKM	530	W	FHS	548	W	FHS	565	W	FHS
513	W	MKM	531	W	FHS	549	W	FHS	566	W	FHS
514	W	MKM	532	W	FHS	550	W	FHS	567	W	FHS
515	W	MKM	533	W	FHS	551	W	FHS	568	W	FHS
516	W	MKM	534	W	FHS	552	W	FHS	569	W	FHS
517	W	MKM	535	W	FHS	553	W	FHS	570	W	FHS
518	W	MKM	536	W	FHS						

TYPE AM70A (SABENA)   2-CAR UNITS

These units were built for use on the Brussels Airport service when this was just a shuttle service. Since the construction of a new station at the airport, services from the south of Brussels now run through to the airport and the Sabena units have been put into the general pool of suburban units.

B + ABD (DMSO–DMBCO).

Built: 1970–1971.
Builder–Mechanical Parts: Ragheno.   **Accommodation:** –/74 1T + 32/12 1T.
Builder–Electrical Parts: ACEC.   **Weight:** 52 + 52 tonnes.
Traction Motors: 4 x 170 kW.   **Length over Couplers:** 23.71 + 23.59 m.
Wheel Arrangement: A1-1A + A1-1A.   **Maximum Speed:** 140 km/h.

595	NK	597	NK	599	NK	600	NK
596	NK	598	NK				

TYPE AM66/70   2-CAR UNITS

Units 601–782 are now being refurbished with around 25 units per year being dealt with at Mechelen works. Changes include new doors and altered seating giving fewer first class seats and smoking accommodation. Used on some IR routes but mostly used for local and peak services. Refurbished units were allocated to Brussels CityRail services before a more specific refurbishment was carried out on Types AM70TH and AM73. All the 601–604 batch are now refurbished.

B + ABD (DMSO–DMBCO).

Built: 1966/70–71.
Builder–Mechanical Parts: BN, Ragheno, BLC, ABR.
Builder–Electrical Parts: ACEC.
Traction Motors: 4 x 170 kW.   **Weight:** 56 + 52 tonnes.
Wheel Arrangement: A1-1A + A1-1A.   **Length over Couplers:** 23.71 + 23.59 m.
Accommodation: –/102 1T + 20/58 1T.   **Maximum Speed:** 140 km/h.

Originally numbered 228.601–664.

601	N	FKR	617	N	FKR	633	N	FKR	649	N	FSRE
602	N	FKR	618	N	FKR	634	N	FKR	650	N	FSRE
603	N	FKR	619	N	FKR	635	N	NK	651	N	FSRE
604	N	FKR	620	N	FKR	636	N	NK	652	N	FSRE
605	N	FKR	621	N	FKR	637	N	NK	653	N	FSRE
606	N	FKR	622	N	FKR	638	N	NK	654	N	FSRE
607	N	FKR	623	N	FKR	639	N	NK	655	N	FSRE
608	N	FKR	624	N	FKR	640	N	NK	657	N	FSRE
609	N	FKR	625	N	FKR	641	N	FSRE	658	N	FSRE
610	N	FKR	626	N	FKR	642	N	FSRE	659	N	FSRE
611	N	FKR	627	N	FKR	643	N	FSRE	660	N	FSRE
612	N	FKR	628	N	FKR	644	N	FSRE	661	N	FSRE
613	N	FKR	629	N	FKR	645	N	FSRE	662	N	FSRE
614	N	FKR	630	N	FKR	646	N	FSRE	663	N	FSRE
615	N	FKR	631	N	FKR	647	N	FSRE	664	N	FSRE
616	N	FKR	632	N	FKR	648	N	FSRE			

TYPE AM70TH   2-CAR UNITS

The "TH" denotes thyristor control, the first Belgian units so fitted. Timken roller bearings. Use as for AM66/70. All units are being refurbished and all except 672 will be renumbered 966–970 for CityRail services.

B + ABD (DMSO–DMBCO).

Built: 1971–1972.
Builder–Mechanical Parts: CWFM.   **Accommodation:** –/104 1T + 28/48 1T.
Builder–Electrical Parts: ACEC.   **Weight:** 56 + 53 tonnes.
Traction Motors: 4 x 170 kW.   **Length over Couplers:** 23.71 + 23.59 m.
Wheel Arrangement: A1-1A + A1-1A.   **Maximum Speed:** 140 km/h.

665		GCR	668		GCR	672	N	GCR	675		GCR
666		GCR	669		GCR	673		GCR	676		GCR
667		GCR	670		GCR	674		GCR			

TYPE AM73/74/78/79   2-CAR UNITS

These are the production series of thyristor-controlled units. Units are currently being refurbished. 677–683 and 707–730 (excluding 709) are receiving a more significant upgrade and a revised CityRail livery. They will be renumbered 971–999 in order as they go through works. Withdrawn 716 donated one car to set 709.

B + ABD (DMSO–DMBCO).

Built: 1972–1980. 677–706 are Type AM73, 707–730 AM74, 731–756 AM78 and 757–782 AM79.
Builder–Mechanical Parts: BN (707–730 CFCF).   **Accommodation:** –/102 1T + 28/48 1T.
Builder–Electrical Parts: ACEC.   **Weight:** 56 + 52 tonnes.
Traction Motors: 4 x 170 kW.   **Length over Couplers:** 23.71 + 23.59 m.
Wheel Arrangement: A1-1A + A1-1A.   **Maximum Speed:** 140 km/h.

No				No				No				No			
677			GCR	702	N	r	GCR	740	N	r	GCR	762	N	r	GCR
678			GCR	703	N	r	GCR	741	N	r	GCR	763	N	r	GCR
680			GCR	704	N	r	GCR	742	N	r	GCR	764	N	r	GCR
682			GCR	705	N	r	GCR	743	N	r	GCR	765	N	r	GCR
684	N	r	GCR	706	N	r	GCR	744	N	r	GCR	766	N	r	GCR
685	N	r	GCR	709	N	r	GCR	745	N	r	GCR	767	N	r	GCR
686	N	r	GCR	710			GCR	746	N	r	GCR	768	N	r	GCR
687	N	r	GCR	714			GCR	747	N	r	GCR	769	N	r	GCR
688	N	r	GCR	718			GCR	748	N	r	GCR	770	N	r	GCR
689	N	r	GCR	719			GCR	749	N	r	GCR	771	N	r	GCR
690	N	r	GCR	722			GCR	750	N	r	GCR	772	N	r	NK
691	N	r	GCR	728			GCR	751	N	r	GCR	773	N	r	NK
692	N	r	GCR	731	N	r	GCR	752	N	r	GCR	774	N	r	NK
693	N	r	GCR	732	N	r	GCR	753	N	r	GCR	775	N	r	NK
694	N	r	GCR	733	N	r	GCR	754	N	r	GCR	776	N	r	NK
695	N	r	GCR	734	N	r	GCR	755	N	r	GCR	777	N	r	NK
696	N	r	GCR	735	N	r	GCR	756	N	r	GCR	778	N	r	NK
697	N	r	GCR	736	N	r	GCR	757	N	r	GCR	779	N	r	NK
698	N	r	GCR	737	N	r	GCR	758	N	r	GCR	780	N	r	NK
699	N	r	GCR	735	N	r	GCR	759	N	r	GCR	781	N	r	NK
700	N	r	GCR	738	N	r	GCR	760	N	r	GCR	782	N	r	NK
701	N	r	GCR	739	N	r	GCR	761	N	r	GCR				

TYPE AM75/76/77   4-CAR UNITS

These thyristor-controlled units are gangwayed within the sets only. Pantographs are fitted to only one of the motor coaches. Pressure ventilation. Used on IR services b, l and n.

AD + B + B + B (DTBFO–PMSO–MSO–DTSO).

Built: 1975–1979. Units 801–820 are AM75, 821–832 are AM76 and 833–844 are AM77.
Builder–Mechanical Parts: BN.
Builder–Electrical Parts: ACEC   **Traction Motors:** 8 x 170 kW.
Weight: 51 + 60 + 60 + 49 tonnes.   **Maximum Speed:** 140 km/h.
Wheel Arrangement: 2-2 + Bo-Bo + Bo-Bo + 2-2.
Accommodation: 56/– 1T + –/100 1T + –/106 1T + –/96 1T.
Length over Couplers: 25.11 + 24.40 + 24.40 + 25.11 m.

Disc and tread brakes.

No		No		No		No	
801	GCR	812	GCR	823	GCR	834	GCR
802	GCR	813	GCR	824	GCR	835	GCR
803	GCR	814	GCR	825	GCR	836	GCR
804	GCR	815	GCR	826	GCR	837	GCR
805	GCR	816	GCR	827	GCR	838	GCR
806	GCR	817	GCR	828	GCR	839	GCR
807	GCR	818	GCR	829	GCR	840	GCR
808	GCR	819	GCR	830	GCR	841	GCR
809	GCR	820	GCR	831	GCR	842	GCR
810	GCR	821	GCR	832	GCR	843	GCR
811	GCR	822	GCR	833	GCR	844	GCR

TYPE AM86/89   2-CAR UNITS

These were the first Belgian EMUs to feature 2+2 seating in second class. Another innovation is the use of polyester sides and front nose which are glued onto the main body. They are designed for eventual one-person operation and rear-view mirrors are fitted which are flush with the side of the vehicle when not in use. They are officially known as "Sprinters", but their unusual front end appearance has led to them being nicknamed "Snorkels". Used on local services around Brussels, Antwerpen, Hasselt and Leuven including Leuven to St. Niklaas. The first class section in the power car was downgraded to second in 2006.

B + AB (MSO–DTCO).

Built: 1988–1991. Units 901–935 are AM86 and 936–952 are AM89.
Builder–Mechanical Parts: BN.
Builder–Electrical Parts: ACEC.
Traction Motors: 4 x 172 kW type AE121N.
Wheel Arrangement: Bo-Bo + 2-2.
Accommodation: –/88 1T + 24/86.
Weight: 59 + 48 tonnes.
Length over Couplers: 26.40 + 26.40 m.
Maximum Speed: 120 km/h.

901	FSRE	914	FSRE	927	FSRE	941	FSRE
902	FSRE	915	FSRE	928	FSRE	942	FSRE
903	FSRE	916	FSRE	929	FSRE	943	FSRE
904	FSRE	917	FSRE	930	FSRE	944	FSRE
905	FSRE	918	FSRE	931	FSRE	945	FSRE
906	FSRE	919	FSRE	933	FSRE	946	FSRE
907	FSRE	920	FSRE	934	FSRE	947	FSRE
908	FSRE	921	FSRE	935	FSRE	948	FSRE
909	FSRE	922	FSRE	936	FSRE	949	FSRE
910	FSRE	923	FSRE	937	FSRE	950	FSRE
911	FSRE	924	FSRE	938	FSRE	951	FSRE
912	FSRE	925	FSRE	939	FSRE	952	FSRE
913	FSRE	926	FSRE	940	FSRE		

TYPE AM70TH   2-CAR CITYRAIL UNITS

AM70TH refurbished for CityRail services and renumbered. For details see 665–676.

960	(665)	R		964	(669)	R		968	(674)	R
961	(666)	R		965	(670)	R		969	(675)	R
962	(667)	R		966	(671)	R	GCR	970	(676)	R
963	(668)	R		967	(673)	R				

TYPE AM73/AM74   2-CAR CITYRAIL UNITS

AM73/AM74 refurbished for CityRail services and renumbered. For details see 677–730.

971	(677)	R		981	(711)	R	GCR	991	(722)	R	
972	(678)	R		982	(712)	R	GCR	992	(723)	R	GCR
973	(679)	R	GCR	983	(713)	R	GCR	993	(724)	R	GCR
974	(680)	R		984	(714)	R		994	(725)	R	GCR
975	(681)	R	GCR	985	(715)	R	GCR	995	(726)	R	GCR
976	(682)	R		986	(717)	R	GCR	996	(727)	R	GCR
977	(683)	R	GCR	987	(718)	R		997		R	
978	(707)	R	GCR	988	(719)	R		998	(729)	R	GCR
979	(708)	R	GCR	989	(720)	R	GCR	999	(730)	R	GCR
980	(710)	R		990	(721)	R					

1.2. ELECTRIC LOCOMOTIVES

All electric locomotives are in the standard blue livery with yellow stripes unless stated otherwise. The standard voltage is 3000 V DC.

CLASS 11   Bo-Bo

These dual voltage locos are a development of Class 21 and are used only on the Brussels–Amsterdam "Benelux" service. SNCB/NMBS provides the locos for these push-pull InterCity services and NS provides the coaching stock. Originally planned to be numbered 1101–1112, the higher numbers were eventually decided on to avoid conflicting with now defunct NS Class 1100. The Benelux service was to be replaced by high speed trains in 2007 but this has slipped to 2009. As Class 11 locos are very unreliable, Bombardier TRAXX Class 186 will be hired to help out in the meantime. Once replaced, Class 11 are to be cascaded to freight between Belgium and the Netherlands, replacing Class 25.5.

Built: 1985–6.
Systems: 1500 V/3000 V DC.
Builder–Mechanical Parts: BN.
Builder–Electrical Parts: ACEC.
Traction Motors: 4 x LE622S frame mounted.
One Hour Rating: 3310 kW.

Maximum Tractive Effort: 234 kN.
Wheel Diameter: 1250 mm.
Weight: 85 tonnes.
Length over Buffers: 18.65 m.
Maximum Speed: 140 km/h.

Electro-pneumatic braking. Rheostatic braking.

1181	B	FSR	1184	B	FSR	1187	B	FSR	1190	B	FSR
1182	B	FSR	1185	B	FSR	1188	B	FSR	1191	B	FSR
1183	B	FSR	1186	B	FSR	1189	B	FSR	1192	B	FSR

CLASS 12   Bo-Bo

Another dual-voltage development of Class 21, these locomotives were once used on passenger services but now work only freight trains from Antwerpen, Gent and Charleroi to Lille, Somain and Aulnoye in northern France.

Built: 1986.
Systems: 3000 V DC, 25 kV AC 50 Hz.
Builder–Mechanical Parts: BN.
Builder–Electrical Parts: ACEC.
Traction Motors: 4 x LE622S frame mounted.
One Hour Rating: 3310 kW.

Maximum Tractive Effort: 234 kN.
Wheel Diameter: 1250 mm.
Weight: 85 tonnes.
Length over Buffers: 18.65 m.
Maximum Speed: 160 km/h.

Electro-pneumatic braking. Rheostatic braking. Thyristor control.

1201	FKR	1204	FKR	1207	FKR	1210	FKR
1202	FKR	1205	FKR	1208	FKR	1211	FKR
1203	FKR	1206	FKR	1209	FKR	1212	FKR

CLASS 13   Bo-Bo

These dual-voltage locomotives were ordered together with 20 identical Class 3000 for CFL. The first ten were built in Belfort, France and the remainder at the Bombardier plant at Brugge. They are general purpose machines with a capability of 200 km/h but are now divided into two subfleets – 1301–1340 work only freight on the "Sibelit" Antwerpen–Luxembourg corridor, with some work to Metz in France. 1341–1360 work Oostende–Brussels–Liège–Eupen and Brussels–Liège–Maastricht passenger services using the Leuven–Liège high speed line. The class is expected to lose all passenger work when the new Class 18 is delivered.

Built: 1997–2000.
Systems: 3000 V DC, 25 kV AC 50 Hz.
Builder–Mechanical Parts: Bombardier.
Builder–Electrical Parts: Alstom.
Traction Motors: 4 x PXA4339B frame mounted.
One Hour Rating: 5200 kW.
Class Specific Livery: S White with blue stripe below and red stripe above bodyside grilles.

Maximum Tractive Effort: 288 kN.
Wheel Diameter: 1160 mm.
Weight: 90 tonnes.
Length over Buffers: 19.11 m.
Maximum Speed: 200 km/h.

Electro-pneumatic braking. Rheostatic braking.

1301	S	FKR	1316	S	FKR	1331	S	FKR	1346	S	FKR
1302	S	FKR	1317	S	FKR	1332	S	FKR	1347	S	FKR
1303	S	FKR	1318	S	FKR	1333	S	FKR	1348	S	FKR
1304	S	FKR	1319	S	FKR	1334	S	FKR	1349	S	FKR
1305	S	FKR	1320	S	FKR	1335	S	FKR	1350	S	FKR
1306	S	FKR	1321	S	FKR	1336	S	FKR	1351	S	FKR
1307	S	FKR	1322	S	FKR	1337	S	FKR	1352	S	FKR
1308	S	FKR	1323	S	FKR	1338	S	FKR	1353	S	FKR
1309	S	FKR	1324	S	FKR	1339	S	FKR	1354	S	FKR
1310	S	FKR	1325	S	FKR	1340	S	FKR	1355	S	FKR
1311	S	FKR	1326	S	FKR	1341	S	FKR	1356	S	FKR
1312	S	FKR	1327	S	FKR	1342	S	FKR	1357	S	FKR
1313	S	FKR	1328	S	FKR	1343	S	FKR	1358	S	FKR
1314	S	FKR	1329	S	FKR	1344	S	FKR	1359	S	FKR
1315	S	FKR	1330	S	FKR	1345	S	FKR	1360	S	FKR

CLASS 15   Bo-Bo

These are triple voltage locos designed for through workings to the Dutch and French systems. The class were once used on services between Paris, Brussels and Amsterdam, but in 1988 were banned from the NS. The introduction of TGV Nord and Thalys services has made them redundant and they are now used on peak services between Gouvy, Welkenraedt, Liège and Brussels. The pantograph at No. 1 end is for DC and that at No. 2 end is for AC.

Built: 1962.
Systems: 1500/3000 V DC, 25 kV AC 50 Hz. **Weight:** 77.7 tonnes.
Builder–Mechanical Parts: BN. **Length over Buffers:** 17.75 m.
Builder–Electrical Parts: ACEC. **Maximum Speed:** 160 km/h.
Traction Motors: 4 x ES541 frame mounted. **Maximum Tractive Effort:** 170 kN.
One Hour Rating: 2780 kW. **Wheel Diameter:** 1250 mm.

Electro-pneumatic braking.

Originally numbered 150.001–003/011/012.

1501	NK	1503	NK	1504	NK	

CLASS 16   Bo-Bo

These four voltage international locos lost their work on Oostende–Brussels–Köln services when Thalys TGV and ICE services were introduced between Brussels and Köln. They were surprisingly retained in service on peak services from Oostende and Welkenraedt to Brussels. They are also sometimes used on dated services such as the Treski to Austria which the class works through to Aachen. Only 1601 and 1602 are now authorised in Germany.

Built: 1966.
Systems: 1500/3000 V DC, 15 kV AC 16.67 Hz, 25 kV AC 50 Hz.
Builder–Mechanical Parts: BN.
Builder–Electrical Parts: ACEC. **Wheel Diameter:** 1250 mm.
Traction Motors: 4 x ES541 frame mounted. **Weight:** 82.6 tonnes.
One Hour Rating: 2780 kW. **Length over Buffers:** 16.65 m.
Maximum Tractive Effort: 196 kN. **Maximum Speed:** 160 km/h.

Electro-pneumatic braking.

Originally numbered 160.001–004/021–024.

1601	FSD	1603	FSD	1605	FSD	1608	FSD
1602	FSD	1604	FSD	1606	FSD		

CLASS 18   Bo-Bo

In late 2006, Belgian Railways ordered 60 new dual-voltage electric locomotives from Siemens, rather than the four-voltage freight locos expected. The new locos will be equipped with ETCS signalling and for push-pull with Type I11 and M6 stock. They will replace Classes 13, 21 and 27 on passenger services, freeing the latter for freight where they will certainly allow withdrawal of Classes 23 and 26. An option exists for a further 60 locos. The choice of Class 18 is confusing as the last of the previous class were still extant but stored at the time of ordering. Class 14 was widely touted before the order and more logical.

Built: 2009–.
Systems: 3000 V DC, 25 kV AC 50 Hz.
Builder: Siemens.
Traction Motors: 4 frame mounted.
One Hour Rating: 6000 kW.
Continuous Rating: 5000 kW.
Maximum Tractive Effort: 304 kN.
Wheel Diameter: 1250 mm.
Weight: 90 tonnes.
Length over Buffers: 19.58 m.
Maximum Speed: 200 km/h.
Class Specific Livery: S White with blue stripe below and red stripe above bodyside grilles.

1801	1816	1831	1846
1802	1817	1832	1847
1803	1818	1833	1848
1804	1819	1834	1849
1805	1820	1835	1850
1806	1821	1836	1851
1807	1822	1837	1852
1808	1823	1838	1853
1809	1824	1839	1854
1810	1825	1840	1855
1811	1826	1841	1856
1812	1827	1842	1857
1813	1828	1843	1858
1814	1829	1844	1859
1815	1830	1845	1860

CLASS 20   Co-Co

These thyristor controlled locos were once the most powerful in Belgium and have had a chequered career with varying defects over the years. Their main use is on the Brussels–Luxembourg artery (EC/IC passenger) as well as Antwerpen–Montzen (freight).

Built: 1975–77.
Builder–Mechanical Parts: BN.
Builder–Electrical Parts: ACEC.
Traction Motors: 6 x LE772G frame mounted.
One Hour Rating: 5150 kW.
Maximum Tractive Effort: 314 kN.
Wheel Diameter: 1250 mm.
Weight: 110 tonnes.
Length over Buffers: 19.50 m.
Max. Speed: 140 km/h.

Electro-pneumatic braking. Separately excited rheostatic braking.

L Equipped to operate into Luxembourg.

2001	L	MKM	2007	L	MKM	2013	MKM	2019	MKM
2002	L	MKM	2008		MKM	2014	MKM	2021	MKM
2003	L	MKM	2009		MKM	2015	MKM	2022	MKM
2004	L	MKM	2010		MKM	2016	MKM	2023	MKM
2005	L	MKM	2011		MKM	2017	MKM	2024	MKM
2006	L	MKM	2012		MKM	2018	MKM	2025	MKM

CLASS 21   Bo-Bo

These are very similar to Class 27 but lower powered. Used on push-pull trains and freights. 2130 was converted to prototype dual-voltage (3000 V DC/25 kV AC) loco 1901 as a development stage for Class 13 then converted back to standard.

Built: 1984–1987.
Builder–Mechanical Parts: BN.
Builder–Electrical Parts: ACEC.
Traction Motors: 4 x LE622S frame mounted.
One Hour Rating: 3310 kW.
Maximum Tractive Effort: 234 kN.
Wheel Diameter: 1250 mm.
Weight: 84 tonnes.
Length over Buffers: 18.65 m.
Maximum Speed: 160 km/h.

Rheostatic braking.

2101	FSD	2107	FSD	2113	FSD	2119	FSD
2102	FSD	2108	FSD	2114	FSD	2120	FSD
2103	FSD	2109	FSD	2115	FSD	2121	FSD
2104	FSD	2110	FSD	2116	FSD	2122	FSD
2105	FSD	2111	FSD	2117	FSD	2123	FSD
2106	FSD	2112	FSD	2118	FSD	2124	FSD

2125	FSD	2134	FSD	2143	FSD	2152	FSD
2126	FSD	2135	FSD	2144	FSD	2153	FSD
2127	FSD	2136	FSD	2145	FSD	2154	FSD
2128	FSD	2137	FSD	2146	FSD	2155	FSD
2129	FSD	2138	FSD	2147	FSD	2156	FSD
2130	FSD	2139	FSD	2148	FSD	2157	FSD
2131	FSD	2140	FSD	2149	FSD	2158	FSD
2132	FSD	2141	FSD	2150	FSD	2159	FSD
2133	FSD	2142	FSD	2151	FSD	2160	FSD

CLASS 22   Bo-Bo

A general purpose locomotive now restricted to a few peak passenger workings and expected to be withdrawn at any moment. 2239–2250 were originally dual voltage (1500/3000 V DC). Plans to sell many Class 22 and 25 to Poland have apparently fallen through.

Built: 1953–54.
Builder–Mechanical Parts: Niv.
Builder–Electrical Parts: SEMG/ACEC.
Traction Motors: 4 x CF729 axle-hung.
One Hour Rating: 1880 kW.

Maximum Tractive Effort: 196 kN.
Wheel Diameter: 1262 mm.
Weight: 87 tonnes.
Length over Buffers: 18.00 m.
Maximum Speed: 130 km/h.

Originally numbered 122.001–038/201/212.

2204	GCR	2221	GCR	2229	GCR	2248	NK
2213	GCR	2223	GCR	2236	GCR	2249	NK
2214	GCR	2224	GCR	2247	NK	2250	NK
2216	GCR	2226	GCR				

CLASS 23   Bo-Bo

Another mixed traffic loco at work all over the system mainly on freight. Can work in multiple with others of the same class and Class 26. Overhauls will continue until 2010 but the arrival of Class 18 and Class 28 locos hired for the Aachen line will at last allow withdrawals to begin.

Built: 1955–57.
Builder–Mechanical Parts: BN.
Builder–Electrical Parts: ACEC/SEMG.
Traction Motors: 4 x CF729 axle-hung.
One Hour Rating: 1880 kW.

Maximum Tractive Effort: 196 kN.
Wheel Diameter: 1262 mm.
Weight: 92 tonnes.
Length over Buffers: 18.00 m.
Maximum Speed: 130 km/h.

Regenerative braking.

Originally numbered 123.001–083.

2383 was fitted with special equipment for banking at Liège. It was renumbered 124 001 and then 2401 before becoming 2383.

2301	FNND	2324	FNND	2344	FNND	2364	FNND
2303	FNND	2325	FNND	2345	FNND	2365	FNND
2304	FNND	2326	FNND	2346	FNND	2366	FNND
2306	FNND	2327	FNND	2347	FNND	2367	FNND
2308	FNND	2328	FNND	2348	FNND	2368	FNND
2309	FNND	2329	FNND	2349	FNND	2369	FNND
2310	FNND	2330	FNND	2350	FNND	2370	FNND
2311	FNND	2331	FNND	2351	FNND	2371	FNND
2312	FNND	2332	FNND	2352	FNND	2372	FNND
2313	FNND	2333	FNND	2353	FNND	2373	FNND
2314	FNND	2334	FNND	2354	FNND	2374	FNND
2315	FNND	2335	FNND	2355	FNND	2375	FNND
2316	FNND	2336	FNND	2356	FNND	2376	FNND
2317	FNND	2337	FNND	2357	FNND	2377	FNND
2318	FNND	2338	FNND	2358	FNND	2378	FNND
2319	FNND	2339	FNND	2359	FNND	2379	FNND
2320	FNND	2340	FNND	2360	FNND	2380	FNND
2321	FNND	2341	FNND	2361	FNND	2381	FNND
2322	FNND	2342	FNND	2362	FNND	2382	FNND
2323	FNND	2343	FNND	2363	FNND	2383	FNND

CLASS 25   Bo-Bo

This class are now only used on a few peak passenger workings plus occasional freights and are expected to be withdrawn very soon.

Built: 1960–61.
Builder–Mechanical Parts: BN.
Builder–Electrical Parts: ACEC/SEMG.
Traction Motors: 4 x CF729 axle-hung.
One Hour Rating: 1880 kW.

Maximum Tractive Effort: 196 kN.
Wheel Diameter: 1262 mm.
Weight: 84 tonnes.
Length over Buffers: 18.00 m.
Maximum Speed: 130 km/h.

Originally numbered 125.001–014.

| 2503 | FNND | 2506 | FNND | 2510 | FNND | 2514 | FNND |
| 2505 | FNND | 2507 | FNND | 2513 | FNND | | |

CLASS 25.5   Bo-Bo

Formerly numbered 2515–22, these locos were modified in 1973/4 to dual voltage for working the push-pull Brussels–Amsterdam service for which they received an additional headlamp and a special dark blue livery. Note that only one pantograph is fitted. They were replaced on these duties by Class 11 and are now used on freights from Belgium to Rotterdam Kijfhoek yard, and between Maastricht and Sittard. In 2007, two locos were on hire to Railion Nederland for use on freight over the route to Venlo and Sittard. They will be replaced by Class 11 once the latter are replaced on the Benelux passenger service.

Built: 1960–61. **Systems:** 1500/3000 V DC.
Builder–Mechanical Parts: BN.
Builder–Electrical Parts: ACEC/SEMG.
Traction Motors: 4 x CF729 axle-hung.
One Hour Rating: 1880 kW.

Maximum Tractive Effort: 196 kN.
Wheel Diameter: 1262 mm.
Weight: 85 tonnes.
Length over Buffers: 18.00 m.
Maximum Speed: 130 km/h.

Class-Specific Livery: S Old Benelux push-pull livery (dark blue with a yellow stripe).

Originally numbered 125.015–016, 140.001–006 (later 125.101–106).
Note: After an accident in 1979, 2557 and 2504 changed identities.

2551	(2515)	S	FNND	2555	(2519)	S	FNND	2557	(2521)	S	FNND
2552	(2516)	S	FNND	2556	(2520)	S	FNND	2558	(2522)	S	FNND
2553	(2517)	S	FNND								

CLASS 26   B-B

These locos feature monomotor bogies by Schneider and have two gear ratios giving maximum speeds of 100/130 km/h. Seen all over Belgium, the class is fitted for multiple working with other members of the class and with Class 23 for heavy freights.

Built: 1964–71.
Builder–Mechanical Parts: BN.
Builder–Electrical Parts: ACEC.
Traction Motors: 2 x 2ES508 frame mount
One Hour Rating: 2580 kW.

Maximum Tractive Effort: 235 kN.
Wheel Diameter: 1150 mm.
Weight: 83 tonnes.
Length over Buffers: 17.25 m.
Maximum Speed: 130 km/h.

2601–2620 originally numbered 126.001–005, 126.101–115.

2601	GCR	2610	GCR	2620	GCR	2628	GCR
2602	GCR	2611	GCR	2621	GCR	2629	GCR
2603	GCR	2612	GCR	2622	GCR	2630	GCR
2604	GCR	2613	GCR	2623	GCR	2631	GCR
2605	GCR	2614	GCR	2624	GCR	2632	GCR
2606	GCR	2615	GCR	2625	GCR	2633	GCR
2607	GCR	2617	GCR	2626	GCR	2634	GCR
2608	GCR	2618	GCR	2627	GCR	2635	GCR
2609	GCR	2619	GCR				

CLASS 27 Bo-Bo

Developed after experience with Class 20, these were the first of the 1980s generation of electric locomotives and heralded a new era, being more powerful than their predecessors. Flexicoil suspension. They are used throughout the network on both passenger and freight work. All locos are being equipped with time division multiplex (MUX) equipment for multiple and push-pull working whilst 2742 to 2760 are also receiving Type GF auto couplers at one end for use with Type M6 stock.

Built: 1981–1984.
Builder–Mechanical Parts: BN.
Builder–Electrical Parts: ACEC.
Traction Motors: 4 x LE921S frame mounted.
One Hour Rating: 4380 kW.

Maximum Tractive Effort: 234 kN.
Wheel Diameter: 1250 mm.
Weight: 85 tonnes.
Length over Buffers: 18.65 m.
Maximum Speed: 160 km/h.

Electro-pneumatic braking. Rheostatic braking.

a   Type GF auto coupler fitted.
m   time division multiplex fitted.

2701	NK	2716	NK	2731	m NK	2746	am NK
2702	NK	2717	NK	2732	NK	2747	NK
2703	NK	2718	NK	2733	m NK	2748	m NK
2704	NK	2719	NK	2734	NK	2749	NK
2705	NK	2720	NK	2735	m NK	2750	am NK
2706	NK	2721	NK	2736	m NK	2751	m NK
2707	NK	2722	m NK	2737	m NK	2752	am NK
2708	NK	2723	m NK	2738	m NK	2753	am NK
2709	NK	2724	NK	2739	m NK	2754	am NK
2710	NK	2725	m NK	2740	m NK	2755	NK
2711	NK	2726	NK	2741	am NK	2756	am NK
2712	NK	2727	NK	2742	am NK	2757	m NK
2713	NK	2728	m NK	2743	am NK	2758	a NK
2714	NK	2729	NK	2744	NK	2759	am NK
2715	NK	2730	m NK	2745	m NK	2760	am NK

CLASS 28 (CLASS 186) Bo-Bo

In late 2007, B-Cargo signed a contract with Angel Trains Cargo for the long-term hire of 40 four voltage (1500/3000 V DC, 15/25 kV AC) locomotives, which are mainly needed to operate over the Antwerpen–Aachen West line which is electrified at 3000 V DC as far as Montzen then at 15 kV AC 16.7 Hz from there, across the border, to Aachen West. The locos will also operate into Germany – at least as far as Köln Gremberg under an arragement with Railion known as COBRA. They will also be capable of operation in the Netherlands and Austria and we assume they will take over all cross-border services. This will free most of Class 20 and 55, some Class 23 and 26 plus all Class 25.5. The locos are Bombardier's TRAXX MS design, version DABNL (Germany, Austria, Belgium, Netherlands) and will be built in 2008/9. The locos are known as Class 186 in Germany and elsewhere but will be numbered as Class 28 by B Cargo. Although no announcement has been made, we assume the locos will be maintained by Antwerpen Noord depot. For details see page 121. The first three locos are on short-term loan for passenger services.

Angel Trains Cargo numbers are shown in brackets.

2801	(E 186 123)	2816	(E 186 193)	2830	(E 186 207)
2802	(E 186 124)	2817	(E 186 194)	2831	(E 186 208)
2803	(E 186 125)	2818	(E 186 195)	2832	(E 186 209)
2804	(E 186 181)	2819	(E 186 196)	2833	(E 186 210)
2805	(E 186 182)	2810	(E 186 197)	2834	(E 186 211)
2806	(E 186 183)	2821	(E 186 198)	2835	(E 186 212)
2807	(E 186 184)	2822	(E 186 199)	2836	(E 186 213)
2808	(E 186 185)	2823	(E 186 200)	2837	(E 186 214)
2809	(E 186 186)	2824	(E 186 201)	2838	(E 186 215)
2810	(E 186 187)	2825	(E 186 202)	2839	(E 186 216)
2811	(E 186 188)	2826	(E 186 203)	2840	(E 186 217)
2812	(E 186 189)	2827	(E 186 204)	2841	(E 186 218)
2813	(E 186 190)	2828	(E 186 205)	2842	(E 186 219)
2814	(E 186 191)	2829	(E 186 206)	2843	(E 186 220)
2815	(E 186 192)				

1.3. DIESEL MULTIPLE UNITS

CLASS 41   2-CAR UNITS

These recent units brought new standards of comfort to Belgian branch line services as they have air conditioning, good seating, information displays etc. Besides replacing ancient Classes 44 & 45 they also eliminated the last diesel locomotive-operated passenger trains in Belgium. They are used on IR trains Antwerpen–Neerpelt plus L trains Dinant–Bertrix–Libramont, Bertrix–Rodange, Rodange–Arlon, Charleroi–Couvin, Gent–Eeklo. Gent–Ronse, Gent–Grammont and P trains Aalst–Burst.

AB–B (DMC–DMS).

Built: 2000–2002.
Builder: Alstom Spain.
Wheel Arrangement: 2-B + B-2.
Engine: One Cummins QSK650R of 485 kW per car.
Transmission: Hydraulic. Voith T311 bre.
Length over Couplers: 24.80 + 24.80 m. **Weight:** 49 + 49 tonnes.
Maximum Speed: 120 km/h. **Accommodation:** 12/64 + –/78 1T.

4101	W	FHS	4125	W	FKR	4149	W	FHS	4173	W	FKR
4102	W	GCR	4126	W	FKR	4150	W	FHS	4174	W	FKR
4103	W	GCR	4127	W	FKR	4151	W	FHS	4175	W	FKR
4104	W	GCR	4128	W	FKR	4152	W	FHS	4176	W	FKR
4105	W	GCR	4129	W	FHS	4153	W	FHS	4177	W	FKR
4106	W	GCR	4130	W	FHS	4154	W	MKM	4178	W	FKR
4107	W	GCR	4131	W	FHS	4155	W	FHS	4179	W	FKR
4108	W	GCR	4132	W	FHS	4156	W	FHS	4180	W	FKR
4109	W	GCR	4133	W	FHS	4157	W	MKM	4181	W	FKR
4110	W	MKM	4134	W	FHS	4158	W	MKM	4182	W	FKR
4111	W	FKR	4135	W	FHS	4159	W	MKM	4183	W	FKR
4112	W	FKR	4136	W	FHS	4160	W	MKM	4184	W	FKR
4113	W	GCR	4137	W	FHS	4161	W	MKM	4185	W	FKR
4114	W	GCR	4138	W	FHS	4162	W	MKM	4186	W	FKR
4115	W	FKR	4139	W	FHS	4163	W	MKM	4187	W	FKR
4116	W	FHS	4140	W	FHS	4164	W	MKM	4188	W	FKR
4117	W	FHS	4141	W	FHS	4165	W	MKM	4189	W	FKR
4118	W	GCR	4142	W	FHS	4166	W	FKR	4190	W	FHS
4119	W	GCR	4143	W	FHS	4167	W	FKR	4191	W	FKR
4120	W	GCR	4144	W	FHS	4168	W	FKR	4192	W	FKR
4121	W	FKR	4145	W	FHS	4169	W	FKR	4193	W	FKR
4122	W	FKR	4146	W	FHS	4170	W	FKR	4194	W	FKR
4123	W	MKM	4147	W	FHS	4171	W	FKR	4195	W	FKR
4124	W	FKR	4148	W	FHS	4172	W	FKR	4196	W	FKR

1.4. DIESEL LOCOMOTIVES

Note: All diesel locomotives are in yellow and green livery except where stated otherwise.

CLASS 52   Co-Co

Classes 52, 53 and 54 are part of a large European family of locomotives. The design originated as Nohab/GM and similar locomotives were found in Denmark (Classes MX and MY), Hungary (Class M61) and Norway (Class Di.3). After many complaints from crews new cabs were fitted to almost all locos which substantially altered their appearance. Classes 52 and 53 were originally differentiated due to having a train heating boiler or not. None now have a boiler and all three classes have now been downgraded to hauling infrastructure trains.

Built: 1955.
Builder–Mechanical Parts: AFB.
Builder–Electrical Parts: GM.
Engine: GM 16-567C of 1265 kW at 835 rpm.
Transmission: Electric. Six axle-hung Smit D19 traction motors.
Train Heating: None.   **Wheel Diameter**: 1010 mm.
Weight: 108 tonnes.   **Length over Buffers**: 18.85 m.
Maximum Tractive Effort: 245 kN.   **Maximum Speed**: 120 km/h.

Multiple working fitted. Rheostatic braking.
The original 5201–13 were originally numbered 202.001–013.

5201		I	MKM	5211		I	MKM	5216	(5317)	I	MKM
5205		I	MKM	5212		I	MKM	5217	(5318)	I	MKM
5209		I	MKM	5215	(5302)	I	MKM				

CLASS 53   Co-Co

These are similar to Class 52 but were originally numbered differently because of having no train heating.

Built: 1956–57.
Builder–Mechanical Parts: AFB.
Builder–Electrical Parts: GM.
Engine: GM 16-567C of 1265 kW at 835 rpm.
Transmission: Electric. Six axle-hung Smit D19 traction motors.
Train Heating: None.   **Weight**: 106.6 tonnes.
Maximum Tractive Effort: 245 kN.   **Length over Buffers**: 18.85 m.
Wheel Diameter: 1010 mm.   **Maximum Speed**: 120 km/h.

Rheostatic braking. Multiple working fitted.
The original 5301–19 were originally numbered 203.001–019.

5301		I	MKM	5307	(5206)	I	MKM	5315		I	MKM
5302	(5203)	I	MKM	5309		I	MKM	5316		I	MKM
5303		I	MKM	5311		I	MKM	5318	(5208)	I	MKM
5305		I	MKM	5312		I	MKM	5320	(5210)	I	MKM
5306		I	MKM	5313		I	MKM				

CLASS 54   Co-Co

Similar to Class 52, but no rheostatic braking and an additional headlight.

Built: 1955–57.
Builder–Mechanical Parts: AFB.
Builder–Electrical Parts: GM.
Engine: GM 16-567C of 1265 kW at 835 rpm.
Transmission: Electric. Six Smit D19 axle-hung traction motors.
Train Heating: None.   **Wheel Diameter**: 1010 mm.
Weight: 108 tonnes.   **Length over Buffers**: 18.85 m.
Maximum Tractive Effort: 245 kN.   **Maximum Speed**: 120 km/h.

Multiple working fitted.

Originally numbered 204.001–007.

| 5401 | I | MKM | 5403 | I | MKM | 5404 | H | FNND | 5407 | I | MKM |

CLASS 55　　　　　　　　　　　　　　　　　　　　　　　　Co-Co

Most of the class is based at Liège for freight use on the Liège–Montzen–Aachen line. A few are fitted with ETH and are painted in blue and yellow livery instead of the standard yellow and green. Their passenger work on the Liège–Luxembourg line disappeared when the line was electrified. Locos at Schaarbeek are fitted with TVM430 cab signalling and adapter couplers for rescue work on the Brussels–Lille high speed line. They are stationed in Brussels and Ath. Their livery has an extra red band. Overhauls of the class finished in 2007. They are expected to be replaced by electric locos when the Montzen–Aachen line is electrified in December 2008.

Built: 1961–62.
Builder–Mechanical Parts: BN.
Builder–Electrical Parts: ACEC/SEMG.
Engine: GM 16-567C of 1435 kW at 835 rpm.
Transmission: Electric. Six axle-hung ACEC D57 traction motors.
Train Heating: None (e Electric. ACEC 300 kW alternator).
Weight: 110 tonnes.
Maximum Tractive Effort: 272 kN.　　　　　**Length over Buffers:** 19.55 m.
Wheel Diameter: 1010 mm.　　　　　　　　**Maximum Speed:** 120 km/h.

Rheostatic braking. Multiple working fitted.
t　Fitted with TVM 430 cab signalling.

Originally numbered 205.001–042.

5501	P	t	FSR	5510	C Y e	NK	5519	C Y e	NK	5532	C		NK		
5503	C		NK	5511	P	t FSR	5523	C		NK	5533	C		NK	
5505	C Y e		NK	5512	P	t FSR	5526	C		NK	5535	C		NK	
5506	P	t	FSR	5514	P	t FSR	5528	C		NK	5537	C		NK	
5507	C		NK	5515	C Y e	NK	5529	C Y e	NK	5538	C		NK		
5508	C		NK	5517	C		NK	5530	C		NK	5539	C		NK
5509	P	t	FSR	5518	C		NK	5531	C Y e	NK	5540	C Y e	NK		

CLASS 62　　　　　　　　　　　　　　　　　　　　　　　　Bo-Bo

Originally a mixed traffic locomotive whose use on passenger trains ceased Class 41 DMUs arrived. Most locomotives have now been transferred to Infrabel – the Infrastructure department. Five locos were sold to private operator ACTS in the Netherlands. Infrabel locomotives are maintained by the depots concerned but normally stable in the engineers' own yards and sidings or at construction sites. Four locomotives are equipped with TBL2 signalling to rescue TGV or ICE sets on the Leuven–Liège line.

Built: 1961–66.
Builder–Mechanical Parts: BN.
Builder–Electrical Parts: ACEC.
Engine: GM 12-567C of 1050 kW at 835 rpm.
Transmission: Electric. Four ACEC DN41.1 axle-hung traction motors.
Train Heating: None.　　　　　　　　　**Wheel Diameter:** 1010 mm.
Weight: 78.6 tonnes.　　　　　　　　　**Length over Buffers:** 16.79 m.
Maximum Tractive Effort: 212 kN.　　　**Maximum Speed:** 120 km/h.

Multiple working fitted.
t　Fitted with TBL2 signalling.
E　Fitted with ETCS.

Originally numbered 212.101–231.

6201	I		FKR	6212	I		FKR	6218	I	G	GCR	6227	P	t NK
6202	I		FKR	6213	I		GCR	6219	I G	FKR	6228	I	FKR		
6203	I		FKR	6214	I		GCR	6221	P		FNND	6229	I	FKR
6204	P		FNND	6215	I		NK	6222	I		FKR	6231	I	GCR
6207	I		FNND	6216	I		NK	6223	I		FSR	6236	I	FNND
6210	I		FKR	6217	I		GCR	6225	P	t	NK	6237	I	FSR

6238	I		FKR	6257	I		NK	6283	P		FNND	6311	I		GCR

6238	I		FKR	6257	I		NK	6283	P		FNND	6311	I		GCR
6241	I		NK	6260	P		FNND	6285	I		GCR	6312	I		FNND
6242	I		GCR	6261	I		GCR	6288	I		NK	6313	P	t	NKR
6243	I		NK	6262	I		GCR	6291	I		FNND	6315	P		FNND
6244	P	G	FNND	6263	I		GCR	6292	I		FNND	6316	I		GCR
6246	P		FNND	6264	I	E	FNND	6294	P		FNND	6317	I		FNND
6247	I		GCR	6267	I		NK	6295	I		FNND	6319	I		NK
6249	I		FSR	6268	P		FNND	6296	P		FNND	6320	I		GCR
6250	P		FNND	6274	I		NK	6297	P		FNND	6323	I		GCR
6251	I		NK	6275	I		GCR	6299	P		FNND	6324	P	t	NK
6253	P		FNND	6277	P		FNND	6304	I		FKR	6328	I		GCR
6254	P		FNND	6278	I		GCR	6305	I		NK	6329	I		NK
6255	I		NK	6281	P		FNND	6306	H		NK	6330	I		FNND
6256	P	G	FNND	6282	I		FSR	6309	I		NK	6331	P		FNND

NOTE RE CLASSES 73–82.

Many of these locomotives carry a name on the cabside. This is the radio call sign for the locomotive when used as a shunter. Names are duplicated within the class but not at individual depots. A locomotive being transferred thus may get a new name if this is already in use at its new depot. The list of "named" locomotives is not complete and in some cases actual observations have shown that the depot records are not correct!

CLASS 73   C

General purpose shunters, sometimes used on trip freights. The introduction of Class 77 and reorganisation of freight services has led to the withdrawal of the earlier 7301–7335 batch. All rod coupled shunters are expected to be withdrawn by 2010.

Built: 1973–74 7336–75; 1976–77 7376–95.
Builder: BN.
Engine: Cockerill 6T240CO of 550 kW at 950 r.p.m.
Transmission: Hydraulic. Voith L217u.
Train Heating: None.   **Weight:** 56 tonnes.
Maximum Tractive Effort: 211 kN.   **Length over Buffers:** 11.40 m.
Wheel Diameter: 1262 mm.
Maximum Speed: 30 km/h shunting/60 km/h main line.

a   Auto-couplers for shunting.
m   Multiple working fitted for use in hump yards.
n   Fitted with snowplough.

7382 and 7394 have been sold to RRF in the Netherlands.

7336	C	a	FSR(S)	MEXICO	7367	C		FKR(S)	BILBAO
7337	C		GCR	MALAGA	7368	C		FKR(S)	CARGO
7338	I		FSR	ALBI	7370	C		FSR(S)	ALPHA
7340	I	n	MKM	COBRA	7371	C		FHS(S)	CAPRI
7341	C		MKM(S)		7373	C	a	FSR(S)	COBRA
7346	C		GCR(S)	Domino	7374	C		GCR	CAPRI
7349	C		GCR(S)	EL PASO	7375	C		FSR(S)	ETNA
7350	I		NK	SAFFIER/JAVA	7376	C		GCR(S)	METEOR
7351	I		NK	ECHO	7377	C	m	GCR	MIMOSA
7352	I		GCR	MIMOSA	7378	C	m	GCR(S)	MISTRAL
7353	C		GCR	FOXTROT	7381	C	m	GCR	
7354	I		FSR	JIVARO	7384	C	m	GCR	
7355	I		FSR	FLORAC	7386	C	m	GCR	
7356	C		FKR(S)	NEVADA	7387	C	m	FSR(S)	PAPYRUS
7358	C		GCR	MAZURKA	7388	C	m	GCR	PIRANA
7359	I		GCR	ALABAMA	7389	C	m	GCR	CONDOR
7361	C		GCR(S)	LIMA	7390	C	m	FSR	SAFFIER
7362	C		GCR	MONACO	7391	C	m	FSR	EDELWEISS
7363	C		GCR	VEGA	7392	C	m	FSR	TANGO
7364	C		GCR	NEW YORK	7393	C	m	FSR	KENIA
7365	C		GCR	ATLAS	7395	C	m	FSR	MISTRAL
7366	C		GCR	BRAVO					

CLASS 74   C

Shunters used in pairs around Antwerpen docks. To be withdrawn by 2010.

Built: 1977.
Builder: BN/CFC.
Engine: ABC 6DXS of 550 kW at 750 r.p.m.
Transmission: Hydraulic. Voith L217u.
Train Heating: None.   **Weight:** 59 tonnes.
Maximum Tractive Effort: 196 kN.   **Length over Buffers:** 11.40 m.
Wheel Diameter: 1262 mm.
Maximum Speed: 30 km/h shunting/60 km/h main line.

Multiple working within class and with Class 82.
ma Master unit.
s Slave unit.

7401	C	s	FNND	POLKA	7406	C	ma	FNND	SIRIUS
7402	C	ma	FNND	MARS	7407	C	s	FNND(S)	SALAMBO
7403	C	s	FNND	TANGO	7408	C	ma	FNND	URANUS
7404	C	ma	FNND	OSIRIS	7409	C		FNND	KIMONO
7405	C	s	FNND	MAZURKA	7410	P		FNND	MIKADO

CLASS 77   B-B

These locomotives, ordered in two batches – 90 then another 80 – are for freight train and shunting use and completely replaced Classes 70, 71, 75 and 80. The class is based on the Vossloh Type G1200 but adapted for Belgian conditions with an ABC engine, built in Gent mainly for canal barges! Eighteen are fitted with radio controls and BSI auto couplers for working at Antwerpen Noord, Kinkempois and Gent Zeehaven yards. Twenty have Dutch and German safety equipment. These locos haul Volvo car parts trains between Gent and Bad Bentheim in Germany via the Netherlands and also reach Moers, Duisburg and Wanne-Eickel. The rest are general purpose locomotives and operate throughout Belgium.

Built: 1999–2005.
Builders: Vossloh/Bombardier.
Engine: ABC Type 60DZC-1000 of 1150 kW at 1000 r.p.m.
Transmission: Hydraulic. Voith L4r4zseU2a.
Train Heating: None.   **Weight:** 87.4 tonnes.
Maximum Tractive Effort: 264 kN.   **Length over Buffers:** 15.59 m.
Wheel Diameter: 1000 mm.   **Maximum Speed:** 100/60 km/h.
Multiple Working: Up to three locos may work in multiple.
Class Specific Livery: S Pale grey with yellow solebars, handrails and ends, blue stripe at bottom of cab and narrow red stripe on bonnets.

a Fitted with autocoupler.
d Equipped to operate in Netherlands and Germany.
h Radio fitted for hump shunting.
r Radio control fitted.

7701	C S ah	FNND	ALIBI		7718	C S ra	FKR	CORDOBA
7702	C S ah	FNND	ALPHA		7719	C S r	FNND	DAKAR
7703	C S ah	FNND	BAKOE		7720	C S r	FNND	DELTA
7704	C S ah	FNND	BAMAKO		7721	C S r	FNND	DIAMANT
7705	C S ah	FNND	BANGKOK		7722	C S r	FNND	DOMINO
7706	C S ah	FNND	BARRACUDA		7723	C S r	FNND	ECHO
7707	C S ah	FNND	BILBAO		7724	C S r	FNND	EDELWEISS
7708	C S ah	FNND	BORNEO		7725	C S r	FNND	EL PASO
7709	C S ah	FNND	BRAVO		7726	C S r	FNND	FLORAC
7710	C S r	NK	BUFFALO		7727	C S r	FNND	GRANADA
7711	C S ra	NK	CALCUTTA		7728	C S r	FNND	JAVA
7712	C S ra	NK	CALYPSO		7729	C S r	FNND	
7713	C S ra	FNND	CAPRI		7730	C S r	FNND	
7714	C S ra	FNND	CARGO		7731	C S r	FNND	
7715	C S ra	FKR	CHICAGO		7732	C S r	FNND	
7716	C S ra	FKR	COBRA		7733	C S r	FNND	
7717	C S ra	FKR	COLUMBIA		7734	C S r	FNND	

7735	C	**S**	r	NK	7769	C	**S**	r	NK	7803	C	**S**	r	FKR	7837	C	**S**	r	FNND
7736	C	**S**	r	NK	7770	C	**S**	r	NK	7804	C	**S**	r	FKR	7838	C	**S**	r	FNND
7737	C	**S**	r	GCR	7771	C	**S**	d	FNND	7805	C	**S**	r	FKR	7839	C	**S**	r	FNND
7738	C	**S**	r	GCR	7772	C	**S**	d	FNND	7806	C	**S**	r	FKR	7840	C	**S**	r	FNND
7739	C	**S**	r	GCR	7773	C	**S**	d	FNND	7807	C	**S**	r	FKR	7841	C	**S**	r	FNND
7740	C	**S**	r	GCR	7774	C	**S**	d	FNND	7808	C	**S**	r	FKR	7842	C	**S**	r	FNND
7741	C	**S**	r	GCR	7775	C	**S**	d	FNND	7809	C	**S**	r	FKR	7843	C	**S**	r	FNND
7742	C	**S**	r	GCR	7776	C	**S**	d	FNND	7810	C	**S**	r	FKR	7844	C	**S**	r	FNND
7743	C	**S**	r	GCR	7777	C	**S**	d	FNND	7811	C	**S**	r	FKR	7845	C	**S**	r	FNND
7744	C	**S**	r	GCR	7778	C	**S**	d	FNND	7812	C	**S**	r	FKR	7846	C	**S**	r	FNND
7745	C	**S**	r	GCR	7779	C	**S**	d	FNND	7813	C	**S**	r	FKR	7847	C	**S**	r	FNND
7746	C	**S**	r	GCR	7780	C	**S**	d	FNND	7814	C	**S**	r	FKR	7848	C	**S**	r	FNND
7747	C	**S**	r	GCR	7781	C	**S**	d	FNND	7815	C	**S**	r	FNND	7849	C	**S**	r	FNND
7748	C	**S**	r	GCR	7782	C	**S**	d	FNND	7816	C	**S**	r	FNND	7850	C	**S**	r	FNND
7749	C	**S**	r	GCR	7783	C	**S**	d	FNND	7817	C	**S**	r	FNND	7851	C	**S**	r	FNND
7750	C	**S**	r	NK	7784	C	**S**	d	FNND	7818	C	**S**	r	FNND	7852	C	**S**	r	FNND
7751	C	**S**	r	NK	7785	C	**S**	d	FNND	7819	C	**S**	r	FKR	7853	C	**S**	r	FNND
7752	C	**S**	r	NK	7786	C	**S**	d	FNND	7820	C	**S**	r	FKR	7854	C	**S**	r	FNND
7753	C	**S**	r	NK	7787	C	**S**	d	FNND	7821	C	**S**	r	FKR	7855	C	**S**	r	FNND
7754	C	**S**	r	NK	7788	C	**S**	d	FNND	7822	C	**S**	r	FKR	7856	C	**S**	r	FNND
7755	C	**S**	r	NK	7789	C	**S**	d	FNND	7823	C	**S**	r	GCR	7857	C	**S**	r	FNND
7756	C	**S**	r	NK	7790	C	**S**	d	FNND	7824	C	**S**	r	GCR	7858	C	**S**	r	FNND
7757	C	**S**	r	NK	7791	C	**S**	r	FKR	7825	C	**S**	r	GCR	7859	C	**S**	r	FNND
7758	C	**S**	r	NK	7792	C	**S**	r	FKR	7826	C	**S**	r	GCR	7860	C	**S**	r	FNND
7759	C	**S**	r	NK	7793	C	**S**	r	FKR	7827	C	**S**	r	GCR	7861	C	**S**	r	FNND
7760	C	**S**	r	NK	7794	C	**S**	r	FKR	7828	C	**S**	r	GCR	7862	C	**S**	r	FNND
7761	C	**S**	r	NK	7795	C	**S**	r	FKR	7829	C	**S**	r	GCR	7863	C	**S**	r	FNND
7762	C	**S**	r	NK	7796	C	**S**	r	FKR	7830	C	**S**	r	GCR	7864	C	**S**	r	FNND
7763	C	**S**	r	NK	7797	C	**S**	r	FKR	7831	C	**S**	r	GCR	7865	C	**S**	r	FNND
7764	C	**S**	r	NK	7798	C	**S**	r	FKR	7832	C	**S**	r	FNND	7866	C	**S**	d	FNND
7765	C	**S**	r	NK	7799	C	**S**	r	FKR	7833	C	**S**	r	FNND	7867	C	**S**	d	FNND
7766	C	**S**	r	NK	7800	C	**S**	r	FKR	7834	C	**S**	r	FNND	7868	C	**S**	d	FNND
7767	C	**S**	r	NK	7801	C	**S**	r	FKR	7835	C	**S**	r	FNND	7869	C	**S**	d	FNND
7768	C	**S**	r	NK	7802	C	**S**	r	FKR	7836	C	**S**	r	FNND	7870	C	**S**	d	FNND

CLASS 80   C

Formerly used in the Brussels area, the last loco is used for shunting in Salzinnes works. A version of the DB Class 360 (V60) built under licence. Many withdrawn locos have been sold abroad, particularly to Italian track maintenance firms.

Built: 1960–1963.
Builder: ABR.
Engine: Maybach GTO6A of 480 kW at 1400 r.p.m.
Transmission: Hydraulic. Voith L37z Ub.
Train Heating: None.
Maximum Tractive Effort: 173 kN.
Wheel Diameter: 1262 mm.

Weight: 52 tonnes.
Length over Buffers: 10.360 m.
Maximum Speed: 30 km/h.

Originally numbered 260.035.

8035	P	FAZ

CLASS 82   C

General purpose shunters, sometimes used for trip workings. To be withdrawn by 2010.

Built: 1965/6 8201–55; 1972/3 8256–75.
Builder: ABR (BN 8241–45/8256–75).
Engine: ABC 6DXS of 480 kW at 750 r.p.m.
Transmission: Hydraulic. Voith L217u.
Train Heating: None.

Weight: 57 (59 m, 56 s) tonnes.
Maximum Tractive Effort: 191 kN.
Wheel Diameter: 1262 mm.
Length over Buffers: 11.170 (11.320 s) m.
Maximum Speed: 60 km/h.

a Fitted with BSI autocoupler.
c Compressed air drier for shunting Eurostar sets at Forest depot.
m Fitted for multiple working within class and with Class 74 around Antwerpen.
n Fitted with snowplough.

8201–55 were originally numbered 262.001–055.

8203	C		FSR(S)	TOLEDO	8242	P		FAZ	ALBATROS
8204	C	c	FSR	NEBRASKA	8243	C		FSR(S)	MIRANDA
8205	C	a	NK	CAPRI	8245	C		NK(S)	DELTA
8209	C		FSR	ALPHA	8248	C		FNND	ETNA
8210	C		FSR	ONTARIO	8250	P		FNND	MEXICO
8211	C		FSR	NAPOLI	8251	C	n	NK(S)	ETNA
8212	C		NK(S)	HERMES	8252	I		NK	ERATO
8214	C		NK	ATLANTA	8253	C		NK(S)	LIMA
8215	C	a	NK	TIRANO	8255	C		NK(S)	POLKA
8216	C		NK	COBRA	8256	C	m	FNND	KATAR
8217	C		FSR	BAKOU	8257	C	m	FNND	KENIA
8218	P		FAZ	ALBI	8258	C	m	NK	LIMA
8219	C		FSR	ATLANTA	8259	C	m	NK	MALAGA
8221	I	n	NK	COLIBRI	8260	C	m	FNND(S)	MEXICO
8223	I	n	NK	BRAVO	8261	C	m	NK	MONACO
8226	C		NK(S)	RUBIS	8262	C	m	FNND	NAPOLI
8227	C		NK	BOLERO	8263	C	m	FNND	NEBRASKA
8228	C		NK(S)	DOMINO	8264	C	m	FNND	NEVADA
8229	C		NK(S)	BUFFALO	8265	C	m	FNND	NEW YORK
8231	C		NK	COLORADO	8266	C	m	FNND	OSAKA
8232	P		FAZ	BOLERO	8268	C	m	FNND	PEKING
8234	C		NK	CONDOR	8269	C	m	NK	PORTO-RICO
8235	C		FNND	PALMA	8270	C	m	FNND	RIMINI
8236	P		FAZ	URANUS	8271	C	m	FNND	SUMATRA
8237	C	a	NK	KASAI	8272	C	m	FSR(S)	TIRANA
8238	C		NK(S)	BORNEO	8274	C	m	FNND(S)	TORONTO
8239	C	a	NK	DAKAR					

CLASS 91   B

The first ten of this class were originally numbered 9001–10. Locos were rebuilt in the late 1970s with more powerful engines and in some cases lengthened frames (marked *) ready for automatic couplers! Many have been made spare by changes in freight workings and have been transferred to departmental use, sold or scrapped. All remaining locos are used as depot or works pilots.

Built: 1961–64.
Builders: Cockerill (9101–10), ABR (9111–9135), BN (9136–60).
Engine: GM 12V71N of 245 kW at 1800 r.p.m.
Transmission: Hydraulic. Esco Power Twin Disc 11500 HS390.
Train Heating: None   **Weight:** 33.8 (35*) tonnes.
Maximum Tractive Effort: 96 kN.   **Length over Buffers:** 6.625 m (8.055 m.*)
Wheel Diameter: 920 mm.
Maximum Speed: 20 km/h shunting/40 km/h main line.

Originally numbered 230.001–010/101–150.

9109	P		FKR		9128	P		GCR		9138	P	§	FKR		9152	P		FKR
9111	P		FHS		9132	P		FKR		9146	P	§	NK		9153	P		MKM
9116	P	§	FHS		9134	P		FHS(S)		9147	P	§	FAZ		9156	P	§	NK
9119	P		FHS		9135	P	§	MKM		9149	P		GCR		9158	P	§	NK
9123	P		FKR		9136	P	§	FKR		9150	P		FKR		9159	P	§	MKM
9124	P		FHS															

1.5. SELF-PROPELLED DEPARTMENTAL STOCK

This series consists mainly of overhead line inspection units. Full details of these are not available.

ES200 SERIES

Built new 1971–72.

ES205   FEO |

ES400 SERIES

Conversions from Class 43 DMUs.

* Unpowered.

ES401 (4307)	FSR	ES404 (4319) **Y** MKM		ES406 (4306)	FKR
ES402 (4325)	GCR	ES405 (4326) * **Y** FNND		ES410 (4315)	NK
ES403 (4328)	GCR				

ES500 SERIES

In generally re-equipping itself, Belgian Railways acquired some new overhead line units which are similar to ÖBB Class X 552. The arrival of these new units allowed older ES 100 and ES 200 cars to be withdrawn.

Built: 1996–99.
Builder: Matisa, Roma, Italy.
Wheel Arrangement: B–2.
Engine: Deutz BF8M1015C of 330 kW.
Auxilary Engine: Deutz BF6M1012 of 93 kW.
Transmission: Hydraulic. Voith T211 rzz.
Weight in Full Working Order: 55 tonnes.
Length over Buffers: 16.04 m.
Wheel Diameter: 840 mm.
Maximum Speed: 100 km/h.

ES501	**Y** GCR	ES505	**Y** FEO	ES509	**Y** FKR	ES513	**Y** FHS
ES502	**Y** FNND	ES506	**Y** GCR	ES510	**Y** GCR	ES514	**Y** FKR
ES503	**Y** FKR	ES507	**Y** FSR	ES511	**Y** NK	ES515	**Y** NK
ES504	**Y** FNND	ES508	**Y** NK	ES512	**Y** FHS		

1.6. LOCO-HAULED COACHING STOCK

DEVELOPMENTS

Belgian Railways had a fleet of around 1300 hauled coaches in late 2007 of which 576 were Type M4, 245 Type M6, 163 TYpe I11, 130 Type M5, 93 Type I10 and 78 Type I6.

There have been major changes to Belgian hauled stock since the last edition of Benelux Railways. All Type M2 stock has been withdrawn, except a short rake of preserved stock, the last being replaced by Class 41 DMUs. The introduction of Type I11 stock and a severe cutback in international services has meant that most Type I6 and I10 former international stock has been cascaded to internal peak hour services and all Type I5 couchettes have been withdrawn. Type M6 double-deck stock has been introduced on some InterCity and peak services, allowing the withdrawal of all Type K4 stock, some of which was sold to Senegal. The refurbishment of Type M4 coaches was almost complete by the end of 2007. The much-loathed Type M5 double-deck stock is to be refurbished from 2008, getting a comprehensive makeover.

Following the first 210 Type M6 double-deck coaches, two further batches totalling 160 coaches were ordered, this time including 50 driving trailers. These started to enter service in late 2007. The first trains to use the driving trailers are IC services between Blankenberge/Knokke and Hasselt/Tongeren. Next will be Antwerpen–Brussels–Charleroi IC services which need to be topped-and-tailed by two locomotives due to tight turnrounds. Class 27 are being fitted with time division multiplex equipment and auto couplers for this work and it is possible to couple two rakes of loco plus M6 stock in multiple in the same way as Class 1700 and DDm stock is multipled in the Netherlands. Unfortunately, initial operation in this mode was unreliable.

NUMBERING

All Belgian stock has the full UIC number painted on the side of the coach in the centre, and its "old" number, duly crossed out, either on the bottom left-hand corner or on the end of the vehicle. All stock has an "old" number, including new stock being delivered! "Old" numbers are used in this section, with a note on the UIC series in the class details.

TYPES

There are now only two basic categories of hauled stock in Belgium:

* Type I stock is for international use with 2+1 seating in open firsts, 2+2 seating in open seconds and six seats in both first and second class compartments. I stock is now also being used on non-international services.
* Type M stock is of an open design and has larger doors placed closer to the middle of the train. Seating in M stock is 2+2 in first class and 3+2 in second. Until now, both the latter types have been to a lower standard than in most other European countries but M6 stock is a major improvement, with 2+2 seating in second class. Type M4 stock is used on several InterCity services but M5 stock is restricted to peak trains.

LIVERIES

* Livery on preserved M2 stock is plain dark green.
* M4/5 stock was introduced in a maroon livery lined in white but refurbished M4 stock was repainted in the new pale grey livery with red doors and blue trim and this was then also applied to refurbished Type I stock.
* Prior to Type I11, all Type I stock was turned out in orange with a white stripe. This had almost disappeared by the end of 2007. A small number of international coaches were painted in the "Memling" livery (for the train of that name which ran from Oostende to Dortmund). This livery is similar to that on "Break" EMUs.
* Type I11 and M6 are in a very pale grey livery with red doors and a black window band.
* Couchettes are dark blue with a pink band.

Ex-WAGONS LITS SLEEPING CAR TYPE   T2

Used only on the Bergland Express between brussels and Austria run by a private company.

Built: 1974–75.
Bogies: Minden-Deutz M6.
Accommodation: 36 berths
Heating: Air conditioned.
UIC Numbers: 71 88 75 70 156–161.
Class Specific Livery: S Dark blue with red band.

Builder: CF.
Length over Buffers: 26.40 m.
Weight: 61 tonnes.
Maximum Speed: 160 km/h.

5108	S	5109	S	5110	S	5151	S	5152	S	5153	S

TYPE I6   CORRIDOR FIRST

Built: 1977.
Bogies: Fiat Y0270.S.
Accommodation: 54/– 2T (48/– 2T*).
Heating: Electric.
UIC Numbers: 61 88 19 70 601–620.

Builder: BN.
Length over Buffers: 26.40 m.
Weight: 43 tonnes.
Maximum Speed: 160 km/h.

* Modified with cycle compartment.

11601	N	11605	N	11609	N	11612	N	11615	N	*	11618	N
11602	N	11606	N	11610	N	11613	N	11616	N		11619	N
11603	N	11607	N	11611	N	11614	N	11617	N		11620	N
11604	N	11608	N									

TYPE I10   OPEN FIRST

Built: 1988.
Bogies: Fiat Y0270.S.
Accommodation: 66/– 2T.
Heating: Electric.
UIC Numbers: 51 88 11 70 001–015.

Builder: BN.
Length over Buffers: 26.40 m.
Weight: 41 tonnes.
Maximum Speed: 160 km/h.

11701	N	11704	N	11707	N	11710	N	11712	N	11714	N
11702	N	11705	N	11708	N	11711	N	11713	N	11715	N
11703	N	11706	N	11709	N						

TYPE I11   OPEN FIRST

Built: 1995–98.
Bogies: ANF Type 36.
Accommodation: 60/– 2T.
Heating: Electric.
UIC Numbers: 61 88 10 90 001–036.

Builder: Bombardier.
Length over Buffers: 26.40 m.
Weight: 45 tonnes.
Maximum Speed: 200 km/h.

Push-pull fitted.

11801	W	11807	W	11813	W	11819	W	11825	W	11831	W
11802	W	11808	W	11814	W	11820	W	11826	W	11832	W
11803	W	11809	W	11815	W	11821	W	11827	W	11833	W
11804	W	11810	W	11816	W	11822	W	11828	W	11834	W
11805	W	11811	W	11817	W	11823	W	11829	W	11835	W
11806	W	11812	W	11818	W	11824	W	11830	W	11836	W

TYPE I6   CORRIDOR SECOND

Built: 1977–78.
Bogies: Fiat Y0270.S.
Accommodation: –/66 2T 1W.
Heating: Electric.
UIC Numbers: 61 88 21 70 601–659.

Builder: BN.
Length over Buffers: 26.40 m.
Weight: 43 tonnes.
Maximum Speed: 160 km/h.

Note: Some of these vehicles have been converted to couchettes and numbered in the 146XX series.

12601	N	12604	N	12607	N	12609	N	12611	N	12614	N
12603	N	12605	N	12608	N	12610	N	12613	N	12615	N

12616	N	12622	N	12630	N	12638	N	12645	N	12653	N
12617	N	12625	N	12631	N	12640	N	12648	N	12654	N
12618	N	12626	N	12634	N	12641	N	12650	N	12656	N
12619	N	12627	N	12635	N	12642	N	12651	N	12658	N
12620	N	12629	N	12636	N	12643	N	12652	N	12659	N
12621	N										

TYPE I10   OPEN SECOND

Built: 1987–88.
Bogies: Fiat Y0270.S.
Accommodation: –/86 2T.
Weight: 41 tonnes. (42.5 tonnes 12746–79).
Heating: Electric. 12746–79 are air conditioned.
UIC Numbers: 51 88 21 70 001–045, 61 88 21 70 046–074.

Builder: BN.
Length over Buffers: 26.40 m.
Maximum Speed: 160 km/h.

12701	N	12714	N	12727	N	12739	N	12751	N	12763	N
12702	N	12715	N	12728	N	12740	N	12752	N	12764	N
12703	N	12716	N	12729	N	12741	N	12753	N	12765	N
12704	N	12717	N	12730	N	12742	N	12754	N	12766	N
12705	N	12718	N	12731	N	12743	N	12755	N	12767	N
12706	N	12719	N	12732	N	12744	N	12756	N	12768	N
12707	N	12720	N	12733	N	12745	N	12757	N	12769	N
12708	N	12721	N	12734	N	12746	N	12758	N	12770	N
12709	N	12722	N	12735	N	12747	N	12759	N	12771	N
12710	N	12723	N	12736	N	12748	N	12760	N	12772	N
12711	N	12724	N	12737	N	12749	N	12761	N	12773	N
12712	N	12725	N	12738	N	12750	N	12762	N	12774	N
12713	N	12726	N									

TYPE I11   OPEN SECOND

Built: 1995–98.
Bogies: ANF Type 36.
Accommodation: –/80 2T.
Heating: Electric.
UIC Numbers: 61 88 20 90 001–106.

Builder: Bombardier.
Length over Buffers: 26.40 m.
Weight: 45 tonnes.
Maximum Speed: 200 km/h.

Push-pull fitted.

12801	W	12819	W	12837	W	12855	W	12873	W	12890	W
12802	W	12820	W	12838	W	12856	W	12874	W	12891	W
12803	W	12821	W	12839	W	12857	W	12875	W	12892	W
12804	W	12822	W	12840	W	12858	W	12876	W	12893	W
12805	W	12823	W	12841	W	12859	W	12877	W	12894	W
12806	W	12824	W	12842	W	12860	W	12878	W	12895	W
12807	W	12825	W	12843	W	12861	W	12879	W	12896	W
12808	W	12826	W	12844	W	12862	W	12880	W	12897	W
12809	W	12827	W	12845	W	12863	W	12881	W	12898	W
12810	W	12828	W	12846	W	12864	W	12882	W	12899	W
12811	W	12829	W	12847	W	12865	W	12883	W	12900	W
12812	W	12830	W	12848	W	12866	W	12884	W	12901	W
12813	W	12831	W	12849	W	12867	W	12885	W	12902	W
12814	W	12832	W	12850	W	12868	W	12886	W	12903	W
12815	W	12833	W	12851	W	12869	W	12887	W	12904	W
12816	W	12834	W	12852	W	12870	W	12888	W	12905	W
12817	W	12835	W	12853	W	12871	W	12889	W	12906	W
12818	W	12836	W	12854	W	12872	W						

TYPE I6   SECOND COUCHETTE

Built: 1977–78. Converted from corridor second.
Builder: BN.
Bogies: Fiat Y0270.S.
Accommodation: –/66 (66 berths) 2T 1W.
Heating: Electric.
UIC Numbers: 61 88 50 70 601–615.

Length over Buffers: 26.40 m.
Weight: 47 tonnes.
Maximum Speed: 160 km/h.

14601	(12602)	C	14606	(12628)	C	14611	(12644)	C
14602	(12606)	C	14607	(12632)	C	14612	(12646)	C
14603	(12612)	C	14608	(12633)	C	14613	(12649)	C
14604	(12623)	C	14609	(12637)	C	14614	(12655)	C
14605	(12624)	C	14610	(12639)	C	14615	(12657)	C

TYPE I10   RESTAURANT CAR

Built: 1987–88. Converted from open seconds.
Bogies: Fiat Y0270.S.
Accommodation: –/48 2T.
Weight: 47 tonnes.
Heating: Electric. Air conditioned.
UIC Numbers: 61 88 88-90 005–008.

Builder: BN.
Length over Buffers: 26.40 m.
Maximum Speed: 200 km/h.

16005	(12775)	N	16007	(12777)	N	16008	(12778)	N
16006	(12776)	N					

TYPE ID   BRAKE VAN

Built: 1978.
Bogies: Fiat YO 332.
Accommodation: None.
Heating: Electric.
UIC Numbers: 51 88 95 70 901–934.

Builder: BN.
Length over Buffers: 26.40 m.
Weight: 39 tonnes.
Maximum Speed: 160 km/h.

17401 has been converted to 00800.

17406	N b	17413	N	17419	N	17425	N	17429	N	17432	N b
17412	N	17414	N	17424	N	17428	N	17431	N b	17433	N b

TYPE I1   EXHIBITION VEHICLES

Built: 1933.
Bogies: Schlieren 27.
Accommodation: None.
Heating: Electric.
Class Specific Livery: S Painted as required.
UIC Numbers: 60 88 99 40 025–030/035–037.

Builder: .
Length over Buffers: 22.30 m.
Weight: 45 tonnes.
Maximum Speed: 140 km/h.

Note: These vehicles are based at Schaarbeek.

17805	S	17807	S	17809	S	17810	S	17816	S	17817	S
17806	S	17808	S								

TYPE I6   BAR

Built: 1978.
Bogies: Fiat 31.
Accommodation: None.
Heating: Electric. Air conditioned.
Computer Number: 61 88 89 70 002-6.

Builder: BN.
Length over Buffers: 26.40 m.
Weight: 48 tonnes.
Maximum Speed: 160 km/h.

17902   N

TYPE I10   BAR

Built: 1988. Converted from second.
Builder: BN.
Bogies: Fiat Y0270.S
Accommodation: –/37 2T.
Weight: 48 tonnes.
Heating: Electric. Air conditioned.
UIC Numbers: 61 88 88 80 003-0.
Class Specific Livery: S Grey and white.

Length over Buffers: 26.40 m.
Maximum Speed: 160 km/h.

17903   (12780)   S

TYPE I11 DRIVING OPEN SECOND

Built: 1995–98.
Bogies: ANF Type 36.
Accommodation: –/58 1T.
Heating: Electric.
UIC Numbers: 61 88 80 90 001–021.

Builder: Bombardier.
Length over Buffers: 26.40 m.
Weight: 45 tonnes.
Maximum Speed: 200 km/h.

Push-pull fitted. Cabs similar to those on Class 13 locomotives.

19801	N	19805	N	19809	N	19813	N	19816	N	19819	N
19802	N	19806	N	19810	N	19814	N	19817	N	19820	N
19803	N	19807	N	19811	N	19815	N	19818	N	19821	N
19804	N	19808	N	19812	N						

TYPE K1 OPEN FIRST

Museum stock for use on historic trains. Others preserved by PFT/TSP.

Built: 1934–35.
Bogies: Pennsylvania.
Accommodation: 64/– 1T.
Heating: Electric.
UIC Numbers: 50 88 18 40 008–030.

Builder: BM/BND.
Length over Buffers: 23.32 m.
Weight: 43.1 tonnes.
Maximum Speed: 140 km/h.

| 21008 | G | 21017 | G | 21023 | G | 21026 | G | 21029 | G | 21030 | G |
| 21015 | G | | | | | | | | | | |

TYPE M2 OPEN FIRST

Built: 1958–60. Museum stock.
Bogies: Schlieren Type 23.
Accommodation: 68/– 1T.
Heating: Dual.
UIC Number: 50 88 18 48 622.

Builder: BN/Ragheno/St. Eloi.
Length over Buffers: 24.00 m.
Weight: 34.5 tonnes.
Maximum Speed: 125 km/h.

| 41022 | |

TYPE M2 OPEN SECOND

Built: 1958–60. Museum stock.
Bogies: Schlieren Type 23.
Accommodation: –/106 1T.
Heating: Dual.
UIC Numbers: 50 88 20 48 606/629/667/751/803/806.

Builder: BN/Ragheno/St. Eloi.
Length over Buffers: 24.00 m.
Weight: 33.6 tonnes.
Maximum Speed: 125 km/h.

| 42306 | 42329 | 42367 | 42451 | 42503 | 42506 |

TYPE M2 OPEN COMPOSITE

Built: 1958–60. Museum stock.
Bogies: Schlieren Type 23.
Accommodation: 36/47 1T.
Heating: Dual.
UIC Number: 50 88 39 48 669.

Builder: BN/Ragheno/St. Eloi.
Length over Buffers: 24.00 m.
Weight: 34.4 tonnes.
Maximum Speed: 125 km/h.

| 43269 | |

TYPE M2 DRIVING BRAKE OPEN SECOND

Built: 1958–60. Push-pull driving trailer. Museum stock.
Builder: BN. Museum stock.
Bogies: Schlieren Type 23.
Accommodation: –/74 1T.
Heating: Dual.
UIC Number: 50 88 87 48 611.

Length over Buffers: 24.00 m.
Weight: 32.4 tonnes.
Maximum Speed: 120 km/h.

| 49911 | |

TYPE M4 OPEN FIRST

Built: 1979–80.
Bogies: Fiat Type Y32.
Accommodation: 72/– 1T).
Heating: Electric.
UIC Numbers: 50 88 19 78 001–049.

Builder: BN.
Length over Buffers: 24.26 m.
Weight: 38 tonnes.
Maximum Speed: 160 km/h.

p Push-pull fitted.

51001	N	51010	N	51018	N	51026	N	51034	N p
51002	N	51011	N	51019	N	51027	N	51035	N p
51003	N	51012	N	51020	N	51028	N	51036	N p
51004	N	51013	N	51021	N	51029	N	51037	N p
51005	N	51014	N	51022	N	51030	N	51038	N p
51006	N	51015	N	51023	N	51031	N	51039	N p
51007	N	51016	N	51024	N	51032	N	51040	N p
51008	N	51017	N	51025	N	51033	N	51041	N
51009	N								

51042	N p
51043	N p
51044	N p
51045	N p
51046	N p
51047	N p
51048	N p
51049	N p

TYPE M5 OPEN FIRST

Push-pull fitted double-deck stock.

Built: 1986–87.
Bogies: .
Accommodation: 142/– 2T.
Heating: Electric.
UIC Numbers: 50 88 16 38 001–015.

Builder: BN.
Length over Buffers: 26.40 m.
Weight: 44 tonnes.
Maximum Speed: 140 km/h.

51501	51504	51507	51510	51512	51514
51502	51505	51508	51511	51513	51515
51503	51506	51509			

TYPE M4 OPEN SECOND

Built: 1980–83.
Bogies: Fiat Type Y32.
Accommodation: –/95 1T.
Heating: Electric.
UIC Numbers: 50 88 20 78 001–430.

Builder: BN.
Length over Buffers: 24.26 m.
Weight: 39 tonnes.
Maximum Speed: 160 km/h.

p Push-pull fitted.

52001	N	52024	N	52048	N	52071	N	52094	N	52117	N
52002	N	52025	N	52049	N	52072	N	52095	N	52118	N
52003	N	52026	N	52050	N	52073	N	52096	N	52119	N
52004	N	52027	N	52051	N	52074	N	52097	N	52120	N
52005	N	52028	N	52052	N	52075	N	52098	N	52121	N
52006	N	52029	N	52053	N	52076	N	52099	N	52122	N
52007	N	52030	N	52054	N	52077	N	52100	N	52123	N
52008	N	52031	N	52055	N	52078	N	52101	N	52124	N
52009	N	52032	N	52056	N	52079	N	52102	N	52125	N
52010	N	52033	N	52057	N	52080	N	52103	N	52126	N
52011	N	52034	N	52058	N	52081	N	52104	N	52127	N
52012	N	52035	N	52059	N	52082	N	52105	N	52129	N
52013	N	52036	N	52060	N	52083	N	52106	N	52130	N
52014	N	52037	N	52061	N	52084	N	52107	N	52131	N
52015	N	52038	N	52062	N	52085	N	52108	N	52132	N
52016	N	52040	N	52063	N	52086	N	52109	N	52133	N
52017	N	52041	N	52064	N	52087	N	52110	N	52134	N
52018	N	52042	N	52065	N	52088	N	52111	N	52135	N
52019	N	52043	N	52066	N	52089	N	52112	N	52136	N
52020	N	52044	N	52067	N	52090	N	52113	N	52137	N
52021	N	52045	N	52068	N	52091	N	52114	N	52138	N
52022	N	52046	N	52069	N	52092	N	52115	N	52139	N
52023	N	52047	N	52070	N	52093	N	52116	N	52140	N

52141	N	52191	N	52239	N	52287	N p	52335	N p	52383	N p
52142	N	52192	N	52240	N	52288	N p	52336	N p	52384	N p
52143	N	52193	N	52241	N	52289	N p	52337	N p	52385	N p
52144	N	52194	N	52242	N	52290	N p	52338	N p	52386	N p
52145	N	52195	N	52243	N	52291	N p	52339	N p	52387	N p
52146	N	52196	N	52244	N	52292	N p	52340	N p	52388	N p
52147	N	52197	N	52245	N	52293	N p	52341	N p	52389	N p
52148	N	52198	N	52246	N	52294	N p	52342	N p	52390	N p
52149	N	52199	N	52247	N	52295	N p	52343	N p	52391	N p
52150	N	52200	N	52248	N p	52296	N p	52344	N p	52392	N p
52152	N	52201	N	52249	N p	52297	N p	52345	N p	52393	N p
52153	N	52202	N	52250	N p	52298	N p	52346	N p	52394	N p
52154	N	52203	N	52251	N p	52299	N p	52347	N p	52395	N p
52155	N	52204	N	52252	N p	52300	N p	52348	N p	52396	N p
52156	N	52205	N	52253	N p	52301	N p	52349	N p	52397	N p
52157	N	52206	N	52254	N p	52302	N p	52350	N p	52398	N p
52158	N	52207	N	52255	N p	52303	N p	52351	N p	52399	N p
52159	N	52208	N	52256	N p	52304	N p	52352	N p	52400	N p
52160	N	52209	N	52257	N p	52305	N p	52353	N p	52401	N p
52161	N	52210	N	52258	N p	52306	N p	52354	N p	52402	N p
52162	N	52211	N	52259	N p	52307	N p	52355	N p	52403	N p
52163	N	52212	N	52260	N p	52308	N p	52356	N p	52404	N p
52164	N	52213	N	52261	N p	52309	N p	52357	N p	52405	N p
52165	N	52214	N	52262	N p	52310	N p	52358	N p	52406	N p
52166	N	52215	N	52263	N p	52311	N p	52359	N p	52407	N p
52167	N	52216	N	52264	N p	52312	N p	52360	N p	52408	N p
52168	N	52217	N	52265	N p	52313	N p	52361	N p	52409	N p
52169	N	52218	N	52266	N p	52314	N p	52362	N p	52410	N p
52170	N	52219	N	52267	N p	52315	N p	52363	N p	52411	N p
52171	N	52220	N	52268	N p	52316	N p	52364	N p	52412	N p
52172	N	52221	N	52269	N p	52317	N p	52365	N p	52413	N p
52173	N	52222	N	52270	N p	52318	N p	52366	N p	52414	N p
52174	N	52223	N	52271	N p	52319	N p	52367	N p	52415	N p
52175	N	52224	N	52272	N p	52320	N p	52368	N p	52416	N p
52176	N	52225	N	52273	N p	52321	N p	52369	N p	52417	N p
52177	N	52226	N	52274	N p	52322	N p	52370	N p	52418	N p
52178	N	52227	N	52275	N p	52323	N p	52371	N p	52419	N p
52179	N	52228	N	52276	N p	52324	N p	52372	N p	52420	N p
52180	N	52229	N	52277	N p	52325	N p	52373	N p	52421	N p
52181	N	52230	N	52278	N p	52326	N p	52374	N p	52422	N p
52182	N	52231	N	52279	N p	52327	N p	52375	N p	52423	N p
52183	N	52232	N	52280	N p	52328	N p	52376	N p	52424	N p
52184	N	52233	N	52281	N p	52329	N p	52377	N p	52425	N p
52185	N	52234	N	52282	N p	52330	N p	52378	N p	52426	N p
52186	N	52235	N	52283	N p	52331	N p	52379	N p	52427	N p
52187	N	52236	N	52284	N p	52332	N p	52380	N p	52428	N p
52188	N	52237	N	52285	N p	52333	N p	52381	N p	52429	N p
52189	N	52238	N	52286	N p	52334	N p	52382	N p	52430	N p
52190	N										

TYPE M5

OPEN SECOND

Push-pull fitted double-deck stock.

Built: 1986–87.
Builder: BN .
Bogies: .
Accommodation: –/146 2T.
Heating: Electric.
UIC Numbers: 50 88 26 38 001–097.

Length over Buffers: 26.40 m.
Weight: 43.8 tonnes.
Maximum Speed: 140 km/h.

52501	52505	52509	52513	52517	52521
52502	52506	52510	52514	52518	52522
52503	52507	52511	52515	52519	52523
52504	52508	52512	52516	52520	52524

▲ Class AM82 "Break" EMU No. 324 in "Memling" livery approaches Brussels Midi on 13 September 2005.

▼ Class AM79 EMU No. 775 approaches Brussels Midi later on the same day. **John P. Robinson (2)**

▲ Type AM75 4-car EMU No. 803 arrives at Brussels Midi on 2 July 2007.   **Colin J. Marsden**

▼ Class AM89 "Snorkel" 2-car EMU 911at Lier with the 13.12 Turnhout–Antwerpen on 6 April 2006.
Brian Denton

▲ Three Class AM96 3-car units led by unit 539 form IC4530, the 09.40 Antwerpen Centraal–Brussels Midi on 9 November 2006.   **Keith Fender**

▼ There is now only one type of DMU operating in Belgium, the Class 41. A pair of them, 4149 and 4138 are seen at Lier on 6 April 2006 with the 14.18 Antwerpen–Neerpelt.   **Brian Denton**

▲ Class 13 No. 1345 heads the 15.36 Antwerpen–Oostende formed of 110 stock through Berchem on 9 September 2006. **Brian Denton**

▼ Class 15 No. 1504 stands at Liège Guillemins on the 16.18 to Gouvy. **W.J. Freebury**

Ⓑ 53

▲ Class 16 No. 1602 heads train P8002, the 16.38 Schaarbeek–Oostende through Brussels Midi on 2 June 2006. **Brian Denton**

▼ SNCB/NMBS Class 20 No. 2016 stabled at Luxembourg station on 4 November 2006. **W.J. Freebury**

Ⓑ

▲ Class 21 No. 2108 approaches Brussels Noord on 7 July 2006 with train IC4518 Brussels Midi–Antwerpen Centraal formed of the new Class 111 stock. **Chris Wilson**

▼ Class 22 No. 2240 at Brussels Midi on 22 March 2006 with the 16.57 Schaarbeek–Braine-le-Comte. **Brian Denton**

▲ A pair of Class 23s Nos. 2347 and 2340 pass through Berchem with a train of iron ore.

Brian Denton

▼ Class 26 2624 stabled at Ronet Yard in June 2006.   **Steve Phillips**

Dual voltage Class 25/5 No. 2551 heads a southbound freight through Lage Zwaluwe (Netherlands).

▲ Class 27 No. 2755 departs Brussels with the 15.53 IC service to Antwerpen on 2 July 2007 formed of the new 111 double-deck stock. **Colin J. Marsden**

▼ Class 53 No. 5301 at Schaarbeek on 27 April 2007 with an engineers' train in connection with the new Leuven–Schaarbeek line. **Keith Fender**

▲ Class 55s Nos. 5523 and 5539 at Bressoux on 8 November 2006 with a Montzen–Kinkempois freight. **Keith Fender**

▼ Class 62 No. 6291 stabled at Lier on 6 April 2006. **Brian Denton**

▲ Class 84 8441 at Antwerpen Noord on 13 November 2004. **Keith Fender**

▼ Class 91 9116 at Hasselt depot on 7 October 2006. **Steve Phillips**

▲ Class 73 7355 at Schaerbeek depot on 7 October 2006. **Steve Phillips (2)**

▼ Class 82 8228 at Kinkempois on 18 June 2006.

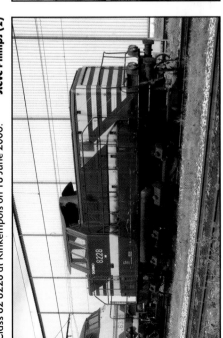

SNCB 7720 is seen working a trip freight from the container terminal to the main yard at Kallo in Antwerpen Dock on 13 June 2007. **Colin J. Marsden**

Ⓑ

▲ Class M4 open first 51009 at Brussels Midi on 31 August 2007 in the new pale grey livery with red doors and blue trim.

▼ Class M5 double-deck open first 52505 at Brussels Midi on the same day in maroon livery.　**Peter Fox (2)**

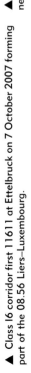

▲ Class I6 corridor first 11611 at Ettelbruck on 7 October 2007 forming part of the 08.56 Liers–Luxembourg.　**Robin Ralston (2)**

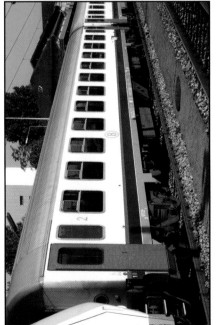

▼ Class I10 open second 12722 on the same train.

▲ CFL 1101 (Type Vossloh G1000 on hire from Angel trains) at Luxembourg depot on 17 June 2006.
Steve Phillips

▶ 2-car EMU No. 2012 at Bettembourg on 1 April 2004.
Colin Boocock

▶ Class 1600 No. 1603 ex-works in Salzinnes Yard on 22 July 2006.
Steve Phillips

▲ Class 800 diesel shunter No. 851 with a trip working through Hollerich on 22 November 2005.
W.J. Freebury

▼ Vossloh Type G1206 No. 1501 (on hire from Angel Trains) shunts at Luxembourg station on 25 March 2006. **Keith Fender**

▲ Class 1800 diesel electric No. 1819 with an eastbound freight at Petange in May 2004.
David Cable

▼ The CFL Class 3000 are identical to the SNCB Class 13. 3007 is seen at Ettelbruck with the 08.58 Liers–Luxembourg formed of Belgian 16 stock on 7 October 2007. **Robin Ralston**

52525	52538	52550	52562	52574	52586
52526	52539	52551	52563	52575	52587
52527	52540	52552	52564	52576	52588
52528	52541	52553	52565	52577	52589
52529	52542	52554	52566	52578	52590
52530	52543	52555	52567	52579	52591
52531	52544	52556	52568	52580	52592
52532	52545	52557	52569	52581	52593
52533	52546	52558	52570	52582	52594
52534	52547	52559	52571	52583	52595
52535	52548	52560	52572	52584	52596
52536	52549	52561	52573	52585	52597
52537					

TYPE M4 BRAKE OPEN FIRST

Built: 1982.
Bogies: Fiat Type Y32.
Accommodation: 56/– 1T.
Heating: Electric.
UIC Numbers: 50 88 81 78 001–033.
Builder: BN .
Length over Buffers: 24.26 m.
Weight: 37.2 tonnes.
Maximum Speed: 160 km/h.

58001	N	58007	N	58013	N	58019	N	58024	N	58029	N
58002	N	58008	N	58014	N	58020	N	58025	N	58030	N
58003	N	58009	N	58015	N	58021	N	58026	N	58031	N
58004	N	58010	N	58016	N	58022	N	58027	N	58032	N
58005	N	58011	N	58017	N	58023	N	58028	N	58033	N
58006	N	58012	N	58018	N						

TYPE M4 DRIVING BRAKE OPEN FIRST

Built: 1983. Push-pull driving trailer.
Builder: BN.
Bogies: Fiat Type Y32.
Accommodation: 48/– 1T.
Heating: Electric.
UIC Numbers: 50 88 81 78 034–065.
Length over Buffers: 24.26 m.
Weight: 39 tonnes.
Maximum Speed: 160 km/h.

58034	N	58040	N	58046	N	58051	N	58056	N	58061	N
58035	N	58041	N	58047	N	58052	N	58057	N	58062	N
58036	N	58042	N	58048	N	58053	N	58058	N	58063	N
58037	N	58043	N	58049	N	58054	N	58059	N	58064	N
58038	N	58044	N	58050	N	58055	N	58060	N	58065	N
58039	N	58045	N								

TYPE M4 BRAKE OPEN SECOND

Built: 1983–84.
Bogies: Fiat Type Y32.
Accommodation: –/64 1T.
Heating: Electric.
UIC Numbers: 50 88 82 78 001–025, 50 88 87 78 026–035.
Builder: BN.
Length over Buffers: 24.26 m.
Weight: 39.5 tonnes.
Maximum Speed: 160 km/h.

k With compartment for catering trolley.
p Converted to push-pull driving trailer.

59901	N	59907	N	59913	N	59919	N	59925	N	59931	N pk
59902	N	59908	N	59914	N	59920	N	59926	N pk	59932	N pk
59903	N	59909	N	59915	N	59921	N	59927	N pk	59933	N pk
59904	N	59910	N	59916	N	59922	N	59928	N pk	59934	N pk
59905	N	59911	N	59917	N	59923	N	59929	N pk	59935	N pk
59906	N	59912	N	59918	N	59924	N	59930	N pk		

TYPE M5   DRIVING OPEN SECOND

Double-deck push-pull driving trailer.

Built: 1986–87.
Bogies: .
Accommodation: –/118 2T.
Heating: Electric.
UIC Numbers: 50 88 82 38 001–018.

Builder: BN.
Length over Buffers: 26.85 m.
Weight: 49.3 tonnes.
Maximum Speed: 140 km/h.

59951	59954	59957	59960	59963	59966
59952	59955	59958	59961	59964	59967
59953	59956	59959	59962	59965	59968

TYPE M6   OPEN FIRST

Type M6 stock represented a massive jump in quality for SNCB/NMBS suburban stock as comfort levels are as good as in I11 international stock, including air conditioning and individual cloth covered seats in all classes. Following the first batch of 35 coaches, 37 more are on order. Of the total of 72, 54 were in service in September 2007

Built: 2001–.
Bogies: Bombardier
Accommodation: 124/– 1T.
Heating: Electric.
UIC Numbers: 50 88 16-72 001–072.

Builder: Alstom/Bombardier.
Length over Buffers: 26.80 m.
Weight: 49.7 tonnes.
Maximum Speed: 160 km/h.

61001	61013	61025	61037	61049	61061
61002	61014	61026	61038	61050	61062
61003	61015	61027	61039	61051	61063
61004	61016	61028	61040	61052	61064
61005	61017	61029	61041	61053	61065
61006	61018	61030	61042	61054	61066
61007	61019	61031	61043	61055	61067
61008	61020	61032	61044	61056	61068
61009	61021	61033	61045	61057	61069
61010	61022	61034	61046	61058	61070
61011	61023	61035	61047	61059	61071
61012	61024	61036	61048	61060	61072

TYPE M6   OPEN SECOND

Following a first batch of 140 coaches, 55 are now on order. These had not started to be delivered in late 2007.

Built: 2001–.
Bogies: Bombardier
Accommodation: –/140 1T.
Heating: Electric.
UIC Numbers: 50 88 26-72 001–195.

Builder: Alstom/Bombardier.
Length over Buffers: 26.80 m.
Weight: 49.9 tonnes.
Maximum Speed: 160 km/h.

62001	62017	62033	62049	62065	62081
62002	62018	62034	62050	62066	62082
62003	62019	62035	62051	62067	62083
62004	62020	62036	62052	62068	62084
62005	62021	62037	62053	62069	62085
62006	62022	62038	62054	62070	62086
62007	62023	62039	62055	62071	62087
62008	62024	62040	62056	62072	62088
62009	62025	62041	62057	62073	62089
62010	62026	62042	62058	62074	62090
62011	62027	62043	62059	62075	62091
62012	62028	62044	62060	62076	62092
62013	62029	62045	62061	62077	62093
62014	62030	62046	62062	62078	62094
62015	62031	62047	62063	62079	62095
62016	62032	62048	62064	62080	62096

62097	62114	62131	62148	62164	62180
62098	62115	62132	62149	62165	62181
62099	62116	62133	62150	62166	62182
62100	62117	62134	62151	62167	62183
62101	62118	62135	62152	62168	62184
62102	62119	62136	62153	62169	62185
62103	62120	62137	62154	62170	62186
62104	62121	62138	62155	62171	62187
62105	62122	62139	62156	62172	62188
62106	62123	62140	62157	62173	62189
62107	62124	62141	62158	62174	62190
62108	62125	62142	62159	62175	62191
62109	62126	62143	62160	62176	62192
62110	62127	62144	62161	62177	62193
62111	62128	62145	62162	62178	62194
62112	62129	62146	62163	62179	62195
62113	62130	62147			

TYPE M6 — DRIVING TRAILER OPEN SECOND

The first batch of M6 stock contained no driving trailers but it was found that they were desirable and 50 are now on order. Of these, seven had been commissioned in September 2007 but introduction was problematic. 19 of the vehicles (we believe 65001 to 65019) will be equipped with Type GF auto couplers for use with Class 27 locos, whilst the others will be used in push-pull mode with either Class 27 or Class 13.

Built: 2006–.
Bogies: Bombardier
Accommodation: –/134.
Heating: Electric.
UIC Numbers: 50 88 80-72 001-050.

Builder: Alstom/Bombardier.
Length over Buffers: 27.09 m.
Weight: 52.8 tonnes.
Maximum Speed: 160 km/h.

a equipped with auto couplers for operation with Class 27 and second rake in multiple.

65001	a	65010	65019	65027	65035	65043
65002		65011	65020	65028	65036	65044
65003		65012	65021	65029	65037	65045
65004	a	65013	65022	65030	65038	65046
65005	a	65014	65023	65031	65039	65047
65006	a	65015	65024	65032	65040	65048
65007		65016	65025	65033	65041	65049
65008		65017	65026	65034	65042	65050
65009		65018				

TYPE M6 — MULTI-PURPOSE OPEN COMPOSITE

The first batch of these totalled 35 and a further 18 are currently being delivered of which nine were in service in September 2007.

Built: 2001–.
Bogies: Bombardier
Accommodation: 25/44 (33) 1T.
Heating: Electric.
UIC Numbers: 50 88 81-72 001-053.

Builder: Alstom/Bombardier.
Length over Buffers: 26.80 m.
Weight: 49.6 tonnes.
Maximum Speed: 160 km/h.

69001	69010	69019	69028	69037	69046
69002	69011	69020	69029	69038	69047
69003	69012	69021	69030	69039	69048
69004	69013	69022	69031	69040	69049
69005	69014	69023	69032	69041	69050
69006	69015	69024	69033	69042	69051
69007	69016	69025	69034	69043	69052
69008	69017	69026	69035	69044	69053
69009	69018	69027	69036	69045	

MISCELLANEOUS DEPARTMENTAL STOCK

00013 60 88 99 70 013-2	Traction department test coach
00014 60 88 99 70 014-0	Brake test coach (ex 16001).
00015 60 88 99 70 015-9	Brake test coach (ex 17401).
00051 60 88 99 69 051-5	Emergency vehicle. Antwerpen Noord breakdown train.
00052 60 88 99 69 052-3	Emergency vehicle. Antwerpen Noord breakdown train.
00053 60 88 99 69 053-1	Emergency vehicle. Antwerpen Noord breakdown train.
00054 60 88 99 69 054-9	Emergency vehicle. Antwerpen Noord breakdown train.
00055 60 88 99 69 055-6	Emergency vehicle. Antwerpen Noord breakdown train.
00056 60 88 99 29 056-3	Emergency vehicle. Antwerpen Noord breakdown train.
00057 60 88 99 00 057-4	Emergency vehicle. Antwerpen Noord breakdown train.
00062 60 88 99 69 102-7	Signalling school coach.
00063 60 88 99 69 103-5	Signalling school coach.
00064 60 88 99 69 104-3	Signalling school coach.
00065 60 88 99 69 105-0	Signalling school coach.
00201 60 88 99 29 201-5	Infrastructure dept. coach (track renewal).
00202 60 88 99 29 202-3	Infrastructure dept. coach (track renewal).
00203 60 88 99 29 203-1	Infrastructure dept. coach (track renewal).
00204 60 88 99 29 204-9	Infrastructure dept. coach (track renewal).
00205 60 88 99 29 205-6	Infrastructure dept. coach (track renewal).
00206 60 88 99 29 206-4	Infrastructure dept. coach (track renewal mess coach).
00207 60 88 99 29 207-2	Infrastructure dept. coach (track renewal mess coach).
00208 60 88 99 29 208-0	Infrastructure dept. coach (track renewal staff dormitory).
00209 60 88 99 29 209-8	Infrastructure dept. coach (track renewal staff dormitory).
00210 60 88 99 29 210-6	Infrastructure dept. coach.
00211 60 88 99 29 211-4	Infrastructure dept. coach.
00212 60 88 99 29 212-2	Infrastructure dept. coach.
00213 60 88 99 29 213-0	Infrastructure dept. coach.
00214 60 88 99 29 214-8	Infrastructure dept. coach.
00215 60 88 99 29 215-5	Infrastructure dept. coach.
00216 60 88 99 29 216-3	Infrastructure dept. coach.
00217 60 88 99 29 217-1	Infrastructure dept. coach.
00218 60 88 99 29 218-9	Infrastructure dept. coach.
00224 60 88 99 29 224-7	Infrastructure dept. coach.
00226 60 88 99 29 226-2	Infrastructure dept. coach.
00801 61 88 82 76 001-2	Ultrasonic test coach (l11 200 km/h) (white).

2. LUXEMBOURG RAILWAYS (CFL)

Luxembourg Railways are known by the abbreviation CFL (Societé Nationale des Chemins de Fer Luxembourgeois). The total length of the system is only 270 km, but this does not mean that the network is uninteresting. CFL operates locomotives and multiple units of types that are also found in neighbouring countries, and Luxembourg Ville station also sees through workings of locomotives from the DB, SNCB/NMBS and SNCF. Electrification is at 25 kV AC 50 Hz and all CFL electric locomotives and multiple units operate on this system. SNCB/NMBS 3000 V DC electrics can also run into Luxembourg Ville station.

NUMBERING SYSTEM

The CFL loco numbering system was based on the horse power of the locomotives. 1801 is an 1800 h.p locomotive, for example. However, some new and smaller locomotives and multiple units are not numbered in accordance with this system.

DEPOTS AND WORKSHOPS

With such a compact system there is no need for many depots. All locomotives and units are allocated to Luxembourg shed which is currently being modernised. There are stabling points at Ettelbruck, Wasserbillig, Troisvierges, Bettembourg yard, Pétange and Esch sur Alzette. Locomotives also stable overnight at branch termini as required. Because of the small fleet only one workshop is required and this is located next to the station at Luxembourg.

DEVELOPMENTS

In 1993, CFL completed electrification of its main lines at 25 kV AC 50 Hz, except for the line to Arlon (B), electrified at 3000 V DC and short freight branches Kleinbettingen–Steinfort and Schieren–Bissen, which remain diesel worked. CFL owns two Class 628.4 2-car DMUs – 628 505 and 506 – which are maintained by DB and shown in the Platform 5 book "German Railways". CFL Class 2200 are identical to SNCF's Class Z 24500 and the classes interwork, CFL sets reaching Nancy.

In the five years to 2007, CFL renewed almost its entire fleet, sold its recent Class 2100 diesel railcars to SNCF and its old Class 250 and 260 EMUs to Romania. Instead of buying new diesels, the company has hired CMI and Vossloh locos.

Like other railways, CFL has been divided into activities and rolling stock with it. In 2006, the company created freight subsidiary CFL Cargo with steel producer Arcelor Mittal which generates most of the domestic rail freight in Luxembourg. The steel company's shunters are now part of the joint fleet. In recent years CFL has expanded outside its borders and now has small subsidiaries in Germany and Denmark. During 2007, diesel locos started to move between Luxembourg and these subsidiaries which complicates compilation of this section. Class 4000 started operation to Köln Gremberg in Germany during 2007 and CFL Cargo started to expand into France during 2008.

SERVICES

Loco-hauled passenger trains and EMUs tend to mix on all routes. Class 2100 EMUs work the short routes to Volmerange and Rumelange while Class 2200 operate most trains into France including to Thionville, Metz and Nancy, and Longwy/Longuyon. Class 4000 is not approved in France. Only Class 3000 can work to Kleinbettingen and Arlon although Class 628.4 DMUs operated some trains to Kleinbettingen in 2006!

LIVERIES

CFL locos, units and hauled stock are generally painted in a bordeaux red with yellow highlights on older locos and white on more recent stock.

2.1. DIESEL LOCOMOTIVES

Note: Self-propelled departmental vehicles are also numbered in this series.

CLASS 100 B

These shunters were part of the Arcelor Mittal internal fleet which became part of CFL Cargo in 2007. We believe only one is serviceable and not likely to stray out of Belval steel works. Originally delivered with numbers 11 to 14. Works numbers 220091 to 220093 and 220097. Yellow livery.

Built: 1966–71.
Builder: MaK. Type G 320 B.
Engine: Mercedes-Benz MB 846 Ab of 259 kW.
Transmission: Hydraulic. Voith L320 U.
Train Heating: None
Maximum Tractive Effort: kN.
Wheel Diameter: 1000 mm.

Weight: 36 tonnes.
Length over Buffers: 8.45 m.
Maximum Speed: 33/60 km/h.

101	102	103	104

CLASS 300 B-B

These heavy shunters were delivered new to Arbed, now Arcelor Mittal, and became part of the CFL Cargo fleet in 2007. They are used mainly within steel works, where they sometimes operate in multiple. However, one of the class was operating in Bettembourg yard in 2007 and there may be more exchanges between the old CFL and Arcelor fleets in future. Delivered numbered D 11 to D 24 (301 to 314) and D 38, 40, 41, 5, and 5, the latter being at various different steelworks in Luxembourg. Works numbers are respectively 800154 to 800160, 800163, 800182, 800173 to 800176, 800170, 800177, 800184, 800185, 800188, and 800189. Yellow livery.

Built: 1966–77.
Builder: MaK. Type G 850 BB.
Engine: MaK 6 M 282 A or 626 kW.
Transmission: Hydraulic. Voith L 306 r or L 5r4.
Train Heating: None.
Maximum Tractive Effort: kN.
Wheel Diameter: 1000 mm.

Weight: 80 tonnes.
Length over Buffers: 12.20 m.
Maximum Speed: 36/60 km/h.

301	305	308	311	314	317
302	306	309	312	315	318
303	307	310	313	316	319
304					

CLASS 500 B

30 of these locos were ordered by Danish State Railways (DSB) as Class MJ but were refused after 16 (501 to 519, there is no 508, 515 or 517) had been built. They are now all hired out by the manufacturer, and considered very good by users. CFL's infrastructure department has hired up to five of the class but had three on hire in late 2007.

Built: 1993–96.
Builder: Cockerill Mechanical Industrie (CMI).
Engine: Caterpillar 3408 BTA of 386 kW.
Transmission: Hydrostatic.
Train Heating: None
Maximum Tractive Effort: 120 kN.
Wheel Diameter: 950 mm.

Weight: 40 tonnes.
Length over Buffers: 8.90 m.
Maximum Speed: 60 km/h.

502	516	518	

CLASS 800 Bo-Bo

These locos are unique to the CFL and are typical American switchers (GM Type SW 1500) of the early 1950s. Only two are still in service, with CFL Cargo, usually shunting or trip working at Bettembourg yard.

Built: 1954.
Builder: AFB.
Engine: GM 8-567B of 600 kW at 835 rpm.
Transmission: Electric. Four GM 4-EMD-D27B axle-hung traction motors.
Train Heating: None
Maximum Tractive Effort: 179 kN.
Wheel Diameter: 1050 mm.
Weight: 74 tonnes.
Length over Buffers: 13.795 m.
Maximum Speed: 80 km/h.

h part of the CFL historic fleet.

| 802 | 804 | 805 h | |

CLASSES 850/900 Bo-Bo

These are from the same family as SNCF Class BB 63500. Used on station pilot and trip freight duties. Now being withdrawn. 853, 909, 910 and 911 were recently sold to RDT 13 in France.

Built: 1956–58.
Builder: B&L.
Engine: SACM MGO V12SH of 615 kW at 1500 r.p.m. (* MGO V12SHR of 690 kW at 1500 r.p.m.).
Transmission: Electric. Four BL 453-29B (* BL 453-29D) axle-hung traction motors.
Train Heating: None.
Maximum Tractive Effort: 174 kN.
Wheel Diameter: 1100 mm.
Weight: 72 tonnes.
Length over Buffers: 14.75 m.
Maximum Speed: 105 km/h.

h part of the CFL historic fleet.

| 851 | | 857 | | 904 | * | | 906 | * | | 907 | * | | 912 | * |
| 856 | h | 858 | | 905 | * | | | | | | | | | |

CLASS 1000 B

Owned by the CFL infrastructure department and used for light shunting duties. 1002 is used as a spares bank.

Built: 1972.
Builder: Jung.
Engine: Deutz F12 L413 of 186 kW at 2150 rpm.
Transmission: Hydraulic. Voith L2r4SU2.
Train Heating: None
Maximum Tractive Effort: 94 kN.
Wheel Diameter: 950 mm.
Weight: 32 tonnes.
Length over Buffers: 7.20 m.
Maximum Speed: 30/60 km/h.

| 1001 | 1003 | 1004 | |

CLASS 1010 B

Owned by the rolling stock department. This shunter has an auto coupler. It is usually found at Luxembourg depot.

Built: 1964.
Builder: Henschel.
Engine: Henschel 6R 1215A of 160 kW at 1800 rpm.
Transmission: Hydraulic. Voith DIWABUS 200S/355.
Train Heating: None
Maximum Tractive Effort: 64 kN.
Wheel Diameter: 850 mm.
Weight: 22 tonnes.
Length over Buffers: 7.10 m.
Maximum Speed: 24 km/h.

1011

CLASS 1020 B

Owned by the rolling stock department. 1024 is fitted with auto couplers and are used at Pétange Wagon Works.

Built: 1952–57.
Builder: Deutz.
Engine: Deutz A8 L614 of 100 kW at 1800 rpm.
Transmission: Hydraulic. Voith L33Y.
Train Heating: None
Maximum Tractive Effort: 64 kN.
Wheel Diameter: 850 mm.
Weight: 22 tonnes.
Length over Buffers: 7.57 m.
Maximum Speed: 53 km/h.

| 1022 | 1023 | 1024 | |

CLASS 1030 B

Owned by the infrastructure department. 1031 is fitted with remote control.

Built: 1988.
Builder: Jenbach.
Engine: MTU 8V 183 TA12 of 267 kW at 2200 rpm.
Transmission: Hydraulic. Voith L2r4SV2.
Train Heating: None
Maximum Tractive Effort: 117 kN.
Wheel Diameter: 950 mm.
Weight: 36 tonnes.
Length over Buffers: 8.55 m.
Maximum Speed: 60 km/h.

| 1031 | 1032 | 1033 | |

CLASS 1050 P.W. TROLLEYS

Owned by the infrastructure department, these permanent way trolleys have a large cabin at one end for the driver and staff and a hydraulic arm at the other. 1051 was formerly numbered 10. 1053 has been withdrawn.

Built: 1980–82.
Builder: Donelli/Geismar.
Engine: Deutz F8 L413F of 173.5 kW. at 1500 rpm.
Transmission: Hydraulic. Clark R 28624-9.
Length over Buffers: 9.90 m.
Wheel Diameter: 850 mm.
Weigh: 36 tonnes.
Maximum Speed: 80 km/h.

| 1051 | 1052 | 1054 | |

CLASS 1060 O.H.L. TROLLEYS

Owned by the infrastructure department. They have a dummy pantograph and a working area above the crew accommodation. They are used for overhead line maintenance.

Built: 1985.
Builder: Donelli/Geismar.
Engine: Deutz F8 L413F of 173.5 kW at 1500 rpm.
Transmission: Hydro-mechanical. MHR 28628-2.
Length over Buffers: 12.14 m.
Wheel Diameter: 850 mm.
Weight: 24 tonnes.
Maximum Speed: 80 km/h.

| 1061 | 1062 | |

CLASS 1100 B-B

These are standard Vossloh G1000 locos on hire from Angel Trains Cargo. They are used for station pilot and light freight duties. Numbering below shows works numbers in brackets. All are in standard Angel Trains Cargo livery of white with a blue cab. All are equipped to operate in Luxembourg and Germany.

Builder: Vossloh
Engine: MTU 8V4000 of 1100 kW.
Transmission: Hydraulic. Voith L4r4.
Maximum Tractive Effort: 259 kN.
Weight: 80 tonnes.

Wheel Diameter: 1000 mm.
Length over Buffers: 14.13 m.
Maximum Speed: 100 km/h.

1101 (5001483)	1103 (5001529)	1105 (5001531)	1106 (5001532)
1102 (5001484)	1104 (5001530)		

CLASS 1150   B-B

LEW Type V100 re-engined with Caterpillar engine of 1082 kW. See page 19 for technical details. Mainly used on freight between Wasserbillig and Germany but may turn up in Luxembourg.

1151 (NEG 03, DB 202 242, works No. 12524).

Note: CFL Cargo Deutschland also has ex NEG 04 (ex DB 202 430, works number 12939).

CLASS 1500   B-B

These are standard Vossloh G1206 locos on hire from Angel Trains Cargo. See page 19 for technical details. They are used for freight duties. Numbering below shows works numbers in brackets. All are in standard Angel Trains Cargo livery of white with a blue cab except where marked. All are equipped to work in both Luxembourg and Germany. 1505 was in use at CFL Cargo Deutschland's Niebüll base in late 2007. 1581/82 were hired in autumn 2007 and are equipped for use in France as well as Luxembourg and Germany. They are the first to receive full UIC numbers. CFL Cargo Deutschland was also hiring Vossloh G1206 1001125 and 1001127 (numbered 1206 008) at Niebüll in late 2007. CFL intends to hire a further three G1206 of which two will be equipped to operate in France. CFL hired a Vossloh G1700, numbering it 1701, from April 2006 but returned the loco in November 2006. 1583 and 1584 hired from MRCE are in black livery.

R all over red livery.

1501 **R** (1001115)	1503 **R** (1001129)	1505 **R** (1001025)	1506
1502 (5001476)	1504 **R** (1001131)		

1581 (5001513, 92 80 1 276 001-5 D-ATLD)	1583 (5001649)
1582 (5001665, 92 80 1 276 002-3 D-ATLD)	1584 (5001731)

CLASS 1800   Co-Co

Identical to SNCB Class 55 except for the coupling of traction motors. Used on a variety of freights within Luxembourg and to Ehrang near Trier in Germany. The class are gradually being withdrawn. 1806 was dispatched to operate for CFL Cargo's subsidiary in Denmark during 2007 and two more are expected to follow.

Built: 1963–64.
Builder–Mechanical Parts: BN.
Builder–Electrical Parts: ACEC/SEM.
Engine: GM 16-567C of 1435 kW at 835 r.p.m.
Transmission: Electric. Six ACEC DS7 axle-hung traction motors.
Train Heating: Steam. Vapor OK 4616.
Maximum Tractive Effort: 272 kN.
Wheel Diameter: 1010 mm.

Weight: 110 tonnes.
Length over Buffers: 19.55 m.
Maximum Speed: 120 km/h.

Rheostatic braking.

i equipped with Indusi safety equipment for operation in Germany.

1801 (S) STADT GÖPPINGEN		1814		
1802 Blankenberge		1815 i	KAUTENBACH 1881–1981
1805 (S) MONDORF-LES-BAINS		1816 i	LAROCHETTE
1806 i COMMUNE DE WALFERDANGE		1817 i	
1807 i COMMUNE DE PÉTANGE		1818 i	
1809		1820	Bettembourg
1810			

2.2. ELECTRIC MULTIPLE UNITS

CLASS 2000   2-CAR UNITS

These EMUs are similar to SNCF Class Z 11500 and used to interwork with the latter into France. Units operate on all lines in Luxembourg.

ABD + B (DMBCO-DTSO).

Built: 1990–92.
Builders: De Dietrich/ANF/Alsthom.
Wheel Arrangement: Bo-Bo + 2-2.
Traction Motors: 4 x TAB 676 B1 of 305 kW each.
Accommodation: 24/60 1T + –/80 1T.   **Length over Couplers:** 25.10 + 25.10 m.
Weight: 64 + 40 tonnes.   **Maximum Speed:** 160 km/h.

* Equipped with SNCF's KVB automatic train control system.
e Equipped with ETCS European train control system.

2001	2005	2009	2013	2017	2020
2002	2006	2010	2014	2018 e	2021 *
2003	2007	2011 e	2015	2019	2022 *
2004	2008	2012 e	2016		

Names

2001	MERSCH	2004	PÉTANGE	2018	TROISVIERGES

CLASS 2200   3-CAR DOUBLE-DECK UNITS

These EMUs are similar to SNCF Class Z 24500 and they interwork with the latter on services to Metz and Nancy. 2207 was severely damaged in a head-on crash at Zoufftgen in November 2006. Units operate on all lines in Luxembourg.

ABD + B (DMBCO-DTSO).

Built: 2005–2007.
Builders: Alstom/Bombardier.
Wheel Arrangement: Bo-2 + Bo-2 + Bo-2.
Traction Motors: 2 x FXA 2851 of 425 kW each per car. Total 2550 kW per unit.
Accommodation: 41/298 3T 1T.   **Length over Couplers:** 27.35 m + 26.40 m + 27.35 m.
Weight: 190 tonnes.   **Maximum Speed:** 160 km/h.

All equipped with SNCF's KVB automatic train control system.

2201	2203	2205	2207 (S)	2209	2211
2202	2204	2206	2208	2210	2212

2206 is named BETTEMBOURG.

FOREIGN TRAINS OPERATING INTO LUXEMBOURG

Luxembourg is such a small country that there is a very large degree of cross-border operation. From Belgium, SNCB/NMBS Class 13 and 20 locomotives work passenger services from Brussels as do Class AM96 EMUs. Class 13 also work freight over the Athus-Meuse line via Virton to Rodange and Bettembourg. Class 41 DMUs operate the Virton–Rodange–Arlon passenger service.

DB Class 181.2 work IC services from Germany and Class 628.4 DMUs operate the frequent service to Trier. Freight generally changes to CFL traction at Ehrang (Trier) but this may well change in future, the most likely locos to be used being Railion Class 185.

From France, TGV Réseau and TGV POS sets now work the service from Paris, Class BB 15000 and BB 26000 electric locos work other long distance passenger services while suburban services are operated by BB 16500 plus push-pull sets, Z 11500 and Z 24500 EMUs, with BB 16500 likely to disappear shortly. Most freight is now worked by Fret SNCF Class BB 27000 and its tri-voltage version BB 37000.

Surprisingly, no open access freight operators have yet to venture into the country but this will probably change soon.

2.3. ELECTRIC LOCOMOTIVES

CLASS 3000 Bo-Bo

These dual-voltage locos were designed to operate in a pool with SNCB/NMBS Class 13 which are identical. They are used on Luxembourg–Liège passenger trains and on Antwerpen–Namur–Bertrix–Rodange–Bettembourg freights over the "Athus-Meuse" line. Otherwise they are used on local passenger services with the new double-deck stock. 3001 was withdrawn after a serious fire. 3005 was on hire to SNCB/NMBS in 2006/7 to haul M6 stock on the Luxembourg–Brussels service.

Built: 1998–2000
Systems: 3000 V DC/25 kV AC 50 Hz (1500 V DC at reduced power)
Builder–Mechanical Parts: Alstom, Bombardier
Builder–Electrical Parts: Alstom (ACEC)
Traction Motors: Four PXA 4339B frame mounted.
One Hour Rating: 5200 kW   **Weight:** 90 tonnes
Maximum Tractive Effort: 288 kN   **Length over Buffers:** 19.11 m.
Wheel Diameter: 1160 mm   **Maximum Speed:** 200 km/h
Train Protection: KVB, TBL, MEMOR.

Multiple working fitted. Equipped with rheostatic and regenerative braking.

Also carry UIC numbers 90 82 3 00 3002 to 3020 plus check digits.

e equipped with ETCS.
p equipped for push-pull operation.

3002	3007	3012 ep	3017 p
3003 ep	3008 p	3013	3018
3004 p	3009 p	3014 p	3019
3005	3010 ep	3015 p	3020
3006	3011 p	3016	

Name: 3002 BLANKENBERGE

CLASS 4000 Bo-Bo

These are Bombardier's TRAXX design and were ordered at the same time as the new double-deck stock. The locos are very similar to a DB Class 185 (first generation) but also have equipment to operate passenger trains. The locos are used all over the CFL network with push-pull double-deck stock as well as on freight to Germany. Initially restricted to Ehrang yard east of Trier, the class started regular freight operation to Köln Gremberg in autumn 2007.

Built: 2004–2006.
Systems: 15 kV AC 16.7 Hz/25 kV AC 50 Hz.
Builder–Mechanical Parts: Bombardier.
Builder–Electrical Parts: Bombardier.
Traction Motors: Four axle hung.
One Hour Rating: 5600 kW.   **Weight:** 84 tonnes.
Maximum Tractive Effort: 300 kN.   **Length over Buffers:** 18.90 m.
Wheel Diameter: 1250 mm.   **Maximum Speed:** 140 km/h.

4001	4006	4011	4016
4002	4007	4012	4017
4003	4008	4013	4018 WILTZ
4004	4009	4014	4019
4005	4010	4015	4020

CLASS 185 Bo-Bo

See details for Class 4000.

These were hired from MRCE Dispolok in April 2008. 185 555 is a first generation loco and can operate into France and Germany. The others are second generation and can only operate within Germany. It is likely they will be rapidly exchanged for others in the 185 551 to 557 batch.

185 555-0	185 563-4	185 566-7	185 567-5

2.4. LOCO-HAULED COACHING STOCK

2.4.1. WEGMANN COACHES

60 coaches were built by Wegmann of Kassel, Germany in 1965–67 and were the backbone of the CFL fleet for almost 40 years. They were all replaced by the new Bombardier double-deck coaches in regular service but a few coaches were retained for tourist services. Most of these are operated in association with the clubs GAR, 1604 and 5519. One coach ran in a service train to Brussels in summer 2007. Those in store will probably be withdrawn. A small number have been sold to German preservation groups BEG, DGEG, EFZ and UEF.

There were originally four types of vehicle – Types B, AB and BD and ABD. The ABD vehicles were identical to the BD vehicles and the AB vehicles were identical to the B vehicles, except for the upholstery on the first class seats.

The livery of all coaches was originally plain dark green, then cream and green. Vehicles are all capable of 140 km/h and are allowed to work into Belgium, the Netherlands and Germany. All coaches are 26.4 m. long over buffers and weigh 28.5 tonnes empty.

D   BICYCLE CARRYING CAR

Converted from a collision-damaged coach in April 1993. Formerly brake composite (A3B9D) and originally brake second (B9D).

Livery: Standard CFL maroon and cream with "Vélos" markings.

51 82 92-40 002-6 (S)   (ex 50 82 81-10 393-9, ex 2182)

B12 (BR§)   OPEN SECOND

Accommodation: –/96 2T.

* Converted from A3B9 (CO).
§ Classified BR and known as the "Rendez-vous" coach. Equipped with a kitchen at the expense of Luxembourg railway enthusiasts group Groupement des Amis du Rail (GAR). Still used in the summer-only Blankenberge Express to Blankenberge on the Belgian coast. Standard CFL livery of maroon and cream with "Rendez-vous" markings. Coach 441 is also equipped to work in the Blankenberge Express.

51 82 22-40 441-1   (ex 50 82 22-10 341-0, ex 2111)
51 82 22-40 452-8 (S) (ex 50 82 22-10 352-7, ex 2122)
51 82 84-40 457-2 §   (ex 50 82 22-40 457-8, ex 2127)
51 82 22-40 461-9 (S) (ex 50 82 22-40 461-0, ex 2131)
51 82 22-40 463-5   (ex 50 82 22-40 363-4, ex 2133)
51 82 22-40 469-2 * (S) (ex 50 82 22-40 469-3, ex 2163)

A3B6D (A6B3D§)   BRAKE OPEN COMPOSITE

All converted from B9D (BSO).

Accommodation: 24/48 1T.

§ Centre compartment is first instead of end compartment.

51 82 81-40 486-4 §   (ex 50 82 81-40 486-5, ex 2187)
51 82 81-40 494-8   (ex 50 82 81-10 394-6, ex 2185)

2.4.2. BOMBARDIER DOUBLE-DECK STOCK

This stock was purchased together with Class 4000 locomotives to replace all the vintage Wegmann stock. Also powered by Class 3000. Air conditioned.

TYPE DABpbdzfa   DRIVING OPEN COMPOSITE

Driving trailers carry the numbers 001 to 018 on their front ends.

Built: 2004–2006.
Builder: Bombardier, Görlitz.
Bogies: Görlitz VIII Do.
Length: 27.27 m.   **Accommodation:** 44/14 (22) 1T.
Weight: 52.5 tonnes.   **Maximum Speed:** 160 km/h.

50 82 86-70 001-0	50 82 86-70 007-7	50 82 86-70 013-5
50 82 86-70 002-8	50 82 86-70 008-5	50 82 86-70 014-3
50 82 86-70 003-6	50 82 86-70 009-3	50 82 86-70 015-0
50 82 86-70 004-4	50 82 86-70 010-1	50 82 86-70 016-8
50 82 86-70 005-1	50 82 86-70 011-9	50 82 86-70 017-6
50 82 86-70 006-9	50 82 86-70 012-7	50 82 86-70 018-4

TYPE DBpza   OPEN SECOND

These were delivered as open composites but the first class seats have already been downgraded to second.

Built: 2004–2006.
Builder: Bombardier, Görlitz.
Bogies: Görlitz VIII Do.
Length: 26.80 m.   **Accommodation:** –/116 (2) 1T.
Weight: 50.2 tonnes   **Maximum Speed:** 160 km/h.

50 82 36-70 019-3	50 82 36-70 024-3	50 82 36-70 029-2
50 82 36-70 020-1	50 82 36-70 025-0	50 82 36-70 030-0
50 82 36-70 021-9	50 82 36-70 026-8	50 82 36-70 031-8
50 82 36-70 022-7	50 82 36-70 027-6	50 82 36-70 032-6
50 82 36-70 023-5	50 82 36-70 028-4	50 82 36-70 033-4

TYPE DBpza   OPEN SECOND

Built: 2004–2006.
Builder: Bombardier, Görlitz.
Bogies: Görlitz VIII Do.
Length: 26.80 m.   **Accommodation:** –/130 (3) 1T.
Weight: 49.6 tonnes   **Maximum Speed:** 160 km/h.

50 82 26-70 034-4	50 82 26-70 052-6	50 82 26-70 069-0
50 82 26-70 035-1	50 82 26-70 053-4	50 82 26-70 070-8
50 82 26-70 036-9	50 82 26-70 054-2	50 82 26-70 071-6
50 82 26-70 037-7	50 82 26-70 055-9	50 82 26-70 072-4
50 82 26-70 038-5	50 82 26-70 056-7	50 82 26-70 073-2
50 82 26-70 039-3	50 82 26-70 057-5	50 82 26-70 074-0
50 82 26-70 040-1	50 82 26-70 058-3	50 82 26-70 075-7
50 82 26-70 041-9	50 82 26-70 059-1	50 82 26-70 076-5
50 82 26-70 042-7	50 82 26-70 060-9	50 82 26-70 077-3
50 82 26-70 043-5	50 82 26-70 061-7	50 82 26-70 078-1
50 82 26-70 044-3	50 82 26-70 062-5	50 82 26-70 079-9
50 82 26-70 045-0	50 82 26-70 063-3	50 82 26-70 080-7
50 82 26-70 046-8	50 82 26-70 064-1	50 82 26-70 081-5
50 82 26-70 047-6	50 82 26-70 065-8	50 82 26-70 082-3
50 82 26-70 048-4	50 82 26-70 066-6	50 82 26-70 083-1
50 82 26-70 049-2	50 82 26-70 067-4	50 82 26-70 084-9
50 82 26-70 050-0	50 82 26-70 068-2	50 82 26-70 085-6
50 82 26-70 051-8		

3. NETHERLANDS RAILWAYS (NS)

THE DUTCH RAILWAY SYSTEM

The Netherlands Railway System is a relatively small one and approximately two thirds of all routes are electrified at 1500 V d.c. with overhead wire collection. Language presents no problem, since most Dutch people speak good English, but restaurant menus are often in Dutch only, so a dictionary or phrase book can still be useful.

The NMa Vervoerkamer (the State Office of Transport Regulation) controls access and use of the railway network.

INFRASTRUCTURE & OPERATIONS

Infrastructure and train operation are now separated in the Netherlands. The national infrastructure manager is **Prorail** which is a company owned by the Dutch State. It was created by the merger of NS Railinfrabeheer, NS Verkeersleiding (traffic control) and a large part of Railned.

Prorail is also infrastructure manager of the HSL-Zuid high speed line (Hoofddorp–Rotterdam West and Rotterdam Lombardijen–Hazeldonk border crossing to Belgium) and the Betuwe route. The daily operation of the freight only Betuwe route is managed by **Keyrail**, of which the shares are owned by Prorail, Port of Rotterdam authorities and Port of Amsterdam authorities. Both HSL-Zuid and Betuwe route infrastructure management are each based on a separate concession.

Most of the sidings are connections between natonal railway network and industries and are owned by **NS Spooraansluitingen**.

Private German railway undertaking **Bentheimer Eisenbahn** owns and manages the line between Coevorden and the Dutch/German border at Laarwald. Preserved railways own their own lines.

The former Zoetemeer Stadslijn and the Den Haag–Rotterdam Hofplein lines are now run as the "RandstadRail" light rail system. The infrastructure management is the responsibility of Haaglanden and Rijnmond, the regional transport authorities of the Den Haag and Rotterdam areas.

SAFETY & CERTIFICATION

The newly established IVW (Inspectie Verkeer en Waterstaat), a department of the Ministry of Transport is now responsible for safety inspection. IVW is also licensing body for railway undertakings, and is also the authority to approve and certify railway vehicles in The Netherlands.

NEDERLANDSE SPOORWEGEN (NS)

NV **Nederlandse Spoorwegen** is now a holding company with legally seperated business units which are:

NS Reizigers (NS passengers). Based on Dutch legislation, NS has been awarded a concession for public transport by train on the defined 'core network'. The concession gives NS an exclusive right for passenger train operations on this network, and comprises all IC services.

NS Internationaal operates international passenger train services. These comprise IC services between Amsterdam/Schiphol and Berlin via Bad Bentheim, ICE services Amsterdam–Frankfurt (and further), and the hourly IC services Amsterdam Centraal and Brussel Zuid/Midi "Benelux" service. These services are marketed as **NS Hispeed**, which will also include domestic high speed services of HSA (High Speed Alliance; the joint venture of NS and KLM for operations of high speed train services on the HSL-Zuid).

NedTrain. is the subsidiary responsible for the maintenance, overhaul and refurbishment of rolling stock. Nedtrain operates several workshops and depots and has the legal status of "railway undertaking".

NS Stations. Operates the commercial space in the stations, such as shops etc.

NS Vastgoed is a propertycompany, the biggest in The Netherlands.

NS Financial services is a rolling stock leasing company based in Dublin. This company owns the majority of the NS rolling stock fleet. It also owns the rolling stock of Syntus and those Railion Nederland locomotives which were owned by NS before it was restructured.

Nedrailways is a subsidiary for business development in railways abroad. Nedrailways operates tendered train services in other countries, making joint bids with strategic local partners.

Nedrailways operates two franchises in the United Kingdom, jointly with Serco (Merseyrail Electrics and Northern Rail), and has bid for tenders in Germany.

NS has a subsidiary for special passenger transport, such as charter trains, and also other events. This subsidiary is **NS Charter Trains**.

RegioNS is an NS subsidiary for the operation of tendered regional train services for which NS as such is excluded from tendering. The company operates train services between Apeldoorn and Zutphen as franchised by the province of Gelderland.

Nedtrain previously had a department for the testing and commissioning rolling stock, activities needed in the framework of approval of rolling stock. This department was turned into another business unit, called Nedtrain Consulting, which was awarded the legal status of Notified Body. This business unit has been sold to Lloyd's Register, and is now called **Lloyd's Register Rail**.

In addition, NS owns the construction company **Strukton** (See section 7.3.)

NS Cargo was NS's former freight operation, but this is now **Railion Benelux** (see section 5), owned by Deutsche Bahn.

PASSENGER TRAINS

The NS timetable is almost entirely regular interval with most routes having half-hourly services and many routes four trains per hour. There are now three types of train category on the NS. Intercity, *Stoptreinen* and *Sneltreinen*. *Stoptreinen* are stopping trains and are generally either EMUs or push-pull double-decker sets. *Sneltreinen* are semi-fast services and are mainly IRM sets. Intercity trains are generally either Koploper EMUs or are loco-hauled, but IRM units are also used on some services. Loco-hauled services are:

Amsterdam–Den Haag HS–Rotterdam–Dordrecht–Roosendaal–Antwerpen Centraal–Brussels. These are push-pull trains with SNCB dual-voltage Class 11 electric locos and ICR stock. Class 186 locos are expected to take over these duties and the trains will not then be push-pull. Through trains to Paris are operated by Thalys units.

Den Haag CS–Rotterdam–Dordrecht–Breda–Tilburg–Eindhoven–Venlo. Loco-hauled with Class 1700/1800. The stock is 11-coach rakes of ex-DB ICK stock.

Amsterdam Centraal–Amersfoort. These trains are loco-hauled with ICL stock (top & tail).

Amsterdam/Hoofddorp–Amersfoort–Enschede. These trains are operated by "Koploper" units or are loco-hauled with ICR stock (push-pull).

Roosendaal–Breda–Tilburg–Nijmegen–Arnhem. ICR stock (push-pull).

Various other trains are loco-hauled, with the situation changing from time to time.

Trains to Germany are loco-hauled with DB IC stock or are operated by ICEs.

NEDTRAIN DEPOTS & WORKSHOPS

Depots (*onderhoudsbedrijven*) are responsible for day-to-day maintenance of vehicles and the particular depots which normally carry out such maintenance are shown as allocations in this section. There are no official depot codes used on NS. Unofficial codes used in this publication will be found in Appendix V on page 176.

The main workshops (*revisiebedrijven*) are at Haarlem (for all units) and Tilburg (for locos and the power units of DMUs) and Amersfoort (for wagons).

There are many places where EMUs stable, but the main locations where units and some locos will be found are: Alkmaar, Amersfoort, Arnhem, Botlek*, Den Haag , Den Helder, Eindhoven, Groningen, Heerlen, Hengelo, Hoofddorp, Kijfhoek Yard*, Lelystad, Maastricht, Maasvlaakte*, Nijmegen, Roosendaal, Rotterdam CS, Sittard, Utrecht, Venlo, Vlissingen, Waalhaven Zuid* and Zwolle.

NUMBERING SYSTEMS

Different numbering series were used for locos and multiple units, but with renumbering and condemnations, numbers do not now duplicate.

LIVERIES

Liveries of most vehicles are based on yellow. Please see Appendix V on Page 176 for details of liveries and livery codes used in this section.

3.1. DIESEL LOCOMOTIVES

CLASS 700   VOSSLOH TYPE G400B   B-B

These new shunters were built to replace NS Reizigers' fleet of ageing Class 600 locos.

Built: 2003–04.
Builder: Vossloh.
Engine: MTU 8V183 TD 13 of 390 kW at 2100 r.p.m.
Transmission: Hydraulic. Voith L2r4z(s)e U2.
Tractive Effort: 130 kN.   **Length over Buffers:** 9.645 m.
Driving Wheel Diameter: 1050 mm.   **Weight:** 40 tonnes.
Maximum Speed: 40 km/h (80 km/h when pulled).
Class Specific Livery: S Lime green with yellow ends.

701	S	TB	704	S	TB	707	S	TB	710	S	TB
702	S	TB	705	S	TB	708	S	TB	711	S	TB
703	S	TB	706	S	TB	709	S	TB	712	S	TB

3.2. ELECTRIC LOCOMOTIVES

CLASS 1700   B-B

This class is virtually identical to Class 1800, (see below) the main difference being the fact that they have thyristor control. As built the locos had auto-couplers on one end for use with the double-decker DD-AR stock as "virtual EMUs". However 50 of them have been replaced with the new mDDM double-deck power cars and have had the auto-couplers removed. The braking system is not suitable for freight train use.

Built: 1990–94.
Builder: GEC-Alsthom.
Traction Motors: 2 x Alsthom TAB 674 C4 frame mounted.
One Hour Rating: 4400 kW.   **Weight:** 83 tonnes.
Maximum Tractive Effort: 294 kN.   **Length over Buffers:** 17.48 m.
Driving Wheel Diameter: 1250 mm.   **Maximum Speed:** 160 km/h.

k Fitted with auto-coupler at one end.

1701	k	LE		1727	k	LE	
1702	k	LE		1728	k	LE	
1703	k	LE		1729		MT	
1704	k	LE		1730		MT	
1705	k	LE	DALFSEN	1731		MT	PURMEREND
1706	k	LE		1732		MT	ZEVENBERGEN
1707	k	LE		1733		MT	
1708	k	LE		1734		MT	
1709	k	LE		1736		MT	GILZE-RIJEN
1710	k	LE		1737		MT	
1711	k	LE	EMMEN	1738		MT	DUIVENDRECHT
1712	k	LE		1739		MT	DAALEN
1713	k	LE		1740		MT	BARN
1714	k	LE	VEENENDAAL	1741		MT	PUTTEN
1715	k	LE		1742		MT	
1716	k	LE		1743		MT	WOLVEGA
1717	k	LE		1744		MT	WIJCHEN
1718	k	LE		1745		MT	
1719	k	LE	VOORHOUT	1746		MT	CASTRICUM
1720	k	LE	BEILEN	1747		MT	
1721	k	LE		1748		MT	
1722	k	LE		1749		MT	
1723	k	LE		1750		MT	
1724	k	LE	Anna Paulowna	1751		MT	
1725	k	LE		1752		MT	
1726	k	LE		1753		MT	

1754	MT	DIEMEN	1768	MT	Boomsterhiem	
1755	MT		1769	MT		
1756	MT		1770	MT		
1757	MT		1771	MT	Abcoude	
1758	MT		1772	MT		
1759	MT		1773	MT	ENKHUIZEN	
1760	MT	AKKRUM	1774	MT	GRAMSBERGEN	
1761	MT		1775	MT		
1762	MT		1776	MT		
1763	MT		1777	MT		
1764	MT		1778	MT		
1765	MT		1779	MT		
1766	MT		1780	MT		
1767	MT		1781	MT		

CLASS 1800 B-B

These locomotives are based on the SNCF Class BB 7200 designed for a maximum speed of 200 km/h but NS locomotives are limited to 160 km/h. They were originally numbered as Class 1600 but the NS Reizigers ones have been renumbered in the 1800 series leaving the Railion ones in the 1600 series.

Built: 1981–83.
Builder: Alsthom.
Traction Motors: 2 x Alsthom TAB 674 C4 frame mounted.
One Hour Rating: 4400 kW. **Weight:** 83 tonnes.
Maximum Tractive Effort: 294 kN. **Length over Buffers:** 17.48 m.
Driving Wheel Diameter: 1250 mm. **Maximum Speed:** 160 km/h.

All push-pull fitted.

1823	MT	HILVERSUM	1842	MT	WEERT
1824	MT	ALKMAAR	1843	MT	HEERLEN
1826	MT	MEPPEL	1844	MT	ROOSENDAAL
1827	MT	GOUDA	1845	MT	MIDDELBURG
1828	MT	APELDOORN	1846	MT	LEEUWARDEN
1829	MT	EDE	1847	MT	DELFT
1830	MT	ZWOLLE	1848	MT	VALKENBURG
1831	MT	VOORBURG	1849	MT	OSS
1832	MT	NIJMEGEN	1850	MT	DEN HAAG
1833	MT	BERGEN OP ZOOM	1851	MT	TILBURG
1834	MT	LELYSTAD	1852	MT	UTRECHT
1835	MT	ENSCHEDE	1853	MT	DEN HELDER
1836	MT	HEERENVEEN	1854	MT	GELEEN
1837	MT	AMERSFOORT	1855	MT	EINDHOVEN
1839	MT	LEIDEN	1856	MT	HOOGEVEEN
1840	MT	STEENWIJK	1857	MT	ROTTERDAM
1841	MT	ALMERE	1858	MT	ZAANDAM

See also Section 6.1 for leased Class 186 locomotives to be used on the Brussels–Amsterdam service.

3.3. DIESEL MULTIPLE UNITS

CLASS DM'90   2-CAR UNITS

These units were introduced to replace the remaining 1950s and 1960s-built DMUs. Assembly was at the Duewag plant in Germany with Talbot providing the bodies and SIG the bogies. They can only work on lines which have been modified with new generation ATB.

mBk+mABk (DMSO–DMCO).

Built: 1995–1999.
Builder: Duewag/Talbot/SIG.
Engine: Cummins NT855R4 of 320 kW at 2000 r.p.m.
Transmission: Hydraulic. Voith 211 rzze.   **Weight:** 47 + 48 tonnes.
Wheel Arrangement: 2-B + B-2.   **Length over Couplers:** 26.17 + 26.17 m.
Accommodation: –/48 1T + 24/37 1T.   **Maximum Speed:** 140 km/h.

Disc brakes. Magnetic track brakes.
d Modified with retractible steps and Indusi for working to Aachen, Germany.

3401	Y	ON	3413	Y	ON	3424	Y	ON	3434	Y	ON
3402	Y	ON	3414	Y	ON	3425	Y	ON	3435	Y	ON
3403	Y	ON	3415	Y	ON	3426	Y	ON	3436	Y	ON
3404	Y	ON	3416	Y	ON	3427	Y	ON	3443	Y	ON
3406	Y	ON	3417	Y	ON	3428	Y	ON	3444	Y	ON
3407	Y	ON	3418	Y	ON	3429	Y	ON	3445	Y	ON
3408	Y	ON	3419	Y	ON	3430	Y	ON	3446	Y	ON
3409	Y	ON	3420	Y	ON	3431	Y d	MS	3447	Y	ON
3410	Y	ON	3421	Y	ON	3432	Y d	MS	3448	Y	ON
3411	Y	ON	3422	Y	ON	3433	Y d	MS	3449	Y	ON
3412	Y	ON	3423	Y	ON						

3.4. ELECTRIC MULTIPLE UNITS

All NS EMUs are gangwayed within the unit only, except for the unrefurbished Plan Z "Koploper" units which have through gangways. All are disc-braked except for Plan V, T and mP which have tread brakes. All have power-operated sliding or folding doors. The various builds of NS EMUs can easily be recognised by their front-end design as follows:

1964 stock ('Mat 64') have short bonnets with the outer cab windows pointed. They are used mainly on stopping services, but also on some Intercity services.
Sprinters were built between 1972 and 1976 and have a slightly sloping front end which curves in at the bottom.
Koplopers were built between 1977 and 1993 and have gangwayed ends with a roof cab.
Regio Runners are double-deck units with a distinctive front-end design.

EMUs are often referred to by their formation code as follows:
EL EMU, D includes guard's/luggage area (dienst), P Post area. 2, 3 or 4 Number of cars.
Example: ELD-2 is a two car EMU with guard's/luggage accommodation.

PLAN V4, V5 & V6   2-CAR UNITS

Mat'64. These sets work *stoptreinen* all over the NS network, as well as some Intercities. They operate as a common fleet with all other Plan V stock.

mABk + mBk (DMCso–DMSso).

Built: 1969–70.
Builder–Mechanical Parts: Werkspoor (441–461), Talbot (462–483).
Builder–Electrical Parts: Smit.
Traction Motors: 4 x Heemaf 145 kW.   **Weight:** 43 + 42 tonnes.
Wheel Arrangement: 2-Bo + Bo-2.   **Length over Couplers:** 26.07 + 26.07 m.
Accommodation: 24/40 1T + –/78.   **Maximum Speed:** 140 km/h.

441–461 are V4, 462–471 are V5 and 472–483 are V6.

441	MT	451	MT	463	MT	474	MT
443	MT	452	MT	464	MT	475	MT
444	MT	453	MT	465	MT	476	MT
445	MT	454	MT	466	MT	478	MT
446	MT	455	MT	467	MT	479	MT
447	MT	456	MT	469	MT	480	MT
449	MT	457	MT	470	MT	482	MT
450	MT	458	MT	471	MT		

PLAN T   4-CAR UNITS

These 4-car units were originally designed for Intercity use for which they were fitted with pantries and a buffet area. They have all been refurbished with new seating and the pantry, restaurant and luggage areas have been removed, as well as two toilets. They operate over a limited area in and around the Randstad in particular between Haarlem CS and Dordrecht. To be withdrawn soon.

Bk + mBD + mAB + Bk (DTSso–MBSO–MCso–DTSo).

Built: 1964–65.
Builder–Mechanical Parts: Werkspoor.
Builder–Electrical Parts: Smit.
Traction Motors: 8 x Heemaf 150 kW.   **Weight:** 39 + 47 + 46 + 36 tonnes.
Wheel Arrangement: 2-2 + Bo-Bo + Bo-Bo + 2-2.
Accommodation: –/80 + –/76 1T + 42/24 1T + –/80.
Length over Couplers: 26.07 + 24.93 + 24.93 + 26.07 m.
Maximum Speed: 140 km/h.

502	AZ	510	AZ	517	AZ	524	AZ
503	AZ	511	AZ	518	AZ	526	AZ
504	AZ	512	AZ	519	AZ	527	AZ
505	AZ	513	AZ	520	AZ	528	AZ
506	AZ	514	AZ	521	AZ	529	AZ
507	AZ	515	AZ	522	AZ	530	AZ
508	AZ	516	AZ	523	AZ(S)	531	AZ
509	AZ						

PLAN V7   2-CAR UNITS

1964 stock. Similar to other Plan V units, but built with post compartment which has since been converted to open saloon containing 16 seats in 4+0 layout.

mABk + mBPk (DMCso–DMPSO).

Built: 1970–72.
Builder–Mechanical Parts: Werkspoor.
Builder–Electrical Parts: Smit.
Traction Motors: 4 x Heemaf 145 kW.   **Weight:** 43 + 42 tonnes.
Wheel Arrangement: 2-Bo + Bo-2.   **Length over Couplers:** 26.07 + 26.07 m.
Accommodation: 24/40 1T + –/80.   **Maximum Speed:** 140 km/h.

801	MT	811	MT	822	MT	832	MT
802	MT	812	MT	823	MT	833	MT
803	MT	813	MT	824	MT	834	MT
804	MT	814	MT	825	MT	835	MT
805	MT	816	MT	827	MT	836	MT
806	MT	817	MT	828	MT	837	MT
807	MT	818	MT	829	MT	838	MT
808	MT	819	MT	830	MT	839	MT
809	MT	820	MT	831	MT	840	MT
810	MT	821	MT				

PLAN V8–V13

2-CAR UNITS

1964 stock. Talbot version of Plan V7.

mABk + mBPk (DMCso–DMPSO).

Built: 1972–76.
Builder–Mechanical Parts: Talbot (Düwag mABk 841–870).
Builder–Electrical Parts: Smit.
Traction Motors: 4 x Heemaf 145 kW.
Wheel Arrangement: 2-Bo + Bo-2.
Accommodation: 24/40 1T + –/64.

Weight: 45 + 43 tonnes.
Length over Couplers: 26.07 + 26.07 m.
Maximum Speed: 140 km/h.

850–870 are V8, 871–888 are V9, 889–920 are V10, 921–935 are V11, 936–950 are V12 and 851–965 are V13.

p   Post compartment converted to passenger accommodation with 12 tip-up seats.

850	p	MT	885	MT	911		MT	939	p	MT
851	p	MT	886	MT	912		MT	940	p	MT
852	p	MT(S)	887	MT	913		MT	941	p	MT
853	p	MT	888	MT	914		MT	942	p	MT
854	p	MT	889	MT	915		MT	943	p	MT
855	p	MT	890	MT	917		MT	944	p	MT
856	p	MT	891	MT	918		MT	945	p	MT
857	p	MT	892	MT	919		MT	946	p	MT
858	p	MT	893	MT	920		MT	947	p	MT
859	p	MT	894	MT	921	p	MT	948	p	MT
860	p	MT	895	MT	922	p	MT	949	p	MT
861	p	MT	896	MT	923	p	MT	950	p	MT
862	p	MT	897	MT	924	p	MT	951	p	MT
863	p	MT	898	MT	925	p	MT	952	p	MT
871		MT(S)	899	MT	926	p	MT	953	p	MT
872		MT	900	MT	927	p	MT	954	p	MT
873		MT	901	MT	928	p	MT	955	p	MT
874		MT	902	MT	929	p	MT	956	p	MT
875		MT	903	MT	930	p	MT	957	p	MT
876		MT	904	MT	931	p	MT	958	p	MT
877		MT	905	MT	932	p	MT	960	p	MT
879		MT	906	MT	933	p	MT	961	p	MT
880		MT	907	MT	934	p	MT	962	p	MT
881		MT	908	MT	935	p	MT	963	p	MT
882	p	MT	909	MT	936	p	MT	964	p	MT
883		MT	910	MT	937	p	MT	965	p	MT
884		MT								

PLAN Y1   SPRINTER SGM 0   2-CAR UNITS

The earliest batch of 'Sprinter' units from which BR's Sprinters took their name, these sets formerly worked on the Den Haag CS–Rotterdam Hofplein line and the Zoetemeer Stadslijn. The rapid acceleration from a standing start was especially useful on these lines which have stations at very close intervals. These two lines have now been transferred to Randstad Rail and have been converted to light rail operation and so the Sprinters have been transferred to other lines. All sets have been modified with first class seating removed, fewer seats and more room for standees. They are branded "City Pendel". They are now starting to be refurbished in a similar manner to the 3-car units.

mABk + mBk (DMCO–DMSO).

Built: 1975–76.
Builder–Mechanical Parts: Talbot.
Builder–Electrical Parts: Oerlikon.
Traction Motors: 8 x Oerlikon 160 kW.
Wheel Arrangement: Bo-Bo + Bo-Bo.

Accommodation: –/40 + –/40.
Weight: 52.5 + 52.5 tonnes.
Length over Couplers: 26.10 + 26.10 m.
Maximum Speed: 125 km/h.

r Refurbished and renumbered units. Numbers in brackets are as unrefurbished.

2111	(2001)	Y	LD	2116	(2006)	Y	LD	2121	(2011)	Y	LD
2112	(2002)	Y	LD	2117	(2007)	Y	LD	2122	(2012)	Y	LD
2113	(2003)	Y	LD	2118	(2008)	Y	LD	2123	(2013)	Y	LD
2114	(2004)	Y	LD	2119	(2009)	Y	LD	2124	(2014)	Y	LD
2115	(2005)	Y	LD	2120	(2010)	Y	LD	2125	(2015)	Y	LD

PLAN Y2   SPRINTER SGM 1   2-CAR UNITS

These sets are similar to Plan Y0, but were built with a toilet and gangways, although the toilets have now been removed. They also previously worked on the Hofpleinlijn and Zoetermeer Stadslijn. Also being refurbished.

mABk + mBk (DMCO–DMSOL).

Built: 1975–76.
Builder–Mechanical Parts: Talbot.
Builder–Electrical Parts: Oerlikon.
Traction Motors: 8 x Oerlikon 160 kW.   **Weight:** 54 + 53 tonnes.
Wheel Arrangement: Bo-Bo + Bo-Bo.   **Length over Couplers:** 26.10 + 26.10 m.
Accommodation: –/40 + –/40.   **Maximum Speed:** 125 km/h.
r Refurbished and renumbered units. Numbers in brackets are as unrefurbished.

2131	(2021)	Y		LD	2136	(2026)	Y		LD	2141	(2031)	S	r	LD
2132	(2022)	Y		LD	2137	(2027)	Y		LD	2142	(2032)	Y		LD
2133	(2023)	S	r	LD	2138	(2028)	Y		LD	2143	(2033)	Y		LD
2134	(2024)	Y		LD	2139	(2029)	Y		LD	2144	(2034)	Y		LD
2135	(2025)	Y		LD	2140	(2030)	Y		LD	2145	(2035)	Y		LD

TYPE S70   SPRINTER LIGHT TRAIN   4-CAR UNITS

New articulated units now being delivered. Based on DB Class 424.

mABk + B + mB + mABk (DMCO–TSO–MSO–DMCO).

Built: 2008 onwards. Bombardier design.
Builder–Mechanical Parts: Bombardier Aachen.
Builder–Electrical Parts: Siemens (heavy parts), Bombardier (electronics).
Traction Motors: 6 Siemens of 250 kW.   **Weight:** 129 tonnes.
Wheel Arrangement: Bo-2-2-Bo-Bo.   **Length over Couplers:** 69.36 m.
Accommodation: 40/144 (38).   **Width:** 2.84 m.
Air Conditioning: Liebherr.   **Floor Height at Entrance:** 800 mm.
Maximum Speed: 140 km/h.

2401	S	LD	2414	S	2427	S	2439	S
2402	S	LD	2415	S	2428	S	2440	S
2403	S		2416	S	2429	S	2441	S
2404	S		2417	S	2430	S	2442	S
2405	S		2418	S	2431	S	2443	S
2406	S		2419	S	2432	S	2444	S
2407	S		2420	S	2433	S	2445	S
2408	S		2421	S	2434	S	2446	S
2409	S		2422	S	2435	S	2447	S
2410	S		2423	S	2436	S	2448	S
2411	S		2424	S	2437	S	2449	S
2412	S		2425	S	2438	S	2450	S
2413	S		2426	S				

TYPE S100   SPRINTER LIGHT TRAIN   6-CAR UNITS

New articulated units now being delivered. Based on DB Class 424.

mABk + mB + B + B + mB + mABk (DMCO–MSO–TSO–TSO–MSO–DMSO).

Built: 2008 onwards. Bombardier design.
Builder: Siemens Krefeld.
Builder–Electrical Parts: Siemens (heavy parts), Bombardier (electronics).
Traction Motors: 8 Siemens of 250 kW.   **Weight:** 176 tonnes.
Wheel Arrangement: Bo-Bo-2-2-2-Bo-Bo.   **Length over Couplers:** 100.54 m.
Accommodation: 56/208 (68).   **Width:** 2.84 m.

Air Conditioning: Liebherr.
Maximum Speed: 140 km/h.

Floor Height at Entrance: 800 mm.

2601	S		2614	S	2626	S	2638	S
2602	S	LD	2615	S	2627	S	2639	S
2603	S		2616	S	2628	S	2640	S
2604	S		2617	S	2629	S	2641	S
2605	S		2618	S	2630	S	2642	S
2606	S		2619	S	2631	S	2643	S
2607	S		2620	S	2632	S	2644	S
2608	S		2621	S	2633	S	2645	S
2609	S		2622	S	2634	S	2646	S
2610	S		2623	S	2635	S	2647	S
2611	S		2624	S	2636	S	2648	S
2612	S		2625	S	2637	S	2649	S
2613	S							

PLAN Y2/Y3   SPRINTER SGM 1/2   3-CAR UNITS

2036–2080 were built as 2-car units but were strengthened with an intermediate trailer, reclassified from Plan Y1 to Plan Y2 and renumbered 2836–2880. 2881–2895 were built as 3-car units and are Plan Y3. The units work on *stoptreinen* in the Randstad area such as Amsterdam–Utrecht, Amsterdam–Haarlem–Uitgeest, Amsterdam–Alkmaar and Rotterdam CS–Hoek van Holland. All sets have now been refurbished at Randers, Denmark and renumbered from the 2800 to the 2900 series.

mBk + AB + mBk (DMSO–TCO–DMSO).

Built: 1978–80 (Plan Y1).1983–84 (Plan Y3 and centre cars of Plan Y2).
Builder–Mechanical Parts: Talbot.
Builder–Electrical Parts: Oerlikon.
Traction Motors: 8 x Oerlikon 160 kW.
Wheel Arrangement: Bo-Bo + 2-2 + Bo-Bo.
Accommodation: –/72 + 40/40 1T + –/72 1T.

Weight: 54 + 36 + 53 tonnes.
Length over Couplers: 26.15 + 26.40 + 26.15 m.
Maximum Speed: 125 km/h.

2936	(2036)	S	LD		2956	(2056)	S	LD		2976	(2076)	S	LD
2937	(2037)	S	LD		2957	(2057)	S	LD		2977	(2077)	S	LD
2938	(2038)	S	LD		2958	(2058)	S	LD		2978	(2078)	S	LD
2939	(2039)	S	LD		2959	(2059)	S	LD		2979	(2079)	S	LD
2940	(2040)	S	LD		2960	(2060)	S	LD		2980	(2080)	S	LD
2941	(2041)	S	LD		2961	(2061)	S	LD		2981		S	*	LD
2942	(2042)	S	LD		2962	(2062)	S	LD		2982		S	LD
2943	(2043)	S	LD		2963	(2063)	S	LD		2983		S	LD
2944	(2044)	S	LD		2964	(2064)	S	LD		2984		S	LD
2945	(2045)	S	LD		2965	(2065)	S	LD		2985		S	LD
2946	(2046)	S	LD		2966	(2066)	S	LD		2986		S	LD
2947	(2047)	S	LD		2967	(2067)	S	LD		2987		S	LD
2948	(2048)	S	LD		2968	(2068)	S	LD		2988		S	LD
2949	(2049)	S	LD		2969	(2069)	S	LD		2989		S	LD
2950	(2050)	S	LD		2970	(2070)	S	LD		2990		S	LD
2951	(2051)	S	LD		2971	(2071)	S	LD		2991		S	LD
2952	(2052)	S	LD		2972	(2072)	S	LD		2992		S	LD
2953	(2053)	S	LD		2973	(2073)	S	LD		2993		S	LD
2954	(2054)	S	LD		2974	(2074)	S	LD		2994		S	LD
2955	(2055)	S	LD		2975	(2075)	S	LD		2995		S	LD

ICM1/2 (PLAN Z0/Z1)   KOPLOPER   3-CAR UNITS

These strikingly modern Intercity units, also known as IC3 units, have raised cabs and through gangways. The coaches in these sets formed the basis for the loco-hauled ICR stock now familiar over many NS routes. These units and the similar 4-car units can be found on Intercity services to Groningen, Leeuwarden, Enschede and Arnhem. The prototype units (4001–7) have now been withdrawn.

mBDk + AB + sBFk (DMSO [kitchenette/pantry]–TCsoL–DTSOL [with cycle space]).

r Units refurbished with interiors similar to the ICR coaching stock operating on the Brussels–Amsterdam services (red leather seats in first class and blue moquette in second class. End gangways sealed. mBFk + AB + sBk (DMSO with cycle space–TCsoL–DTSOL with conductor room).

Built: 1977*/83–89.
Builder–Mechanical Parts: Talbot.
Builder–Electrical Parts: Oerlikon.
Traction Motors: 4 x Oerlikon 312 kW.
Gangways: Large gangways at both ends with cabs on top.
Wheel Arrangement: Bo-Bo + 2-2 + 2-2.
Accommodation: –/54 + 35/31 2T + –/63 1T + bicycle space.
r –/68 + bicycle space + 35/27 (3) 1TD + –/68.
Weight: 59 (r 60) + 42 + 42 tonnes.
Length over Couplers: 27.05 + 26.50 + 27.05 m.
Maximum Speed: 160 km/h.

4011	I	r	ON	4033	I	ON	4055	I	ON	4077	I	ON
4012	I	r	ON	4034	I	ON	4056	I	ON	4078	I	ON
4013	I	r	ON	4035	I	ON	4057	I	ON	4079	I	ON
4014	I	r	ON	4036	I	ON	4058	I	ON	4080	I	ON
4015	I	r	ON	4037	I	ON	4059	I	ON	4081	I	ON
4016	I	r	ON	4038	I	ON	4060	I	ON	4082	I	ON
4017	I	r	ON	4039	I	ON	4061	I	ON	4083	I	ON
4018	I	r	ON	4040	I	ON	4062	I	ON	4084	I	ON
4019	I	r	ON	4041	I	ON	4063	I	ON	4085	I	ON
4020	I	r	ON	4042	I	ON	4064	I	ON	4086	I	ON
4021	I	r	ON	4043	I	ON	4065	I	ON	4087	I	ON
4022	I	ON	4044	I	ON	4066	I	ON	4088	I	ON
4023	I	r	ON	4045	I	ON	4067	I	ON	4089	I	ON
4024	I	r	ON	4046	I	ON	4068	I	ON	4090	I	ON
4025	I	r	ON	4047	I	ON	4069	I	ON	4091	I	ON
4026	I	r	ON	4048	I	ON	4070	I	ON	4092	I	ON
4027	I	ON	4049	I	ON	4071	I	ON	4093	I	ON
4028	I	ON	4050	I	ON	4072	I	ON	4094	I	ON
4029	I	ON	4051	I	ON	4073	I	ON	4095	I	ON
4030	I	ON	4052	I	ON	4074	I	ON	4096	I	ON
4031	I	ON	4053	I	ON	4075	I	ON	4097	I	ON
4032	I	ON	4054	I	ON	4076	I	ON			

ICM3 (PLAN Z2)   KOPLOPER   4-CAR UNITS

These units are a four-car version of the IC3s and are used on the same services.

mBDk + B + A + sBFk (DMSO (kitchenette/pantry)–MSOL–TFsoL–DTSOL).

Built: 1990 onwards.
Builder–Mechanical Parts: Talbot.
Builder–Electrical Parts: Oerlikon.
Traction Motors: 6 x Oerlikon 312 kW.
Gangways: Large gangways at both ends with cabs on top.
Wheel Arrangement: Bo-Bo + Bo-2 + 2-2 + 2-2.
Accommodation: –/55 + –/80 1T + 59/– 2T + –/63 1T.
Weight: 59 + 50 + 42 + 42 tonnes.
Length over Couplers: 27.05 + 26.50 + 26.50 + 27.05 m.
Maximum Speed: 160 km/h.
Non-Standard Livery: N Olympic games (orange).

Note: 4231 was numbered 4444 for a time when it had extra first class accommodation.

4201	N	ON	4210	I	ON	4219	I	ON	4228	I	ON
4202	I	ON	4211	I	ON	4220	I	ON	4229	I	ON
4203	I	ON	4212	I	ON	4221	I	ON	4230	I	ON
4204	I	ON	4213	I	ON	4222	I	ON	4231	I	ON
4205	I	ON	4214	I	ON	4223	I	ON	4232	I	ON
4206	I	ON	4215	I	ON	4224	I	ON	4233	I	ON
4207	I	ON	4216	I	ON	4225	I	ON	4234	I	ON
4208	I	ON	4217	I	ON	4226	I	ON	4235	I	ON
4209	I	ON	4218	I	ON	4227	I	ON	4236	I	ON

4237	I	ON	4241	N	ON	4245	I	ON	4248	I	ON
4238	I	ON	4242	I	ON	4246	I	ON	4249	I	ON
4239	I	ON	4243	I	ON	4247	I	ON	4250	I	ON
4240	N	ON	4244	I	ON						

VIRM   REGIO RUNNER   4/6-CAR UNITS

These double-decker units were originally known as IRM (*Inter-Regio Materieel*). They work various Intercity services over a wide area. They were built as 3 and 4-car units, but in 2001–05 all units had an extra intermediate transformer trailer (Type ABv6) added and 4-car units had an intermediate power car (mBv7) added alsc, so that all are now either 4 or 6-car dual voltage units. They are now known as VIRM (V=*Verlengte* (lengthened). Unit numbers were 82xx series for three-car units and 84xx series for four-car units. They are now 94xx series for the 4-car units and 86xx series for the 6-car units. The set number is determined by the ABv3/4 car. Thus 9403 contains 380 8003. The set numbers are in a sequence of the last 2 numbers and change if a 4-car is converted to a 6-car or vice-versa. So 9408 became 8608 when it became a 6-car unit and 8643 became 9443 when it became a 4-car unit.

An extra batch was built from 2003–2005 and these have unit numbers in the 95xx and 87xx series.

A new batch of 4-car units is under construction.

mBvk1/2 [+ ABv5 + mBv7] + ABv6 + ABv3/4 + mBvk1/2 (DMSO[–TCO–MSO]–TSO–TCO–DMSO).

Built: 1994–96/2001–05.
Builder–Mechanical Parts: VIRM1 – Talbot (De Dietrich), VIRM2/3 Bombardier Talbot.
Builder–Electrical Parts: Holec.
Systems: 1500 V DC/25 kV AC 25 Hz.
Wheel Arrangement: 2-Bo + 2-2 [+ 2-2 + 2-Bo] + 2-2 + Bo-2.
Traction Motors: 2 x Holec-Riddekerk DMKT 60/45 of 302 kW continuous rating per motor car.
Accommodation: –/97(4) [+ 46/48(4) 1T –/94(5)]+ 46/52 1T + 23/80 1T + –/97(4).
Weight: 62.2 [+ ? + ?] + 52.4 (+ ?) + 62.2 tonnes.
Length over Couplers: 27.28 [+ 26.50 + 26.50] + 26.50 + 26.50 + 27.28 m.
Maximum Speed: 160 km/h.
Non-Standard Livery: N Olympic games (orange).

Note: 290 8611 and 290 8718 (ex 9528) have been scrapped and 290 8539 (ex 9420) has accident damage.

NUMBERING.

Set formations vary from time to time. The individual car numbers are listed here together with set formations as far as is known at time of going to press. The individual car numbers are quite small and in one corner at solebar level.

INDIVIDUAL CARS.

mBvk.

290 8501	I	ON	290 8521	I	ON	290 8541	I	ON	290 8561	I	ON
290 8502	I	ON	290 8522	I	ON	290 8542	I	ON	290 8562	I	ON
290 8503	I	ON	290 8523	I	ON	290 8543	I	ON	290 8563	I	ON
290 8504	I	ON	290 8524	I	ON	290 8544	I	ON	290 8564	I	ON
290 8505	I	ON	290 8525	I	ON	290 8545	I	ON	290 8565	I	ON
290 8506	I	ON	290 8526	I	ON	290 8546	I	ON	290 8566	I	ON
290 8507	I	ON	290 8527	I	ON	290 8547	I	ON	290 8567	I	ON
290 8508	I	ON	290 8528	I	ON	290 8548	I	ON	290 8568	I	ON
290 8509	I	ON	290 8529	I	ON	290 8549	I	ON	290 8569	I	ON
290 8510	I	ON	290 8530	I	ON	290 8550	I	ON	290 8570	I	ON
290 8511	I	ON	290 8531	I	ON	290 8551	I	ON	290 8571	I	ON
290 8512	I	ON	290 8532	I	ON	290 8552	I	ON	290 8572	I	ON
290 8513	I	ON	290 8533	I	ON	290 8553	I	ON	290 8573	I	ON
290 8514	I	ON	290 8534	I	ON	290 8554	I	ON	290 8574	I	ON
290 8515	I	ON	290 8535	I	ON	290 8555	I	ON	290 8575	I	ON
290 8516	I	ON	290 8536	I	ON	290 8556	I	ON	290 8576	I	ON
290 8517	I	ON	290 8537	I	ON	290 8557	I	ON	290 8577	I	ON
290 8518	I	ON	290 8538	I	ON	290 8558	I	ON	290 8578	I	ON
290 8519	I	ON	290 8539	I	ON	290 8559	I	ON	290 8579	I	ON
290 8520	I	ON	290 8540	I	ON	290 8560	I	ON	290 8580	I	ON

290 8581	I	ON	290 8625	I	ON	290 8669	I	ON	290 8712	N	ON
290 8582	I	ON	290 8626	I	ON	290 8670	I	ON	290 8713	I	ON
290 8583	I	ON	290 8627	I	ON	290 8671	I	ON	290 8714	I	ON
290 8584	I	ON	290 8628	I	ON	290 8672	I	ON	290 8715	I	ON
290 8585	I	ON	290 8629	I	ON	290 8673	I	ON	290 8716	I	ON
290 8586	I	ON	290 8630	I	ON	290 8674	I	ON	290 8717	I	ON
290 8587	I	ON	290 8631	I	ON	290 8675	I	ON	290 8718	I	ON
290 8588	I	ON	290 8632	I	ON	290 8676	I	ON	290 8719	I	ON
290 8589	I	ON	290 8633	I	ON	290 8677	I	ON	290 8720	I	ON
290 8590	I	ON	290 8634	I	ON	290 8678	I	ON	290 8721	I	ON
290 8591	I	ON	290 8635	I	ON	290 8679	I	ON	290 8722	I	ON
290 8592	I	ON	290 8636	I	ON	290 8680	I	ON	290 8723	I	ON
290 8593	I	ON	290 8637	I	ON	290 8681	I	ON	290 8724	I	ON
290 8594	I	ON	290 8638	I	ON	290 8682	I	ON	290 8725	I	ON
290 8595	I	ON	290 8639	I	ON	290 8683	I	ON	290 8726	I	ON
290 8596	I	ON	290 8640	I	ON	290 8684	I	ON	290 8727	I	ON
290 8597	I	ON	290 8641	I	ON	290 8685	I	ON	290 8728	I	ON
290 8598	I	ON	290 8642	I	ON	290 8686	I	ON	290 8729	I	ON
290 8599	I	ON	290 8643	I	ON	290 8687	I	ON	290 8730	I	ON
290 8600	I	ON	290 8644	I	ON	290 8688	I	ON	290 8731	I	ON
290 8601	I	ON	290 8645	I	ON	290 8689	I	ON	290 8732	I	ON
290 8602	I	ON	290 8646	I	ON	290 8690	I	ON	290 8733	I	ON
290 8603	I	ON	290 8647	I	ON	290 8691	I	ON	290 8734	I	ON
290 8604	I	ON	290 8648	I	ON	290 8692	I	ON	290 8735	I	ON
290 8605	I	ON	290 8649	I	ON	290 8693	I	ON	290 8736	I	ON
290 8606	I	ON	290 8650	I	ON	290 8694	I	ON	290 8737	I	ON
290 8607	I	ON	290 8651	I	ON	290 8695	I	ON	290 8738	I	ON
290 8608	I	ON	290 8652	I	ON	290 8696	I	ON	290 8739	I	ON
290 8609	I	ON	290 8653	I	ON	290 8697	I	ON	290 8740	I	ON
290 8610	I	ON	290 8654	I	ON	290 8698	I	ON	290 8741	I	ON
290 8611	I	ON	290 8655	I	ON	290 8699	I	ON	290 8742	I	ON
290 8612	I	ON	290 8656	I	ON	290 8700	I	ON	290 8743	I	ON
290 8613	I	ON	290 8657	I	ON	290 8701	N	ON	290 8744	I	ON
290 8614	I	ON	290 8658	I	ON	290 8702	N	ON	290 8745	I	ON
290 8615	I	ON	290 8659	I	ON	290 8703	I	ON	290 8746	I	ON
290 8616	I	ON	290 8660	I	ON	290 8704	I	ON	290 8747	I	ON
290 8617	I	ON	290 8661	I	ON	290 8705	I	ON	290 8748	I	ON
290 8618	I	ON	290 8662	I	ON	290 8706	I	ON	290 8749	I	ON
290 8619	I	ON	290 8663	I	ON	290 8707	I	ON	290 8750	I	ON
290 8620	I	ON	290 8664	I	ON	290 8708	I	ON	290 8751	I	ON
290 8621	I	ON	290 8665	I	ON	290 8709	I	ON	290 8752	I	ON
290 8622	I	ON	290 8666	I	ON	290 8710	I	ON	290 8753	I	ON
290 8623	I	ON	290 8667	I	ON	290 8711	N	ON	290 8754	I	ON
290 8624	I	ON	290 8668	I	ON						

mBv7.

260 8801	I	ON	260 8819	I	ON	260 8837	I	ON	260 8855	I	ON
260 8802	I	ON	260 8820	I	ON	260 8838	I	ON	260 8856	I	ON
260 8803	I	ON	260 8821	I	ON	260 8839	I	ON	260 8857	I	ON
260 8804	I	ON	260 8822	I	ON	260 8840	I	ON	260 8858	I	ON
260 8805	I	ON	260 8823	I	ON	260 8841	I	ON	260 8859	I	ON
260 8806	I	ON	260 8824	I	ON	260 8842	I	ON	260 8860	I	ON
260 8807	I	ON	260 8825	I	ON	260 8843	I	ON	260 8861	I	ON
260 8808	I	ON	260 8826	I	ON	260 8844	I	ON	260 8862	I	ON
260 8809	I	ON	260 8827	I	ON	260 8845	I	ON	260 8863	I	ON
260 8810	I	ON	260 8828	I	ON	260 8846	I	ON	260 8864	I	ON
260 8811	I	ON	260 8829	I	ON	260 8847	I	ON	260 8865	I	ON
260 8812	I	ON	260 8830	I	ON	260 8848	I	ON	260 8866	I	ON
260 8813	I	ON	260 8831	I	ON	260 8849	I	ON	260 8867	I	ON
260 8814	I	ON	260 8832	I	ON	260 8850	I	ON	260 8868	I	ON
260 8815	I	ON	260 8833	I	ON	260 8851	I	ON	260 8869	I	ON
260 8816	I	ON	260 8834	I	ON	260 8852	I	ON	260 8870	I	ON
260 8817	I	ON	260 8835	I	ON	260 8853	I	ON	260 8871	I	ON
260 8818	I	ON	260 8836	I	ON	260 8854	I	ON	260 8872	I	ON

260 8873	I	ON	260 8875	I	ON	260 8877	I	ON	260 8879	I	ON
260 8874	I	ON	260 8876	I	ON	260 8878	I	ON	260 8880	I	ON

ABv3/4.

380 8001	I	ON	380 8033	I	ON	380 8065	I	ON	380 8116	I	ON
380 8002	I	ON	380 8034	I	ON	380 8066	I	ON	380 8117	I	ON
380 8003	I	ON	380 8035	I	ON	380 8067	I	ON	380 8118	I	ON
380 8004	I	ON	380 8036	I	ON	380 8068	I	ON	380 8119	I	ON
380 8005	I	ON	380 8037	I	ON	380 8069	I	ON	380 8120	N	ON
380 8006	I	ON	380 8038	I	ON	380 8070	I	ON	380 8121	I	ON
380 8007	I	ON	380 8039	I	ON	380 8071	I	ON	380 8122	I	ON
380 8008	I	ON	380 8040	I	ON	380 8072	I	ON	380 8123	I	ON
380 8009	I	ON	380 8041	I	ON	380 8073	I	ON	380 8124	I	ON
380 8010	I	ON	380 8042	I	ON	380 8074	I	ON	380 8125	N	ON
380 8011	I	ON	380 8043	I	ON	380 8075	I	ON	380 8126	I	ON
380 8012	I	ON	380 8044	I	ON	380 8076	I	ON	380 8127	I	ON
380 8013	I	ON	380 8045	I	ON	380 8077	I	ON	380 8128	I	ON
380 8014	I	ON	380 8046	I	ON	380 8078	I	ON	380 8129	I	ON
380 8015	I	ON	380 8047	I	ON	380 8079	I	ON	380 8130	I	ON
380 8016	I	ON	380 8048	I	ON	380 8080	I	ON	380 8131	I	ON
380 8017	I	ON	380 8049	I	ON	380 8081	I	ON	380 8132	I	ON
380 8018	I	ON	380 8050	I	ON	380 8101	I	ON	380 8133	I	ON
380 8019	I	ON	380 8051	I	ON	380 8102	I	ON	380 8134	I	ON
380 8020	I	ON	380 8052	I	ON	380 8103	I	ON	380 8135	I	ON
380 8021	I	ON	380 8053	I	ON	380 8104	I	ON	380 8136	I	ON
380 8022	I	ON	380 8054	I	ON	380 8105	I	ON	380 8137	I	ON
380 8023	I	ON	380 8055	I	ON	380 8106	I	ON	380 8138	I	ON
380 8024	I	ON	380 8056	I	ON	380 8107	I	ON	380 8139	I	ON
380 8025	I	ON	380 8057	I	ON	380 8108	I	ON	380 8140	I	ON
380 8026	I	ON	380 8058	I	ON	380 8109	I	ON	380 8141	I	ON
380 8027	I	ON	380 8059	I	ON	380 8110	I	ON	380 8142	I	ON
380 8028	I	ON	380 8060	I	ON	380 8111	I	ON	380 8143	I	ON
380 8029	I	ON	380 8061	I	ON	380 8112	I	ON	380 8144	I	ON
380 8030	I	ON	380 8062	I	ON	380 8113	I	ON	380 8145	I	ON
380 8031	I	ON	380 8063	I	ON	380 8114	I	ON	380 8146	I	ON
380 8032	I	ON	380 8064	I	ON	380 8115	I	ON			

ABv5.

380 8201	I	ON	380 8221	I	ON	380 8241	I	ON	380 8261	I	ON
380 8202	I	ON	380 8222	I	ON	380 8242	I	ON	380 8262	I	ON
380 8203	I	ON	380 8223	I	ON	380 8243	I	ON	380 8263	I	ON
380 8204	I	ON	380 8224	I	ON	380 8244	I	ON	380 8264	I	ON
380 8205	I	ON	380 8225	I	ON	380 8245	I	ON	380 8265	I	ON
380 8206	I	ON	380 8226	I	ON	380 8246	I	ON	380 8266	I	ON
380 8207	I	ON	380 8227	I	ON	380 8247	I	ON	380 8267	I	ON
380 8208	I	ON	380 8228	I	ON	380 8248	I	ON	380 8268	I	ON
380 8209	I	ON	380 8229	I	ON	380 8249	I	ON	380 8269	I	ON
380 8210	I	ON	380 8230	I	ON	380 8250	I	ON	380 8270	I	ON
380 8211	I	ON	380 8231	I	ON	380 8251	I	ON	380 8271	I	ON
380 8212	I	ON	380 8232	I	ON	380 8252	I	ON	380 8272	I	ON
380 8213	I	ON	380 8233	I	ON	380 8253	I	ON	380 8273	I	ON
380 8214	I	ON	380 8234	I	ON	380 8254	I	ON	380 8274	I	ON
380 8215	I	ON	380 8235	I	ON	380 8255	I	ON	380 8275	I	ON
380 8216	I	ON	380 8236	I	ON	380 8256	I	ON	380 8276	I	ON
380 8217	I	ON	380 8237	I	ON	380 8257	I	ON	380 8277	I	ON
380 8218	I	ON	380 8238	I	ON	380 8258	I	ON	380 8278	I	ON
380 8219	I	ON	380 8239	I	ON	380 8259	I	ON	380 8279	I	ON
380 8220	I	ON	380 8240	I	ON	380 8260	I	ON	380 8280	I	ON

ABv6.

380 8301	I	ON	380 8305	I	ON	380 8309	I	ON	380 8313	I	ON
380 8302	I	ON	380 8306	I	ON	380 8310	I	ON	380 8314	I	ON
380 8303	I	ON	380 8307	I	ON	380 8311	I	ON	380 8315	I	ON
380 8304	I	ON	380 8308	I	ON	380 8312	I	ON	380 8316	I	ON

380 8317	I	ON	380 8345	I	ON	380 8373	I	ON	380 8401	N	ON
380 8318	I	ON	380 8346	I	ON	380 8374	I	ON	380 8402	I	ON
380 8319	I	ON	380 8347	I	ON	380 8375	I	ON	380 8403	I	ON
380 8321	I	ON	380 8348	I	ON	380 8376	I	ON	380 8404	I	ON
380 8321	I	ON	380 8349	I	ON	380 8377	I	ON	380 8405	I	ON
380 8322	I	ON	380 8350	I	ON	380 8378	I	ON	380 8406	N	ON
380 8323	I	ON	380 8351	I	ON	380 8379	I	ON	380 8407	I	ON
380 8324	I	ON	380 8352	I	ON	380 8380	I	ON	380 8408	I	ON
380 8325	I	ON	380 8353	I	ON	380 8381	I	ON	380 8409	I	ON
380 8326	I	ON	380 8354	I	ON	380 8382	I	ON	380 8410	I	ON
380 8327	I	ON	380 8355	I	ON	380 8383	I	ON	380 8411	I	ON
380 8328	I	ON	380 8356	I	ON	380 8384	I	ON	380 8412	I	ON
380 8329	I	ON	380 8357	I	ON	380 8385	I	ON	380 8413	I	ON
380 8330	I	ON	380 8358	I	ON	380 8386	I	ON	380 8414	I	ON
380 8331	I	ON	380 8359	I	ON	380 8387	I	ON	380 8415	I	ON
380 8332	I	ON	380 8360	I	ON	380 8388	I	ON	380 8416	I	ON
380 8333	I	ON	380 8361	I	ON	380 8389	I	ON	380 8417	I	ON
380 8334	I	ON	380 8362	I	ON	380 8390	I	ON	380 8418	I	ON
380 8335	I	ON	380 8363	I	ON	380 8391	I	ON	380 8419	I	ON
380 8336	I	ON	380 8364	I	ON	380 8392	I	ON	380 8420	I	ON
380 8337	I	ON	380 8365	I	ON	380 8393	I	ON	380 8421	I	ON
380 8338	I	ON	380 8366	I	ON	380 8394	I	ON	380 8422	I	ON
380 8339	I	ON	380 8367	I	ON	380 8395	I	ON	380 8423	I	ON
380 8340	I	ON	380 8368	I	ON	380 8396	I	ON	380 8424	I	ON
380 8341	I	ON	380 8369	I	ON	380 8397	I	ON	380 8425	I	ON
380 8342	I	ON	380 8370	I	ON	380 8398	I	ON	380 8426	I	ON
380 8343	I	ON	380 8371	I	ON	380 8399	I	ON	380 8427	I	ON
380 8344	I	ON	380 8372	I	ON	380 8400	I	ON			

SET FORMATIONS:

First series.

9401	I	ON	290 8571			380 8316	380 8001	290 8658
9402	I	ON	290 8503			380 8355	380 8002	290 8504
9403	I	ON	290 8505			380 8312	380 8003	290 8506
9404	I	ON	290 8507			380 8347	380 8004	290 8508
9405	I	ON	290 8509			380 8308	380 8005	290 8721
9406	I	ON	290 8511			380 8378	380 8006	290 8580
9407	I	ON	290 8513			380 8314	380 8007	290 8514
8608	I	ON	290 8515	380 8240	260 8809	380 8328	380 8008	290 8541
9409	I	ON	290 8517			380 8323	380 8009	290 8518
8610	I	ON	290 8705	380 8227	260 8865	380 8310	380 8010	290 8540
9411	I	ON	290 8521			380 8305	380 8011	290 8522
9412	I	ON	290 8641			380 8303	380 8012	290 8584
9413	I	ON	290 8525			380 8309	380 8013	290 8526
8614	I	ON	290 8527	380 8246	260 8810	380 8329	380 8014	290 8528
8615	I	ON	290 8637	380 8220	260 8846	380 8374	380 8015	290 8530
9416	I	ON	290 8665			380 8306	380 8016	290 8532
9417	I	ON	290 8646			380 8339	380 8017	290 8544
9418	I	ON	290 8535			380 8343	380 8018	290 8536
9419	I	ON	290 8537			380 8307	380 8019	290 8538
9420	I	ON	290 8510			380 8386	380 8020	290 8684
8621	I	ON	290 8516	380 8211	260 8843	380 8371	380 8021	290 8542
9422	I	ON	290 8543			380 8313	380 8022	290 8613
9423	I	ON	290 8545			380 8377	380 8023	290 8546
8624	I	ON	290 8585	380 8214	260 8801	380 8335	380 8024	290 8548
8625	I	ON	290 8733	380 8262	260 8845	380 8348	380 8025	290 8577
9426	I	ON	290 8550			380 8376	380 8026	290 8552
9427	I	ON	290 8529			380 8381	380 8027	290 8568
8628	I	ON	290 8555	380 8203	260 8814	380 8334	380 8028	290 8556
8629	I	ON	290 8557	380 8202	260 8838	380 8336	380 8029	290 8651
9430	I	ON	290 8559			380 8365	380 8030	290 8560
9431	I	ON	290 8561			380 8304	380 8031	290 8562
8632	I	ON	290 8633	380 8204	260 8862	380 8373	380 8032	290 8620

8633	I	ON	290 8565	380 8205	260 8847	380 8418	380 8033	290 8566
9434	I	ON	290 8567			380 8315	380 8034	290 8623
8635	I	ON	290 8569	380 8206	260 8827	380 8352	380 8035	290 8570
8636	I	ON	290 8583	380 8207	260 8802	380 8336	380 8036	290 8572
8637	I	ON	290 8573	380 8208	260 8842	380 8370	380 8037	290 8632
8638	I	ON	290 8575	380 8209	260 8834	380 8361	380 8038	290 8576
8639	I	ON	290 8687	380 8210	260 8841	380 8369	380 8039	290 8578
8640	I	ON	290 8501	380 8247	260 8803	380 8337	380 8040	290 8502
8641	I	ON	290 8581	380 8212	260 8821	380 8344	380 8041	290 8648
8642	I	ON	290 8523	380 8213	260 8825	380 8349	380 8042	290 8626
9443	I	ON	290 8547			380 8311	380 8043	290 8586
8644	I	ON	290 8587	380 8215	260 8826	380 8350	380 8044	290 8588
8645	I	ON	290 8589	380 8216	260 8831	380 8357	380 8045	290 8590
8646	I	ON	290 8591	380 8217	260 8823	380 8346	380 8046	290 8592
8647	I	ON	290 8593	380 8218	260 8805	380 8322	380 8047	290 8594
8648	I	ON	290 8595	380 8219	260 8807	380 8325	380 8048	290 8596
8649	I	ON	290 8597	380 8221	260 8816	380 8320	380 8049	290 8598
9450	I	ON	290 8636			380 8380	380 8050	290 8600
8651	I	ON	290 8601	380 8222	260 8813	380 8333	380 8051	290 8602
8652	I	ON	290 8603	380 8223	260 8837	380 8364	380 8052	290 8604
8653	I	ON	290 8605	380 8228	260 8828	380 8345	380 8053	290 8534
8654	I	ON	290 8607	380 8225	260 8817	380 8321	380 8054	290 8608
8655	I	ON	290 8624	380 8226	260 8832	380 8358	380 8055	290 8610
8656	I	ON	290 8599	380 8239	260 8818	380 8340	380 8056	290 8643
8657	I	ON	290 8609	380 8224	260 8822	380 8353	380 8057	290 8614
8658	I	ON	290 8553	380 8201	260 8804	380 8338	380 8058	290 8554
8659	I	ON	290 8617	380 8230	260 8811	380 8330	380 8059	290 8618
8660	I	ON	290 8619	380 8231	260 8815	380 8319	380 8060	290 8564
8661	I	ON	290 8627	380 8232	260 8835	380 8362	380 8061	290 8533
8662	I	ON	290 8645	380 8233	260 8839	380 8367	380 8062	290 8634
8663	I	ON	290 8625	380 8234	260 8830	380 8356	380 8063	290 8524
8664	I	ON	290 8612	380 8238	260 8840	380 8368	380 8064	290 8628
8665	I	ON	290 8629	380 8236	260 8844	380 8372	380 8065	290 8630
8666	I	ON	290 8631	380 8237	260 8808	380 8326	380 8066	290 8574
8667	I	ON	290 8621	380 8235	260 8833	380 8360	380 8067	290 8606
8668	I	ON	290 8723	380 8265	260 8824	380 8412	380 8068	290 8724
9469	I	ON	290 8653			380 8318	380 8069	290 8512
8670	I	ON	290 8639	380 8241	260 8806	380 8324	380 8070	290 8640
8671	I	ON	290 8519	380 8243	260 8819	380 8341	380 8071	290 8520
8672	I	ON	290 8635	380 8242	260 8812	380 8332	380 8072	290 8644
9473	I	ON	290 8657			380 8331	380 8073	290 8622
8674	I	ON	290 8647	380 8244	260 8836	380 8363	380 8074	290 8622
8675	I	ON	290 8649	380 8245	260 8829	380 8354	380 8075	290 8650
8676	I	ON	290 8558	380 8229	260 8820	380 8342	380 8076	290 8652
9477	I	ON	290 8638			380 8351	380 8077	290 8654
9478	I	ON	290 8655			380 8302	380 8078	290 8656
9479	I	ON	290 8615			380 8359	380 8079	290 8616
9480	I	ON	290 8659			380 8379	380 8080	290 8660
9481	I	ON	290 8661			380 8382	380 8081	290 8662

Second series.

8701	I	ON	290 8689	380 8257	260 8848	380 8395	380 8101	290 8690
9502	I	ON	290 8663			380 8317	380 8102	290 8551
8703	I	ON	290 8691	380 8258	260 8849	380 8396	380 8103	290 8692
9504	I	ON	290 8531			380 8383	380 8104	290 8666
8705	I	ON	290 8671	380 8259	260 8850	380 8409	380 8105	290 8672
9506	I	ON	290 8673			380 8387	380 8106	290 8674
8707	I	ON	290 8698	380 8248	260 8851	380 8388	380 8107	290 8676
9508	I	ON	290 8677			380 8389	380 8108	290 8678
8709	I	ON	290 8679	380 8256	260 8852	380 8390	380 8109	290 8680
9510	I	ON	290 8670			380 8391	380 8110	290 8682
8711	I	ON	290 8683	380 8251	260 8853	380 8384	380 8111	290 8722
9512	I	ON	290 8685			380 8385	380 8112	290 8686
8713	I	ON	290 8549	380 8249	260 8854	380 8392	380 8113	290 8688

9514	I	ON	290 8667			380 8393	380 8114	290 8668
8715	I	ON	290 8669	380 8254	260 8855	380 8394	380 8115	290 8717
9516	I	ON	290 8693			380 8327	380 8116	290 8694
8717	I	ON	290 8695	380 8252	260 8856	380 8398	380 8117	290 8696
9518	I	ON	290 8697			380 8399	380 8118	290 8642
8719	I	ON	290 8699	380 8255	260 8857	380 8400	380 8119	290 8700
9520	N	ON	290 8701			380 8401	380 8120	290 8702
8721	I	ON	290 8715	380 8250	260 8858	380 8402	380 8121	290 8704
9522	I	ON	290 8681			380 8403	380 8122	290 8706
8723	I	ON	290 8707	380 8253	260 8859	380 8404	380 8123	290 8708
9524	I	ON	290 8709			380 8405	380 8124	290 8710
9525	N	ON	290 8711			380 8406	380 8125	290 8712
8726	I	ON	290 8713	380 8260	260 8860	380 8407	380 8126	290 8714
8727	I	ON	290 8675	380 8261	260 8861	380 8408	380 8127	290 8716
9528	I	ON	Set not formed.					
8729	I	ON	290 8719	380 8263	260 8863	380 8410	380 8129	290 8720
8730	I	ON	290 8579	380 8264	260 8864	380 8397	380 8130	290 8664
8731	I	ON	Set not formed.					
8732	I	ON	290 8725	380 8266	260 8866	380 8413	380 8132	290 8726
8733	I	ON	290 8727	380 8267	260 8867	380 8414	380 8133	290 8728
8734	I	ON	290 8729	380 8268	260 8868	380 8415	380 8134	290 8730
8735	I	ON	290 8731	380 8269	260 8869	380 8416	380 8135	290 8732
8736	I	ON	290 8703	380 8270	260 8870	380 8417	380 8136	290 8734
8737	I	ON	290 8736	380 8271	260 8871	380 8375	380 8137	290 8735
8738	I	ON	290 8737	380 8272	260 8872	380 8419	380 8138	290 8738
8739	I	ON	290 8739	380 8273	260 8873	380 8411	380 8139	290 8740
8740	I	ON	290 8741	380 8274	260 8874	380 8421	380 8140	290 8742
8741	I	ON	290 8743	380 8275	260 8875	380 8422	380 8141	290 8744
8742	I	ON	290 8745	380 8276	260 8876	380 8423	380 8142	290 8746
8743	I	ON	290 8747	380 8277	260 8877	380 8424	380 8143	290 8748
8744	I	ON	290 8749	380 8278	260 8878	380 8425	380 8144	290 8750
8745	I	ON	290 8751	380 8279	260 8879	380 8426	380 8145	290 8752
8746	I	ON	290 8753	380 8280	260 8880	380 8427	380 8146	290 8754

Third series. Under construction. Sets assumed to be correct formation

9547	I	ON	290 8755			380 8428	380 8147	290 8756
9548	I	ON	290 8757			380 8429	380 8148	290 8758
9549	I	ON	290 8759			380 8430	380 8149	290 8760
9550	I		290 8761			380 8431	380 8150	290 8762
9551	I		290 8763			380 8432	380 8151	290 8764
9552	I		290 8765			380 8433	380 8152	290 8766
9553	I		290 8767			380 8434	380 8153	290 8768
9554	I		290 8769			380 8435	380 8154	290 8770
9555	I		290 8771			380 8436	380 8155	290 8772
9556	I		290 8773			380 8437	380 8156	290 8774
9557	I		290 8775			380 8438	380 8157	290 8776
9558	I		290 8777			380 8439	380 8158	290 8778
9559	I		290 8779			380 8440	380 8159	290 8780
9560	I		290 8781			380 8441	380 8160	290 8782
9561	I		290 8783			380 8442	380 8161	290 8784
9562	I		290 8785			380 8443	380 8162	290 8786
9563	I		290 8787			380 8444	380 8163	290 8788
9564	I		290 8789			380 8445	380 8164	290 8790
9565	I		290 8791			380 8446	380 8165	290 8792
9566	I		290 8793			380 8447	380 8166	290 8794
9567	I		290 8795			380 8448	380 8167	290 8796
9568	I		290 8797			380 8449	380 8168	290 8798
9569	I		290 8799			380 8450	380 8169	290 8800
9570	I		290 8801			380 8451	380 8170	290 8802
9571	I		290 8803			380 8452	380 8171	290 8804
9572	I		290 8805			380 8453	380 8172	290 8806
9573	I		290 8807			380 8454	380 8173	290 8808
9574	I		290 8809			380 8455	380 8174	290 8810
9575	I		290 8811			380 8456	380 8175	290 8812

9576 I	290 8813	380 8457	380 8176	290 8814
9577 I	290 8815	380 8458	380 8177	290 8816
9578 I	290 8817	380 8459	380 8178	290 8818
9579 I	290 8819	380 8460	380 8179	290 8820
9580 I	290 8821	380 8461	380 8180	290 8822
9581 I	290 8823	380 8462	380 8181	290 8824
9582 I	290 8825	380 8463	380 8182	290 8826
9583 I	290 8827	380 8464	380 8183	290 8828
9584 I	290 8829	380 8465	380 8184	290 8830
9585 I	290 8831	380 8466	380 8185	290 8832
9586 I	290 8833	380 8467	380 8186	290 8834
9587 I	290 8835	380 8468	380 8187	290 8836
9588 I	290 8837	380 8469	380 8188	290 8838
9589 I	290 8839	380 8470	380 8189	290 8840
9590 I	290 8841	380 8471	380 8190	290 8842
9591 I	290 8843	380 8472	380 8191	290 8844
9592 I	290 8845	380 8473	380 8192	290 8846
9593 I	290 8847	380 8474	380 8193	290 8848
9594 I	290 8849	380 8475	380 8194	290 8850
9595 I	290 8851	380 8476	380 8195	290 8852
9596 I	290 8853	380 8477	380 8196	290 8854

Spare mBvk1/2: 290 8539, 290 8563.
Spare ABv3/4: 380 8128, 380 8131.
Spare ABv6: 380 8301, 380 8420.
4 reserve bodies, one to become new 290 8718 and another may become new 290 8539.

3.5. TRAMS

TYPE HANNOVER   3-SECTION CARS

NS has an ex-Hannover car on hire from HTM for the Houten–Houten Castellum line. It has been modified to work on 1500 V DC.

Built: 1975.
Builder: Duewag.
Traction Motors: 2 x 217 kW.   **Seating Type:** 2+1.
Wheel Arrangement: B-2-2-B.   **Accommodation:** 46.
Length over Couplers: 27.0 m.   **Weight:** 38.80 tonnes.
Width: 2.40 m.   **Maximum Speed:** 80 km/h.
Non-Standard Livery: N Yellow with light green and light blue doors and two blue bands in the middle.

6016 **N** |

BOMBARDIER TYPE A32   3-SECTION CARS

These bi-directional tram-trains are on lease from HTM (Den Haag) and provide a service between Gouda and Alphen aan den Rijn for which special low platforms have been provided. It is eventually intended to extend this service into the city of Leiden. The trams are a development of those in Stockholm.

Built: 2002–03.
Builder–Mechanical Parts: Bombardier, Wien.
Builder-Electrical Parts: Bombardier, Sweden.
Traction Motors: 4 Alstom 4LXA of three-phase asynchronous of 120 kW.
Seating Type: 2+2.   **Floor Height:** 350/400/580 mm.
Wheel Arrangement: Bo-2-Bo.   **Accommodation:** 70 (8) + 106 standees.
Length over Couplers: 30.40 m.   **Weight:** 38.9 tonnes.
Width: 2.65 m.   **Maximum Speed:** 80 km/h.
Non-Standard Livery: N Yellow and white with light blue around cabs.

6101 **N**	6103 **N**	6105 **N**		6106 **N**
6102 **N**	6104 **N**			

3.6. LOCO-HAULED COACHING STOCK

NUMBERING SYSTEM

Intercity loco-hauled coaches and original double-decker stock are numbered according to the UIC system (see appendix A). The new double deckers have a different numbering system which is similar to that used on the IRM 'Regio Runner' EMUs.

SET NUMBERS

NS ICR and ICK coaches have been formed into sets of one, two or three coaches, with the four-digit set number painted on the side of the coach. Thus an ICK rake will consist of three sets of B-A-B pus one set of B-BD. Various formations are used on different ICR services. ICL stock has not been allocated to sets.

3.6.1. ICR STOCK

Locomotive hauled coaching stock on the NS is generally referred to by its "Plan", which combines the information which in Britain would be provided by the mark and the lot number. The NS type code consists of the "Plan" plus the type code as described in the introductory section of this book.

After A or B comes the number of compartments (or windows in open stock) for each class type, e.g. B10– a second class coach with 10 windows.

ICR stock (*Intercity Rijtuigen*) comes in three varieties, Internal, *Buurland* and Benelux.

Internal stock. As its title suggests, this stock can only work in the Netherlands and has fixed steps for high platforms. Train heating is 1000 V 50 Hz and 1500 V DC only.

Buurland stock. This stock has folding steps for working into Germany, Belgium and Luxembourg. (*Buurland* refers to neighbouring countries). Train heating – all voltages. There are at present no regular workings of this stock outside the Netherlands, except for the Brussels service (see below).

Benelux stock is similar to Buurland stock, except that it also has special jumper cables for push-pull working on the Brussels–Amsterdam "Benelux" service. Push-pull working will cease when new Class 186 locos take over this service from the Belgian Class 11s. Previously the service reversed in Antwerpen Centraal, but with the opening of the new tunnel this became unnecessary. In 2009 this stock will be used on the new high speed Amsterdam–Brussels service via the new high speed line (*HSL Zuid*), this operation being known as *HSL Priodienst*. This service was supposed to be operated by new high speed units from AnsaldoBreda in Italy, but they are extremely late and it is not known when they will appear.

All ICR coaches (except Benelux driving trailers) have now been refurbished and fitted with jumpers for push-pull working, although these are of a different type to the Benelux ones. They have power-operated swing-plug doors, pressure ventilation and disc brakes and are 26.40 m long. Most coaches have red leather seats in first class and mustard-coloured moquette in second class.

Benelux stock (including some "Buurland" coaches) has now been painted in a new livery in anticipation of the *HSL Priodienst* service and the second class coach seats finished in an attractive blue moquette.

The easiest way to record the number of an ICR coach is by its serial number. These do not duplicate except that there are two each of 437, 438 and 439 and also the Benelux driving trailers duplicate Internal open seconds. These are subject to early withdrawal or conversion and are shown at the end of the ICR list, which is presented in serial number order.

PLAN ICR-BDs DRIVING OPEN SECOND (CONDUCTOR)

Buurland stock. Rebuilt from BKDs.

Built: 1981–88.
Builder: Talbot.
Maximum Speed: 160 km/h.

Accommodation: –/52 (2) 1TD.
Weight: 40 tonnes.

50 84 82-70 001-2 (50 84 82-70 901-3) **l**	MT	50 84 82-70 005-3 (50 84 82-70 932-8) **l** MT
50 84 82-70 002-0 (50 84 82-70 927-8) **l**	MT	50 84 82-70 006-1 (50 84 82-70 933-6) **l** MT
50 84 82-70 003-8 (50 84 82-70 907-0) **l**	MT	50 84 82-70 007-9 (50 84 82-70 934-4) **l** MT
50 84 82-70 004-6 (50 84 82-70 931-0) **l**	MT	50 84 82-70 008-7 (50 84 82-70 935-1) **l** MT

50 84 82-70 009-5 (50 84 82-70 936-9) I | MT | 50 84 82-70 016-0 (50 84 82-70 945-0) I | MT
50 84 82-70 010-3 (50 84 82-70 937-7) I | MT | 50 84 82-70 017-8 (50 84 82-70 946-8) I | MT
50 84 82-70 011-1 (50 84 82-70 908-8) I | MT | 50 84 82-70 018-6 (50 84 82-70 947-6) I | MT
50 84 82-70 012-9 (50 84 82-70 941-9) I | MT | 50 84 82-70 019-4 (50 84 82-70 948-4) I | MT
50 84 82-70 013-7 (50 84 82-70 942-7) I | MT | 50 84 82-70 020-2 (50 84 82-70 916-1) I | MT
50 84 82-70 014-5 (50 84 82-70 943-5) I | MT | 50 84 82-70 021-0 (50 84 82-70 926-0) I | MT
50 84 82-70 015-2 (50 84 82-70 944-3) I | MT | 50 84 82-70 022-8 (50 84 82-70 928-6) I | MT

50 84 82-70 023-6 (50 84 20-70 823-4, 50 84 20-70 219-5) I MT
50 84 82-70 024-4 (50 84 20-70 855-6, 50 84 20-70 245-0) I MT
50 84 82-70 025-1 (50 84 20-70 812-7, 50 84 20-70 210-4) I MT
50 84 82-70 026-9 (50 84 20-70 842-4, 50 84 20-70 234-4) I MT
50 84 82-70 027-7 (50 84 20-70 826-7, 50 84 20-70 222-9) I MT
50 84 82-70 028-5 (50 84 20-70 841-6, 50 84 20-70 233-6) I MT
50 84 82-70 029-3 (50 84 20-70 867-1, 50 84 20-70 255-9) I MT
50 84 82-70 030-1 (50 84 20-70 825-9, 50 84 20-70 221-1) I MT
50 84 82-70 031-9 (50 84 20-70 856-4, 50 84 20-70 246-8) I MT
50 84 82-70 032-7 (50 84 20-70 827-5, 50 84 20-70 223-7) I MT

PLAN ICR2-B10   OPEN SECOND

Internal stock.

Built: 1982–84.
Builder: Talbot.   **Accommodation:** –/84 1T.
Maximum Speed: 160 km/h.   **Weight:** 40 tonnes.

50 84 20-77 101-8 (50 84 20-77 701-5) I | MT | 50 84 20-77 128-1 (50 84 20-77 741-1) I | MT
50 84 20-77 102-6 (50 84 20-77 702-3) I | MT | 50 84 20-77 129-9 (50 84 20-77 742-9) I | MT
50 84 20-77 103-4 (50 84 20-77 703-1) I | MT | 50 84 20-77 130-7 (50 84 20-77 743-7) I | MT
50 84 20-77 104-2 (50 84 20-77 704-9) I | MT | 50 84 20-77 131-5 (50 84 20-77 744-5) I | MT
50 84 20-77 105-9 (50 84 20-77 705-6) I | MT | 50 84 20-77 132-3 (50 84 20-77 745-2) I | MT
50 84 20-77 106-7 (50 84 20-77 706-4) I | MT | 50 84 20-77 133-1 (50 84 20-77 746-0) I | MT
50 84 20-77 107-5 (50 84 20-77 708-0) I | MT | 50 84 20-77 134-9 (50 84 20-77 747-8) I | MT
50 84 20-77 108-3 (50 84 20-77 711-4) I | MT | 50 84 20-77 135-6 (50 84 20-77 748-6) I | MT
50 84 20-77 109-1 (50 84 20-77 712-2) I | MT | 50 84 20-77 136-4 (50 84 20-77 751-0) I | MT
50 84 20-77 110-9 (50 84 20-77 713-0) I | MT | 50 84 20-77 137-2 (50 84 20-77 752-8) I | MT
50 84 20-77 111-7 (50 84 20-77 714-8) I | MT | 50 84 20-77 138-0 (50 84 20-77 753-6) I | MT
50 84 20-77 112-5 (50 84 20-77 715-5) I | MT | 50 84 20-77 139-8 (50 84 20-77 755-1) I | MT
50 84 20-77 113-3 (50 84 20-77 717-1) I | MT | 50 84 20-77 140-6 (50 84 20-77 756-9) I | MT
50 84 20-77 114-1 (50 84 20-77 718-9) I | MT | 50 84 20-77 141-4 (50 84 20-77 758-5) I | MT
50 84 20-77 115-8 (50 84 20-77 721-3) I | MT | 50 84 20-77 142-2 (50 84 20-77 761-9) I | MT
50 84 20-77 116-6 (50 84 20-77 722-1) I | MT | 50 84 20-77 143-0 (50 84 20-77 762-7) I | MT
50 84 20-77 117-4 (50 84 20-77 723-9) I | MT | 50 84 20-77 144-8 (50 84 20-77 763-5) I | MT
50 84 20-77 118-2 (50 84 20-77 724-7) I | MT | 50 84 20-77 145-5 (50 84 20-77 764-3) I | MT
50 84 20-77 119-0 (50 84 20-77 726-2) I | MT | 50 84 20-77 146-3 (50 84 20-77 765-0) I | MT
50 84 20-77 120-8 (50 84 20-77 727-0) I | MT | 50 84 20-77 147-1 (50 84 20-77 766-8) I | MT
50 84 20-77 121-6 (50 84 20-77 732-0) I | MT | 50 84 20-77 148-9 (50 84 20-77 767-6) I | MT
50 84 20-77 122-4 (50 84 20-77 733-8) I | MT | 50 84 20-77 149-7 (50 84 20-77 768-4) I | MT
50 84 20-77 123-2 (50 84 20-77 734-6) I | MT | 50 84 20-77 150-5 (50 84 20-77 771-8) I | MT
50 84 20-77 124-0 (50 84 20-77 735-3) I | MT | 50 84 20-77 151-3 (50 84 20-77 772-6) I | MT
50 84 20-77 125-7 (50 84 20-77 736-1) I | MT | 50 84 20-77 152-1 (50 84 20-77 773-4) I | MT
50 84 20-77 126-5 (50 84 20-77 737-9) I | MT | 50 84 20-77 153-9 (50 84 20-77 774-2) I | MT
50 84 20-77 127-3 (50 84 20-77 738-7) I | MT | 50 84 20-77 154-7 (50 84 20-77 775-9) I | MT

50 84 20-77 155-4 (50 84 20-77 731-2, 50 84 20-77 006-9) I MT
50 84 20-77 156-2 (50 84 20-77 754-4, 50 84 20-77 007-7) I MT

PLAN ICR1-B10   OPEN SECOND

Buurland stock. 261–272 were rebuilt from firsts.

Built: 1981–83.
Builder: Talbot.   **Accommodation:** –/84 1T.
Maximum Speed: 160 km/h.   **Weight:** 40 tonnes.

† Modified for HSL-Zuid use.

50 84 20-70 201-3 (50 84 20-70 801-0) I	MT	50 84 20-70 239-3 (50 84 20-70 847-3) I	MT
50 84 20-70 202-1 (50 84 20-70 802-8) I	MT	50 84 20-70 240-1 (50 84 20-70 848-1) I	MT
50 84 20-70 203-9 (50 84 20-70 803-6) I	MT	50 84 20-70 241-9 (50 84 20-70 851-5) H †	WG
50 84 20-70 204-7 (50 84 20-70 804-4) I	MT	50 84 20-70 242-7 (50 84 20-70 852-3) I	MT
50 84 20-70 205-4 (50 84 20-70 805-1) I	MT	50 84 20-70 243-5 (50 84 20-70 853-1) I	MT
50 84 20-70 206-2 (50 84 20-70 806-9) I	MT	50 84 20-70 244-3 (50 84 20-70 854-9) I	MT
50 84 20-70 207-0 (50 84 20-70 807-7) H †	WG	50 84 20-70 247-6 (50 84 20-70 857-2) I	MT
50 84 20-70 208-8 (50 84 20-70 808-5) I	MT	50 84 20-70 248-4 (50 84 20-70 858-0) I	MT
50 84 20-70 209-6 (50 84 20-70 811-9) H †	WG	50 84 20-70 249-2 (50 84 20-70 861-4) I	MT
50 84 20-70 211-2 (50 84 20-70 813-5) I	MT	50 84 20-70 250-0 (50 84 20-70 862-2) I	MT
50 84 20-70 212-0 (50 84 20-70 814-3) I	MT	50 84 20-70 251-8 (50 84 20-70 863-0) I	MT
50 84 20-70 213-8 (50 84 20-70 815-0) I	MT	50 84 20-70 252-6 (50 84 20-70 864-8) I	MT
50 84 20-70 214-6 (50 84 20-70 816-8) I	MT	50 84 20-70 253-4 (50 84 20-70 865-5) I	MT
50 84 20-70 215-3 (50 84 20-70 817-6) I	MT	50 84 20-70 254-2 (50 84 20-70 866-3) I	MT
50 84 20-70 216-1 (50 84 20-70 818-4) H †	WG	50 84 20-70 256-7 (50 84 20-70 868-9) I	(U)
50 84 20-70 217-9 (50 84 20-70 821-8) H †	WG	50 84 20-70 257-5 (50 84 20-70 871-3) H †	WG
50 84 20-70 218-7 (50 84 20-70 822-6) H †	WG	50 84 20-70 258-3 (50 84 20-70 872-1) I	MT
50 84 20-70 220-3 (50 84 20-70 824-2) I	MT	50 84 20-70 259-1 (50 84 20-70 873-9) I	MT
50 84 20-70 225-2 (50 84 20-70 831-7) I	MT	50 84 20-70 260-9 (50 84 20-70 874-7) I	MT
50 84 20-70 226-0 (50 84 20-70 832-5) I	MT	50 84 20-70 261-7 (50 84 10-70 668-5) H †	WG
50 84 20-70 227-8 (50 84 20-70 833-3) I	MT	50 84 20-70 262-5 (50 84 10-70 672-7) I	MT
50 84 20-70 228-6 (50 84 20-70 834-1) I	MT	50 84 20-70 264-1 (50 84 10-70 674-3) I	MT
50 84 20-70 229-4 (50 84 20-70 835-8) I	MT	50 84 20-70 265-8 (50 84 10-70 675-0) I	MT
50 84 20-70 230-2 (50 84 20-70 836-6) H †	WG	50 84 20-70 266-6 (50 84 10-70 676-8) I	MT
50 84 20-70 231-0 (50 84 20-70 837-4) I	MT	50 84 20-70 267-4 (50 84 10-70 678-4) I	MT
50 84 20-70 232-8 (50 84 20-70 838-2) I	MT	50 84 20-70 268-2 (50 84 10-70 681-8) I	MT
50 84 20-70 235-1 (50 84 20-70 843-2) I	MT	50 84 20-70 269-0 (50 84 10-70 682-6) H †	WG
50 84 20-70 236-9 (50 84 20-70 844-0) I	MT	50 84 20-70 270-8 (50 84 10-70 683-4) I	MT
50 84 20-70 237-7 (50 84 20-70 845-7) I	MT	50 84 20-70 271-6 (50 84 10-70 684-2) I	MT
50 84 20-70 238-5 (50 84 20-70 846-5) I	MT	50 84 20-70 272-4 (50 84 10-70 686-7) I	MT

PLAN ICR2-A10   SEMI-OPEN FIRST

Internal stock. These vehicles consist of two six-seat compartments plus an open saloon with 47 seats. Refurbished with red leather seats.

Built: 1982–84.
Builder: Talbot.
Maximum Speed: 160 km/h.
Accommodation: –/59 1T.
Weight: 40 tonnes.

50 84 10-77 301-6	(50 84 20-77 725-4, 50 84 20-77 011-9)	I	MT
50 84 10-77 302-4	(50 84 20-77 728-8, 50 84 20-77 012-7)	I	MT
50 84 10-77 303-2	(50 84 20-77 707-2, 50 84 29-77 008-6)	I	MT
50 84 10-77 304-0	(50 84 20-77 757-7, 50 84 29-77 009-4)	I	MT
50 84 10-77 305-7	(50 84 20-77 716-3, 50 84 20-77 010-1)	I	MT

50 84 10-77 306-5 (50 84 10-77 601-9) I	MT	50 84 10-77 322-2 (50 84 10-77 622-5) I	MT
50 84 10-77 307-3 (50 84 10-77 602-7) I	MT	50 84 10-77 323-0 (50 84 10-77 623-3) I	WG
50 84 10-77 308-1 (50 84 10-77 603-5) I	MT	50 84 10-77 324-8 (50 84 10-77 624-1) I	MT
50 84 10-77 309-9 (50 84 10-77 604-3) I	MT	50 84 10-77 325-5 (50 84 10-77 625-8) I	MT
50 84 10-77 310-7 (50 84 10-77 605-0) I	MT	50 84 10-77 326-3 (50 84 10-77 626-6) I	MT
50 84 10-77 311-5 (50 84 10-77 611-8) I	MT	50 84 10-77 327-1 (50 84 10-77 627-4) I	MT
50 84 10-77 312-3 (50 84 10-77 612-6) I	MT	50 84 10-77 328-9 (50 84 10-77 628-2) I	MT
50 84 10-77 313-1 (50 84 10-77 613-4) I	MT	50 84 10-77 329-7 (50 84 10-77 608-4) I	MT
50 84 10-77 314-9 (50 84 10-77 614-2) I	MT	50 84 10-77 330-5 (50 84 10-77 636-5) I	MT
50 84 10-77 315-6 (50 84 10-77 615-9) I	MT	50 84 10-77 331-3 (50 84 10-77 631-6) I	MT
50 84 10-77 316-4 (50 84 10-77 616-7) I	MT	50 84 10-77 332-1 (50 84 10-77 632-4) I	MT
50 84 10-77 317-2 (50 84 10-77 617-5) I	MT	50 84 10-77 333-9 (50 84 10-77 633-2) I	MT
50 84 10-77 318-0 (50 84 10-77 618-3) I	MT	50 84 10-77 334-7 (50 84 10-77 634-0) I	MT
50 84 10-77 319-8 (50 84 10-77 606-8) I	MT	50 84 10-77 335-4 (50 84 10-77 635-7) I	MT
50 84 10-77 320-6 (50 84 10-77 607-6) I	MT	50 84 10-77 336-2 (50 84 10-77 637-3) I	MT
50 84 10-77 321-4 (50 84 10-77 621-7) I	MT		

PLAN ICR1-A10 (ICR4-A10*)   SEMI-OPEN FIRST

Buurland stock. These vehicles consist of two six-seat compartments plus an open saloon with 47 seats. Refurbished with red leather seats.
Built: 1981–83.
Builder: Talbot.   **Accommodation:** –/59 1T.
Maximum Speed: 160 km/h.   **Weight:** 40 tonnes.

† Modified for HSL-Zuid use.

50 84 10-70 349-2 (50 84 10-70 673-5) I	MT	50 84 10-70 360-9 (50 84 10-70 666-9) I	MT
50 84 10-70 350-0 (50 84 10-70 671-9) I	MT	50 84 10-70 361-7 (50 84 10-70 667-7) I	WG
50 84 10-70 351-8 (50 84 10-70 651-1) H	WG	50 84 10-70 362-5 (50 84 10-70 677-6) I	WG
50 84 10-70 352-6 (50 84 10-70 653-7) I	MT	50 84 10-70 363-3 (50 84 10-70 641-2) I	MT
50 84 10-70 353-4 (50 84 10-70 656-0) H	WG	50 84 10-70 364-1 (50 84 10-70 642-0) I	MT
50 84 10-70 354-2 (50 84 10-70 657-8) I	MT	50 84 10-70 365-8 (50 84 10-70 643-8) I	MT
50 84 10-70 355-9 (50 84 10-70 658-6) I	MT	50 84 10-70 366-6 (50 84 10-70 644-6) I	MT
50 84 10-70 356-7 (50 84 10-70 662-8) I	MT	50 84 10-70 367-4 (50 84 10-70 645-3) I	MT
50 84 10-70 357-5 (50 84 10-70 663-6) I	MT	50 84 10-70 368-2 (50 84 10-70 646-1) I	WG
50 84 10-70 358-3 (50 84 10-70 664-4) I	MT	50 84 10-70 369-0 (50 84 10-70 685-9) I	MT
50 84 10-70 359-1 (50 84 10-70 665-1) I	MT		

50 84 10-70 370-8	(50 84 10-70 655-2, 50 84 10-70 004-3)	H †	WG
50 84 10-70 371-6	(50 84 10-70 661-0, 50 84 10-70 005-0)	H †	WG
50 84 10-70 372-4	(50 84 10-70 652-9, 50 84 18-70 002-9)	H †	WG
50 84 10-70 373-2	(50 84 10-70 654-5, 50 84 18-70 003-7)	H †	WG
50 84 10-70 374-0	(50 84 10-70 431-8, 50 84 10-70 561-2)	H †*	WG
50 84 10-70 375-7	(50 84 10-70 432-6, 50 84 10-70 562-0)	H †*	WG
50 84 10-70 376-5	(50 84 10-70 433-4, 50 84 10-70 563-8)	H †*	WG
50 84 10-70 377-3	(50 84 10-70 564-6)	H †*	WG
50 84 10-70 378-1	(50 84 10-70 647-9, 50 84 10-70 565-3)	I *	MT
50 84 10-70 379-9	(50 84 10-70 648-7, 50 84 10-70 566-1)	I *	MT
50 84 10-70 380-7	(50 84 10-70 691-7, 50 84 10-70 567-9)	I *	MT

PLAN ICR3-B10   OPEN SECOND

Benelux stock. Not renumbered when refurbished. Modified for HSL-Zuid use.

Built: 1981–83.
Builder: Talbot.   **Accommodation:** –/84 1T.
Maximum Speed: 160 km/h.   **Weight:** 40 tonnes.

50 84 20-70 401-9 H	WG	50 84 20-70 407-6 H	WG	50 84 20-70 415-9 H	WG
50 84 20-70 402-7 H	WG	50 84 20-70 408-4 H	WG	50 84 20-70 416-7 H	WG
50 84 20-70 403-5 H	WG	50 84 20-70 411-8 H	WG	50 84 20-70 417-5 H	WG
50 84 20-70 404-3 H	WG	50 84 20-70 412-6 H	WG	50 84 20-70 418-3 H	WG
50 84 20-70 405-0 H	WG	50 84 20-70 413-4 H	WG	50 84 20-70 421-7 H	WG
50 84 20-70 406-8 H	WG	50 84 20-70 414-2 H	WG	50 84 20-70 422-5 H	WG

PLAN ICR-BD   OPEN SECOND (CONDUCTOR)

Buurland stock. These vehicles were rebuilt from BKDs.

Built: 1981–88.
Builder: Talbot.   **Accommodation:** –/72 (4) 1T.
Maximum Speed: 160 km/h.   **Weight:** 41 tonnes.

50 84 82-70 432-9 (50 84 82-70 952-6) I	MT	50 84 82-70 436-0 (50 84 82-70 905-4) I	MT
50 84 82-70 433-7 (50 84 82-70 902-1) I	MT	50 84 82-70 437-8 (50 84 82-70 906-2) I	MT
50 84 82-70 434-5 (50 84 82-70 903-9) I	MT	50 84 82-70 438-6 (50 84 82-70 953-4) I	MT
50 84 82-70 435-2 (50 84 82-70 904-7) I	MT	50 84 82-70 439-4 (50 84 82-70 938-5) I	MT

PLAN ICR-BF   BICYCLE SECOND

Buurland stock. Rebuilt from BKDs.

Built: 1981–88.
Builder: Talbot.   **Accommodation:** –/72 (4) 1T.
Maximum Speed: 160 km/h.   **Weight:** 41 tonnes.

50 84 29-70 437-4 (50 84 82-70 911-2) I	MT	50 84 29-70 444-0 (50 84 82-70 921-1) I	MT
50 84 29-70 438-2 (50 84 82-70 912-0) I	MT	50 84 29-70 445-7 (50 84 82-70 922-9) I	MT
50 84 29-70 439-0 (50 84 82-70 913-8) I	MT	50 84 29-70 446-5 (50 84 82-70 923-7) I	MT
50 84 29-70 440-8 (50 84 82-70 914-6) I	MT	50 84 29-70 447-3 (50 84 82-70 924-5) I	MT
50 84 29-70 441-6 (50 84 82-70 915-3) I	MT	50 84 29-70 448-1 (50 84 82-70 925-2) I	MT
50 84 29-70 442-4 (50 84 82-70 917-9) I	MT	50 84 29-70 449-9 (50 84 82-70 951-8) I	MT
50 84 29-70 443-2 (50 84 82-70 918-7) I	MT	50 84 29-70 450-7 (50 84 82-70 954-2) I	MT

PLAN ICR3-A10   SEMI-OPEN FIRST

Benelux stock. These vehicles consist of two six-seat compartments plus an open saloon with 47 seats. Refurbished with red leather seats. Not renumbered when refurbished. Modified for HSL-Zuid use.

Built: 1986.
Builder: Talbot.   **Accommodation:** –/59 1T.
Maximum Speed: 160 km/h.   **Weight:** 41 tonnes.

50 84 10-70 481-3 **H**	WG	50 84 10-70 485-4 **H**	WG	50 84 10-70 488-8 **H**	WG
50 84 10-70 482-1	WG	50 84 10-70 486-2 **H**	WG	50 84 10-70 491-2 **H**	WG
50 84 10-70 483-9 **H**	WG	50 84 10-70 487-0 **H**	WG	50 84 10-70 492-0 **H**	WG
50 84 10-70 484-7 **H**	WG				

PLAN ICR-BF   BICYCLE SECOND

Buurland stock. These vehicles were rebuilt from BKDs.

Built: 1981–88.
Builder: Talbot.   **Accommodation:** –/72 (4) 1T.
Maximum Speed: 160 km/h.   **Weight:** 44 tonnes.

50 84 29-70 493-7	(50 84 82-70 955-9)	I	MT
50 84 29-70 494-5	(50 84 82-70 956-7)	I	MT
50 84 29-70 495-2	(50 84 82-70 958-3)	I	MT
50 84 29-70 496-0	(50 84 82-70 957-5, 50 84 82-70 001-2)	I	MT
50 84 29-70 497-8	(50 84 82-70 591-2)	I	MT
50 84 29-70 498-6	(50 84 82-70 592-0)	I	MT
50 84 29-70 499-4	(50 84 82-70 593-8)	I	MT

PLAN ICR3-B10   OPEN SECOND

Buurland stock. Rebuilt from Benelux open composites.

Built: 1981–83.
Builder: Talbot.   **Accommodation:** –/84 1T.
Maximum Speed: 160 km/h.   **Weight:** 40 tonnes.

† Modified for HSL-Zuid use.

50 84 20-70 541-2 (50 84 30-70 061-9) I	MT	50 84 20-70 546-1 (50 84 30-70 066-8) **H** † WG
50 84 20-70 542-0 (50 84 30-70 062-7) I	MT	50 84 20-70 547-9 (50 84 30-70 067-6) I	MT
50 84 20-70 543-8 (50 84 30-70 063-5) I	MT	50 84 20-70 548-7 (50 84 30-70 068-4) **H** † WG
50 84 20-70 544-6 (50 84 30-70 064-3) I	MT	50 84 20-70 549-5 (50 84 30-70 071-8) I	MT
50 84 20-70 545-3 (50 84 30-70 065-0) I	MT	50 84 20-70 550-3 (50 84 30-70 072-6) I	MT

PLAN ICR4-B10   OPEN SECOND

Buurland stock. Through-wired for Benelux service if required. Not renumbered when refurbished. Modified for HSL-Zuid use.

Built: 1988.
Builder: Talbot.   **Accommodation:** –/84 1T.
Maximum Speed: 160 km/h.   **Weight:** 40 tonnes.

50 84 20-70 571-9	**H**	WG	50 84 20-70 581-8 (50 84 20-70 423-3) **H**	WG
50 84 20-70 572-7	**H**	WG	50 84 20-70 582-6 (50 84 20-70 424-1) **H**	WG
50 84 20-70 573-5	**H**	WG	50 84 20-70 583-4 (50 84 20-70 425-8) **H**	WG
50 84 20-70 574-3	**H**	WG	50 84 20-70 584-2 (50 84 20-70 426-6) **H**	WG
50 84 20-70 575-0	**H**	WG	50 84 20-70 585-9 (50 84 20-70 427-4) **H**	WG

PLAN ICR3-BD   OPEN SECOND (CONDUCTOR)
Benelux stock. Rebuilt from BKDs. Not renumbered. Modified for HSL-Zuid use.

Built: 1986/8.
Builder: Talbot.   **Accommodation:** –/55 (5) 1TD.
Maximum Speed: 160 km/h.   **Weight:** 41 tonnes.

50 84 82-70 971-6	H	WG	50 84 82-70 974-0	H	WG	50 84 82-70 978-1	H		WG
50 84 82-70 972-4	H	WG	50 84 82-70 976-5	I	WG	50 84 82-70 981-5	H		WG
50 84 82-70 973-2	I	WG	50 84 82-70 977-3	H	WG	50 84 82-70 982-3	H	*	WG

PLAN ICR3-Bvs   BENELUX   DRIVING OPEN SECOND
Benelux stock. Not refurbished.

Built: 1986.
Builder: Talbot.   **Accommodation:** –/64 1T.
Maximum Speed: 160 km/h.   **Weight:** 41 tonnes.

50 84 28-70 101-7	B	WG	50 84 28-70 105-8	B	WG	50 84 28-70 111-6	B	WG
50 84 28-70 102-5	B	WG	50 84 28-70 106-6	B	WG	50 84 28-70 112-4	B	WG
50 84 28-70 103-3	B	WG	50 84 28-70 107-4	B	WG	50 84 28-70 113-2	B	WG
50 84 28-70 104-1	B	WG	50 84 28-70 108-2	B	WG			

ROYAL SALOON
Converted from ICR4-A10 semi-open first built 1988.

Converted: 1994.
Builder: Talbot.
Maximum Speed: 160 km/h.   **Weight:** 41 tonnes.
Non-standard livery: N NS plain Intercity royal blue.

61 84 89-70 003-8   (50 84 10-70 647-9)   **N**   MT

3.6.2. ICK STOCK
This is stock bought by NS from DB. All vehicles are 26.40 m long.

ICK-A12   COMPARTMENT FIRST
Ex-DB compartment seconds. Every two compartments converted into one large 9-seat compartment.

Built: 1981–88.
Builder: Various. Rebuilt PFA.   **Accommodation:** 54/– (3) 1T.
Maximum Speed: 160 km/h.   **Weight:** 39 tonnes.

50 84 12-37 001-9	I	MT	50 84 12-37 013-4	I	MT	50 84 12-37 025-8	I	MT
50 84 12-37 002-7	I	MT	50 84 12-37 014-2	I	MT	50 84 12-37 026-6	I	MT
50 84 12-37 003-5	I	MT	50 84 12-37 015-9	I	MT	50 84 12-37 027-4	I	MT
50 84 12-37 004-3	I	MT	50 84 12-37 016-7	I	MT	50 84 12-37 028-2	I	MT
50 84 12-37 005-0	I	MT	50 84 12-37 017-5	I	MT	50 84 12-37 029-0	I	MT
50 84 12-37 006-8	I	MT	50 84 12-37 018-3	I	MT	50 84 12-37 030-8	I	MT
50 84 12-37 007-6	I	MT	50 84 12-37 019-1	I	MT	50 84 12-37 031-6	I	MT
50 84 12-37 008-4	I	MT	50 84 12-37 020-9	I	MT	50 84 12-37 032-4	I	MT
50 84 12-37 009-2	I	MT	50 84 12-37 021-7	I	MT	50 84 12-37 033-2	I	MT
50 84 12-37 010-0	I	MT	50 84 12-37 022-5	I	MT	50 84 12-37 034-0	I	MT
50 84 12-37 011-8	I	MT	50 84 12-37 023-3	I	MT	50 84 12-37 035-7	I	MT
50 84 12-37 012-6	I	MT	50 84 12-37 024-1	I	MT	50 84 12-37 036-5	I	MT

ICK-B12   COMPARTMENT SECOND
These coaches have twelve compartments.

Built: 1981–88.
Builder: Various. Rebuilt PFA.   **Accommodation:** –/72 (3) 1T.
Maximum Speed: 160 km/h.   **Weight:** 39 tonnes.

50 84 22-37 901-8 I	MT	50 84 22-37 934-9 I	MT	50 84 22-37 966-1 I	MT
50 84 22-37 902-6 I	MT	50 84 22-37 935-6 I	MT	50 84 22-37 967-9 I	MT
50 84 22-37 903-4 I	MT	50 84 22-37 936-4 I	MT	50 84 22-37 968-7 I	MT
50 84 22-37 904-2 I	MT	50 84 22-37 937-2 I	MT	50 84 22-37 969-5 I	MT
50 84 22-37 905-9 I	MT	50 84 22-37 938-0 I	MT	50 84 22-37 970-3 I	MT
50 84 22-37 906-7 I	MT	50 84 22-37 939-8 I	MT	50 84 22-37 971-1 I	MT
50 84 22-37 907-5 I	MT	50 84 22-37 940-6 I	MT	50 84 22-37 972-9 I	MT
50 84 22-37 908-3 I	MT	50 84 22-37 941-4 I	MT	50 84 22-37 973-7 I	MT
50 84 22-37 909-1 I	MT	50 84 22-37 942-2 I	MT	50 84 22-37 974-5 I	MT
50 84 22-37 910-9 I	MT	50 84 22-37 943-0 I	MT	50 84 22-37 975-2 I	MT
50 84 22-37 911-7 I	MT	50 84 22-37 944-8 I	MT	50 84 22-37 976-0 I	MT
50 84 22-37 912-5 I	MT	50 84 22-37 945-5 I	MT	50 84 22-37 977-8 I	MT
50 84 22-37 913-3 I	MT	50 84 22-37 946-3 I	MT	50 84 22-37 978-6 I	MT
50 84 22-37 914-1 I	MT	50 84 22-37 947-1 I	MT	50 84 22-37 979-4 I	MT
50 84 22-37 915-8 I	MT	50 84 22-37 948-9 I	MT	50 84 22-37 980-2 I	MT
50 84 22-37 916-6 I	MT	50 84 22-37 949-7 I	MT	50 84 22-37 981-0 I	MT
50 84 22-37 917-4 I	MT	50 84 22-37 950-5 I	MT	50 84 22-37 982-8 I	MT
50 84 22-37 918-2 I	MT	50 84 22-37 951-3 I	MT	50 84 22-37 983-6 I	MT
50 84 22-37 919-0 I	MT	50 84 22-37 952-1 I	MT	50 84 22-37 984-4 I	MT
50 84 22-37 920-8 I	MT	50 84 22-37 953-9 I	MT	50 84 22-37 985-1 I	MT
50 84 22-37 921-6 I	MT	50 84 22-37 954-7 I	MT	50 84 22-37 986-9 I	MT
50 84 22-37 922-4 I	MT	50 84 22-37 955-4 I	MT	50 84 22-37 987-7 I	MT
50 84 22-37 923-2 I	MT	50 84 22-37 956-2 I	MT	50 84 22-37 988-5 I	MT
50 84 22-37 924-0 I	MT	50 84 22-37 957-0 I	MT	50 84 22-37 989-3 I	MT
50 84 22-37 925-7 I	MT	50 84 22-37 958-8 I	MT	50 84 22-37 990-1 I	MT
50 84 22-37 926-5 I	MT	50 84 22-37 959-6 I	MT	50 84 22-37 991-9 I	MT
50 84 22-37 928-1 I	MT	50 84 22-37 960-4 I	MT	50 84 22-37 992-7 I	MT
50 84 22-37 929-9 I	MT	50 84 22-37 961-2 I	MT	50 84 22-37 993-5 I	MT
50 84 22-37 930-7 I	MT	50 84 22-37 962-0 I	MT	50 84 22-37 994-3 I	MT
50 84 22-37 931-5 I	MT	50 84 22-37 963-8 I	MT	50 84 22-37 995-0 I	MT
50 84 22-37 932-3 I	MT	50 84 22-37 964-6 I	MT	50 84 22-37 996-8 I	MT
50 84 22-37 933-1 I	MT	50 84 22-37 965-3 I	MT		

ICK-BD   OPEN SECOND (CONDUCTOR)

Built: 1981–88. These coaches have seven compartments.
Builder: Various. Rebuilt PFA.   **Accommodation:** –/45 (10) 1TD.
Maximum Speed: 160 km/h.   **Weight:** 39 tonnes.

50 84 82-37 052-7 I	MT	50 84 82-37 058-4 I	MT	50 84 82-37 064-2 I	MT
50 84 82-37 053-5 I	WG	50 84 82-37 059-2 I	MT	50 84 82-37 065-9 I	MT
50 84 82-37 054-3 I	MT	50 84 82-37 060-0 I	MT	50 84 82-37 066-7 I	MT
50 84 82-37 055-0 I	WG	50 84 82-37 061-8 I	MT	50 84 82-37 067-5 I	MT
50 84 82-37 056-8 I	MT	50 84 82-37 062-6 I	WG	50 84 82-37 068-3 I	WG
50 84 82-37 057-6 I	MT	50 84 82-37 063-4 I	WG		

COMPARTMENT FIRST   A9

Ex DB Type Avmz. These coaches were originally obtained for use on the short-lived Amsterdam–Milano Overnight Express and now work with ICM stock (see below).

Built: 1974–75.
Builders: Orenstein & Koppel (250), Wegmann (others).
Bogies: Minden-Deutz MD36.   **Accommodation:** 54/– 2T.
Maximum Speed: 200 km/h.   **Weight:** 44 tonnes.

61 84 19-90 250-6 I	WG	61 84 19-90 254-8 I	WG	61 84 19-90 257-1 I	WG
61 84 19-90 251-4 I	WG	61 84 19-90 255-5 I	WG	61 84 19-90 258-9 I	WG
61 84 19-90 252-2 I	WG	61 84 19-90 256-3 I	WG	61 84 19-90 259-7 I	WG
61 84 19-90 253-0 I	WG				

3.6.3. ICL STOCK

The following vehicles are on loan from DB until the new build of IRM units is delivered. Most have been repainted into NS InterCity livery, but at the time of writing, some were still carrying DB IR livery (turquoise and pale blue) with a few in DB IC livery (white with red band).

SEMI-OPEN FIRST TYPE   Aimz ICL

Rebuilt for DB InterRegio services from DB Types Am and ABm. Consist of five 5-seat compartments and two saloons together seating 25.

Rebuilt: 2002.
Builder: PFA Weiden.   **Accommodation:** 54/– 2T.
Maximum Speed: 200 km/h.   **Weight:** 42 tonnes.

50 84 10-91 200-2 I	WG	50 84 10-91 217-6 I	WG	50 84 10-91 701-9 I	WG
50 84 10-91 204-4 I	WG	50 84 10-91 218-4 I	WG	50 84 10-91 702-7 I	WG
50 84 10-91 205-1 I	WG	50 84 10-91 221-8 I	WG	50 84 10-91 703-5 I	WG
50 84 10-91 211-9 I	WG	50 84 10-91 223-4 I	WG	50 84 10-91 704-3 I	WG
50 84 10-91 213-5 I	WG	50 84 10-91 224-2 I	WG	50 84 10-91 705-0 I	WG
50 84 10-91 215-0 I	WG	50 84 10-91 700-1 I	WG		

SEMI-OPEN SECOND TYPE Bimz   ICL

Rebuilt for DB InterRegio services from DB Types Am and ABm. Consist of five 5-seat compartments and two saloons together seating 35.

Rebuilt: 2002.
Builder: PFA Weiden.   **Accommodation:** –/60 2T.
Maximum Speed: 200 km/h.   **Weight:** 42 tonnes.

50 84 22-91 068-9 I	WG	50 84 22-91 234-7 I	WG	50 84 22-91 324-6 I	WG
50 84 22-91 085-3 I	WG	50 84 22-91 238-8 I	WG	50 84 22-91 325-3 I	WG
50 84 22-91 089-5 I	WG	50 84 22-91 239-6 I	WG	50 84 22-91 326-1 I	WG
50 84 22-91 090-3 I	WG	50 84 22-91 248-7 I	WG	50 84 22-91 330-3 I	WG
50 84 22-91 091-1 I	WG	50 84 22-91 251-1 I	WG	50 84 22-91 335-2 I	WG
50 84 22-91 094-5 I	WG	50 84 22-91 252-9 I	WG	50 84 22-91 337-8 I	WG
50 84 22-91 096-0 I	WG	50 84 22-91 256-0 I	WG	50 84 22-91 338-6 I	WG
50 84 22-91 105-9 I	WG	50 84 22-91 260-2 I	WG	50 84 22-91 339-4 I	WG
50 84 22-91 106-7 I	WG	50 84 22-91 265-1 I	WG	50 84 22-91 340-2 I	WG
50 84 22-91 110-9 I	WG	50 84 22-91 271-9 I	WG	50 84 22-91 342-8 I	WG
50 84 22-91 118-2 I	WG	50 84 22-91 272-7 I	WG	50 84 22-91 344-4 I	WG
50 84 22-91 126-5 I	WG	50 84 22-91 274-3 I	WG	50 84 22-91 345-1 I	WG
50 84 22-91 165-3 I	WG	50 84 22-91 276-8 I	WG	50 84 22-91 347-7 I	WG
50 84 22-91 172-9 I	WG	50 84 22-91 280-0 I	WG	50 84 22-91 700-7 I	WG
50 84 22-91 177-8 I	WG	50 84 22-91 285-9 I	WG	50 84 22-91 702-3 I	WG
50 84 22-91 179-4 I	WG	50 84 22-91 289-1 I	WG	50 84 22-91 704-9 I	WG
50 84 22-91 180-2 I	WG	50 84 22-91 291-7 I	WG	50 84 22-91 706-4 I	WG
50 84 22-91 200-8 I	WG	50 84 22-91 294-1 I	WG	50 84 22-91 707-2 I	WG
50 84 22-91 203-2 I	WG	50 84 22-91 296-6 I	WG	50 84 22-91 708-0 I	WG
50 84 22-91 208-1 I	WG	50 84 22-91 297-4 I	WG	50 84 22-91 709-8 I	WG
50 84 22-91 211-5 I	WG	50 84 22-91 307-1 I	WG	50 84 22-91 710-6 I	WG
50 84 22-91 213-1 I	WG	50 84 22-91 308-9 I	WG	50 84 22-91 712-2 I	WG
50 84 22-91 214-9 I	WG	50 84 22-91 310-5 I	WG	50 84 22-91 713-0 I	WG
50 84 22-91 215-6 I	WG	50 84 22-91 311-3 I	WG	50 84 22-91 714-8 I	WG
50 84 22-91 218-0 I	WG	50 84 22-91 313-9 I	WG	50 84 22-91 715-5 I	WG
50 84 22-91 223-0 I	WG	50 84 22-91 314-7 I	WG	50 84 22-91 716-3 I	WG
50 84 22-91 225-5 I	WG	50 84 22-91 316-2 I	WG	50 84 22-91 717-1 I	WG
50 84 22-91 230-5 I	WG	50 84 22-91 317-0 I	WG	50 84 22-91 718-9 I	WG
50 84 22-91 231-3 I	WG	50 84 22-91 319-6 I	WG	50 84 22-91 719-7 I	WG
50 84 22-91 232-1 I	WG	50 84 22-91 323-8 I	WG	50 84 22-91 720-5 I	WG

SEMI-OPEN SECOND TYPE Bimdz   ICL

Rebuilt for DB InterRegio services from DB Types Am and ABm. Consist of four 5-seat compartments plus a bike compartment and two saloons together seating 35.

Rebuilt: 2002.
Builder: PFA Weiden.   **Accommodation:** –/55 2T.
Maximum Speed: 200 km/h.   **Weight:** 42 tonnes.

50 84 84-90 003-2 I	WG	50 84 84-90 018-0 I	WG	50 84 84-90 028-9 I	WG
50 84 84-90 007-3 I	WG	50 84 84-90 019-8 I	WG	50 84 84-90 029-7 I	WG
50 84 84-90 008-1 I	WG	50 84 84-90 026-3 I	WG	50 84 84-90 701-1 I	WG

3.6.4. ORIGINAL DOUBLE-DECK STOCK (DDM1)

The double-decker stock operates on outer suburban trains around Amsterdam. The driving coaches are named after endangered species. Certain coaches were modified to work in loco-hauled Intercity trains, but these are now back in use in DDM1 sets.

Note: These coaches also carry set numbers as follows:

101–115 6901–15.   401–472 6801–72.   615–675 6615–75.

DOUBLE DECK DRIVING OPEN SECOND   (Bvs)

Built: 1985–86.
Builder: Talbot.   **Length over Buffers:** 26.89 m.
Accommodation: –/98 (9) 1T (64 (8) upper deck, 34 (1) lower deck, 4 at ends).
Maximum Speed: 140 km/h.   **Weight:** tonnes.

50 84 26-37 101-1	AZ	Kondor	50 84 26-37 108-6	AZ	Olifant
50 84 26-37 102-9	AZ	Ooieveer	50 84 26-37 111-0	AZ	Tijger
50 84 26-37 103-7	AZ	Bison	50 84 26-37 112-8	AZ	Cheeta
50 84 26-37 104-5	AZ	Walvis	50 84 26-37 113-6	AZ	Dolfijn
50 84 26-37 105-2	AZ	Neushoorn	50 84 26-37 114-4	AZ	Otter
50 84 26-37 106-0	AZ	Arend	50 84 26-37 115-1	AZ	Panda
50 84 26-37 107-8	AZ	Zeehond			

DOUBLE DECK SECOND   Bv

Built: 1985–86.
Builder: Talbot.   **Length over Buffers:** 26.40 m.
Accommodation: –/136 (16) 1T (64 (8) upper deck, 64 (8) lower deck, 8 at ends).
Maximum Speed: 140 km/h.   **Weight:** 59 tonnes.

* Numbered 501-508/511-516 for a time when converted for Intercity service.
† Converted from ABv 26-37 605.

50 84 26-37 401-5	*	AZ	50 84 26-37 415-5	*	AZ	50 84 26-37 428-8		AZ
50 84 26-37 402-3	*	AZ	50 84 26-37 416-3	*	AZ	50 84 26-37 431-2		AZ
50 84 26-37 403-1	*	AZ	50 84 26-37 417-1		AZ	50 84 26-37 432-0		AZ
50 84 26-37 404-9	*	AZ	50 84 26-37 418-9		AZ	50 84 26-37 433-8		AZ
50 84 26-37 405-6	*	AZ	50 84 26-37 421-3		AZ	50 84 26-37 434-6		AZ
50 84 26-37 406-4	*	AZ	50 84 26-37 422-1		AZ	50 84 26-37 435-3		AZ
50 84 26-37 407-2	*	AZ	50 84 26-37 423-9		AZ	50 84 26-37 436-1		AZ
50 84 26-37 408-0	*	AZ	50 84 26-37 424-7		AZ	50 84 26-37 437-9		AZ
50 84 26-37 411-4	*	AZ	50 84 26-37 425-4		AZ	50 84 26-37 438-7		AZ
50 84 26-37 412-2	*	AZ	50 84 26-37 426-2		AZ	50 84 26-37 441-1		AZ
50 84 26-37 413-0	*	AZ	50 84 26-37 427-0		AZ	50 84 26-37 472-6	†	AZ
50 84 26-37 414-8	*	AZ						

DOUBLE DECK COMPOSITE   ABv

Built: 1985–86.
Builder: Talbot.   **Length over Buffers:** 26.40 m.
Accommodation: 64/60 (16) 1T (32/24 (8) upper deck, 32/24 (8) lower deck, 12 at ends).
Maximum Speed: 140 km/h.   **Weight:** 59 tonnes.

* Rebuilt from second class coaches 470/1/3–6, originally composites 603/4/6–8.

50 84 26-37 612-7		AZ	50 84 26-37 623-4		AZ	50 84 26-37 633-3		AZ
50 84 26-37 613-5		AZ	50 84 26-37 624-2		AZ	50 84 26-37 634-1		AZ
50 84 26-37 614-3		AZ	50 84 26-37 625-9		AZ	50 84 26-37 635-8		AZ
50 84 26-37 615-0		AZ	50 84 26-37 626-7		AZ	50 84 26-37 670-5	*	AZ
50 84 26-37 616-8		AZ	50 84 26-37 627-5		AZ	50 84 26-37 671-3	*	AZ
50 84 26-37 617-6		AZ	50 84 26-37 628-3		AZ	50 84 26-37 673-9	*	AZ
50 84 26-37 618-4		AZ	50 84 26-37 631-7		AZ	50 84 26-37 674-7	*	AZ
50 84 26-37 621-8		AZ	50 84 26-37 632-5		AZ	50 84 26-37 675-4	*	AZ
50 84 26-37 622-6		AZ						

3.6.5. DOUBLE-DECK STOCK TYPE DD-AR

This double-deck stock works in suburban trains all around the Randstad area. The numbering system strays away from the normally mandatory UIC system. The coaches work as "virtual EMUs", i.e. in sets of fixed formation originally consisting of a Class 1700 locomotive, a composite, one or two seconds and a driving second. For this purpose the locomotive is fitted with an auto-coupler at one end. However fifty "mDDM" power cars have now been delivered and these have released 50 Class 1700s for Intercity use. Set numbers consist of a `7', a digit denoting the formation and the last two digits of the driving trailer. Thus 7345 would be a three car set with the driving trailer 7045, 7445 would be a four-car set with the driving trailer 7045 and 7845 would be am mDDm-powered four-car set with the driving trailer 7045. Formations are changed from time to time.

DOUBLE DECK DRIVING OPEN SECOND   Bvs

Built: 1992–94.   **Builder:** Talbot.
Accommodation: –/120 1T. (64 upper deck, 52 lower deck and 4 in ends).
Length over Buffers: 26.89 m.   **Weight:** 53 tonnes.

270 7001	LD	270 7021	LD	270 7041	LD	270 7061	LD
270 7002	LD	270 7022	LD	270 7042	LD	270 7062	LD
270 7003	LD	270 7023	LD	270 7043	LD	270 7063	LD
270 7004	LD	270 7024	LD	270 7044	LD	270 7064	LD
270 7005	LD	270 7025	LD	270 7045	LD	270 7065	LD
270 7006	LD	270 7026	LD	270 7046	LD	270 7066	LD
270 7007	LD	270 7027	LD	270 7047	LD	270 7067	LD
270 7008	LD	270 7028	LD	270 7048	LD	270 7068	LD
270 7009	LD	270 7029	LD	270 7049	LD	270 7069	LD
270 7010	LD	270 7030	LD	270 7050	LD	270 7070	LD
270 7011	LD	270 7031	LD	270 7051	LD	270 7071	LD
270 7012	LD	270 7032	LD	270 7052	LD	270 7072	LD
270 7013	LD	270 7033	LD	270 7053	LD	270 7073	LD
270 7014	LD	270 7034	LD	270 7054	LD	270 7074	LD
270 7015	LD	270 7035	LD	270 7055	LD	270 7075	LD
270 7016	LD	270 7036	LD	270 7056	LD	270 7076	LD
270 7017	LD	270 7037	LD	270 7057	LD	270 7077	LD
270 7018	LD	270 7038	LD	270 7058	LD	270 7078	LD
270 7019	LD	270 7039	LD	270 7059	LD	270 7079	LD
270 7020	LD	270 7040	LD	270 7060	LD		

DOUBLE DECK SECOND   Bv

Built: 1992–94.   **Builder:** Talbot.
Accommodation: –/140 1T. (64 upper deck, 64 lower deck and 12 in ends).
Length over Buffers: 26.40 m.   **Weight:** 46 tonnes.

280 7201	LD	280 7220	LD	280 7239	LD	280 7258	LD
280 7202	LD	280 7221	LD	280 7240	LD	280 7259	LD
280 7203	LD	280 7222	LD	280 7241	LD	280 7260	LD
280 7204	LD	280 7223	LD	280 7242	LD	280 7261	LD
280 7205	LD	280 7224	LD	280 7243	LD	280 7262	LD
280 7206	LD	280 7225	LD	280 7244	LD	280 7263	LD
280 7207	LD	280 7226	LD	280 7245	LD	280 7264	LD
280 7208	LD	280 7227	LD	280 7246	LD	280 7265	LD
280 7209	LD	280 7228	LD	280 7247	LD	280 7266	LD
280 7210	LD	280 7229	LD	280 7248	LD	280 7267	LD
280 7211	LD	280 7230	LD	280 7249	LD	280 7268	LD
280 7212	LD	280 7231	LD	280 7250	LD	280 7269	LD
280 7213	LD	280 7232	LD	280 7251	LD	280 7270	LD
280 7214	LD	280 7233	LD	280 7252	LD	280 7271	LD
280 7215	LD	280 7234	LD	280 7253	LD	280 7272	LD
280 7216	LD	280 7235	LD	280 7254	LD	280 7273	LD
280 7217	LD	280 7236	LD	280 7255	LD	280 7274	LD
280 7218	LD	280 7237	LD	280 7256	LD	280 7275	LD
280 7219	LD	280 7238	LD	280 7257	LD	280 7276	LD

280 7277	LD	280 7284	LD	280 7291	LD	280 7297	LD
280 7278	LD	280 7285	LD	280 7292	LD	280 7298	LD
280 7279	LD	280 7286	LD	280 7293	LD	280 7299	LD
280 7280	LD	280 7287	LD	280 7294	LD	280 7300	LD
280 7281	LD	280 7288	LD	280 7295	LD	280 7301	LD
280 7282	LD	280 7289	LD	280 7296	LD	280 7302	LD
280 7283	LD	280 7290	LD				

DOUBLE DECK COMPOSITE   ABv

Built: 1992–94.   **Builder:** Talbot.
Accommodation: 64/60 1T. (32/24 upper deck, 32/24 lower deck and 12 in ends).
Length over Buffers: 26.40 m.   **Weight:** 46 tonnes.

380 7501	LD	380 7521	LD	380 7540	LD	380 7559	LD
380 7502	LD	380 7522	LD	380 7541	LD	380 7560	LD
380 7503	LD	380 7523	LD	380 7542	LD	380 7561	LD
380 7504	LD	380 7524	LD	380 7543	LD	380 7562	LD
380 7505	LD	380 7525	LD	380 7544	LD	380 7563	LD
380 7506	LD	380 7526	LD	380 7545	LD	380 7564	LD
380 7507	LD	380 7527	LD	380 7546	LD	380 7565	LD
280 7508	LD	380 7528	LD	380 7547	LD	380 7566	LD
380 7509	LD	380 7529	LD	380 7548	LD	380 7567	LD
380 7510	LD	380 7530	LD	380 7549	LD	380 7568	LD
380 7511	LD	380 7531	LD	380 7550	LD	380 7569	LD
380 7512	LD	380 7532	LD	380 7551	LD	380 7570	LD
380 7513	LD	380 7533	LD	380 7552	LD	380 7571	LD
380 7514	LD	380 7534	LD	380 7553	LD	380 7572	LD
380 7515	LD	380 7535	LD	380 7554	LD	380 7573	LD
380 7516	LD	380 7536	LD	380 7555	LD	380 7574	LD
380 7517	LD	380 7537	LD	380 7556	LD	380 7575	LD
380 7518	LD	380 7538	LD	380 7557	LD	380 7576	LD
380 7519	LD	380 7539	LD	380 7558	LD	380 7577	LD
380 7520	LD						

DOUBLE DECK MOTOR COMPOSITE   mABk

These vehicles are also known as mDDM (motor dubbeldek materiel).

Built: 1997–78.
Builder–Mechanical Parts: De Dietrich.
Builder–Electrical Parts: Adtranz.
Traction Motors: 6 Adtranz Holec asynchronous of 200 kW.
Wheel Arrangement: Bo-Bo-Bo.
Maximum Speed: 140 km/h.
Accommodation: 16/48 (upper deck only).
Length over Buffers: 21.39 m.
Weight: 76 tonnes.

390 7701	LD	390 7714	LD	390 7727	LD	390 7739	LD
390 7702	LD	390 7715	LD	390 7728	LD	390 7740	LD
390 7703	LD	390 7716	LD	390 7729	LD	390 7741	LD
390 7704	LD	390 7717	LD	390 7730	LD	390 7742	LD
390 7705	LD	390 7718	LD	390 7731	LD	390 7743	LD
390 7706	LD	390 7719	LD	390 7732	LD	390 7744	LD
390 7707	LD	390 7720	LD	390 7733	LD	390 7745	LD
390 7708	LD	390 7721	LD	390 7734	LD	390 7746	LD
390 7709	LD	390 7722	LD	390 7735	LD	390 7747	LD
390 7710	LD	390 7723	LD	390 7736	LD	390 7748	LD
390 7711	LD	390 7724	LD	390 7737	LD	390 7749	LD
390 7712	LD	390 7725	LD	390 7738	LD	390 7750	LD
390 7713	LD	390 7726	LD				

4. DUTCH PRIVATE PASSENGER TRAIN OPERATING COMPANIES

The Dutch Ministry of Transport is responsible for some of the unprofitable services in the Netherlands, but the responsibility, powers and finances for some of the unprofitable regional lines has been delegated to regional authorities. These services have been tendered with some lines continuing to be operated by NS and others by private operators.

4.1. ARRIVA TRAINS NEDERLAND

Arriva Trains Nederland operates a network of non-electrified lines in the Groningen and Leeuwarden areas, including a service to Leer in Germany. The company has replaced its fleet of hired-in "Wadlopers" with a new fleet of Stadler GTWs which are known as "Spurts". It also operates the Geldermalsen–Dordrecht line with Plan V EMUs leased from NS Financial Services which will be replaced with new GTW EMUs on order from Stadler.

Lines operated:

- Groningen–Delfzijl
- Groningen–Rodeschool
- Groningen–Leer (Germany)
- Groningen–Leeuwarden
- Leeuwarden–Harlingenhafen
- Leeuwarden–Stavoren
- Geldermalsen–Dordrecht

Depot: Leeuwarden

GTW 2/6 & GTW2/8   3/4-SECTION DMUS

These units have 2+2 seating in both classes.

Built: 2006–07.   **Builder**: Stadler.
Engine: 12 cylinder MTU 12V183 TDE2 of 550 kW at 2100 r.p.m.
Transmission: Electric. Two Adtranz Type 6R1A 4548 three phase asynchronous traction motors.
Floor Height: 830/996 mm.
Maximum Speed: 140 km/h.

Disc brakes. Magnetic track brakes.

* Fitted with retractable steps for operating into Germany.

GTW2/6. 3-section units. AB + B (DTCO–M–DTSO),

Length over Couplers: 18.195 + 4.500 + 18.195 m.
Wheel Arrangement: 2-Bo-2.   **Weight**: 68 tonnes.
Accommodation: 16/32 (7) 1TD + –/56. († 16/20 (12) 1TD + –/56 with space for more bikes).

228	*	JAN UITHAM	236		TONNY VAN LEEUWEN
229	*	SJOUKJE DIJKSTRA	237	†	MARIANNE TIMMER
230	*	EDE STAAL	238	†	FOPPE INNE BROUWER
231		HOTZE SCHUIL	239	†	PIET OBERMAN
232		FOPPE DE HAAN	240	†	EISE EISINGA
233		LIESBETH LIST	241	†	GER VADERS
234		FEDDE SCHURER	242	†	SAMUEL VAN HOUTEN
235		JAN DE ROOS	243	†	EGBERT WAGENBORG

GTW2/8. 4-section units. AB + B + B (DTCO–TSO–M–DTSO).

Length over Couplers: 18.195 + 4.500 + 15.047 + 18.195 m.
Wheel Arrangement: 2-2-Bo-2.   **Weight**: 87 tonnes.
Accommodation: 16/32 (7) 1TD + –/56 + –/56 († 16/20 (12) 1TD + –/56 + –/56 with space for more bikes).

301	*† RIEMER EN ANNIE	308	HEIKE KAMERLINGH ONNES
302	*† BASTIAAN JAN ADER	309	HENDRIK NICOLAAS WERKMAN
303	*† TINY MULDER	310	ABE LENSTRA
304	*† HANS ALDERS	311	HANS WIEGEL
305	*† UBBO EMMIUS	312	M. VASALIS
306	GERRIT KROL	313	ALETTA H. JACOBS
307	FRITS ZERNIKE	314	JOPIE HUISMAN

315	ABEL TASMAN	322	TITUS BRANDSMA
316	WIM DUISENBERG	323	WILLEM ALBERT SCHOLTEN
317	WILLEM BARENTSZ	324	SICCO MANSHOLT
318	NIENKE VAN HICHTUM	325	J.J. NOOITGEDAGT
319	MARTE RÖLING	326	M.C.ESCHER
320	CEES BIJLSTRA	327	JELLE ZIJLSTRA
321	PIET PAALTJENS		

GTW 2/6 & GTW2/8   3/4-SECTION EMUS

Built: 2008 for Dordrecht–Geldermalsen. Details as for DMUs (above) except engine replaced by electrical equipment.
Weight: ?

GTW2/6. 3-section unit.

407

GTW2/8. 4-section units.

501	504
502	505
503	506

PLAN V8   2-CAR EMUS

For details see NS section.

864	866	867	868	869	870
865					

4.2. CONNEXXION

Connexxion operates the Amersfoort–Ede-Wageningen line with a fleet of new Protos electric units plus the Almelo–Mariënberg line with two LINT 41s hired from Syntus. The company also operate the Utrecht light rail system.

Lines operated:

- Amersfoort–Ede-Wageningen
- Almelo–Mariënberg
- Utrecht–Nieuwegein/Ijsselstein (trams)

2-SECTION ARTICULATED TRAMS

Built: 1981–83.
Builder–Mechanical Parts: SIG, Neuhausen, Switzerland.
Builder–Electrical Parts: BBC.
Traction Motors: Two BBC 228 kW.
Length over Couplers: 29.80 m.
Width: 2.65 mm.
Floor Height: 920 mm.
Wheel Arrangement: B-2-B.
Accommodation: 80 + 160 standees.
Weight: 37.5 tonnes.
Maximum Speed: 80 km/h.

Disc brakes. Magnetic track brakes.

5001	5006	5011	5016	5020	5024
5002	5007	5012	5017	5021	5025
5003	5008	5013	5018	5022	5026
5004	5009	5014	5019	5023	5027
5005	5010	5015			

PROTOS   2-CAR EMUS

AB + B (DTCO–DTSO).

Built: 2007.
Builder: Fahrzeug Technik Dessau.
Traction Motors: Two of 335 kW per car.
Length over Couplers: 27.25 + 27.25 m.
Floor Height: 810 /1020 mm.
Wheel Arrangement: 2-Bo + Bo-2.
Accommodation: 16/68 (62) + –/76 (10).These units have 2+2 seating in both classes.
Weight: 56 + 59 tonnes.
Maximum Speed: 160 km/h.

Disc brakes. Magnetic track brakes.

| 5031 | 5032 | 5033 | 5034 | 5035 | |

CORADIA LINT 41   2-SECTION ARTICULATED DMU

Units hired from Syntus (See below).

44 | 45   Hennie Kuiper

4.3. SYNTUS

Syntus operates a number of non-electrified routes in the Gelderland province and has bougjht a fleet of Alstom Lint 41 DMUs for this purpose. It also has some DM'90 units hired from NS Financial Services.

Lines operated:

* Tiel–Arnhem   DM'90
* Arnhem–Winterswijk   DM'90
* Winterswijk–Zutphen

* Hengelo–Oldenzaal
* Hengelo–Zutphen

Depot: Winterswijk

CORADIA LINT 41   2-SECTION ARTICULATED DMU

mBk+mBk (DMSO–DMSO).

Built: 2000–01.
Builder: Alstom Salzgitter, Germany (formerly LHB).
Engine: Two 6 cylinder MTU 6R 183TD 13H engines of 315 kW at 1900 r.p.m.
Transmission: Hydrodynamic.
Length over Couplers: 20.905 + 20.905 m.
Floor Height: 780 mm.
Wheel Arrangement: B-2-B.
Accommodation: –/68 (5) + –/68 (5)
Weight: 68 tonnes.
Maximum Speed: 120 km/h.

Disc brakes. Magnetic track brakes.

21	Masha Bijlsma		33	Berend van Hackfort
22	Hans Keuper		34	Wim Rijkenbarg
23	Ernst Daniel Smit (U)		35	
24	Hendrickje Stoffels		36	
25	Spoorjan Willink		37	Gerard te Broke
26	Gerrit Komrij		38	Jovink en the Voederbietels
27	A.C.W. Staring		39	Monique Wolbert
28	Bennie Jolink		40	Johan de Bondt
29	Sandra Vanreijs		41	Tante Riek
30	Nout Wellink		42	Bert Haanstra
32			43	Willem Wilmink

CLASS DM'90   2-CAR UNITS

mBk+mBk (DMSO–DMSO).

Units hired from NS Financial services. Details as for NS section except:

Accommodation: 48 (22) + –/68 (1)

50	(3450)	52	(3452)	54	(3441)	56	(3440)	58	(3439)	59	(3437)
51	(3451)	53	(3453)	55	(3442)	57	(3438)				

4.4. VEOLIA

Veolia operates two lines in the Limburg area. The Maastricht–Kerkrade line is operated with Plan V units hired from NS Financial Services. However it is replacing these with new GTW EMUs on order from Stadler.

Lines operated:

• Roermond–Nijmegen
• Maastricht–Kerkrade

Depot: Boxtel (Operated by Voith)

GTW 2/6 & GTW2/8   3/4-SECTION DMUS

These units have 2+2 seating in first class and 3+2 in second class.

Built: 2007–8.   **Builder:** Stadler.
Engine: 12 cylinder MTU 12V183 TDE2 of 550 kW at 2100 r.p.m.
Transmission: Electric. Two Adtranz Type 6R1A 4548 three phase asynchronous traction motors.
Floor Height: 830/996 mm.
Maximum Speed: 140 km/h.

Disc brakes. Magnetic track brakes.

GTW2/6. 3-section units. AB + B (DTCO–M–DTSO),

Length over Couplers: 18.195 + 4.500 + 18.195 m.
Wheel Arrangement: 2-Bo-2.   **Weight:** 68 tonnes.
Accommodation: 16/27 (11) 1TD + –/66.

201		206	
202	Pater Karel	207	
203		208	
204	Mat Vestjens	209	
205		210	

GTW2/8. 4-section units. AB + B + B (DTCO–TSO–M–DTSO).

Length over Couplers: 18.195 + 4.500 + 15.047 + 18.195 m.
Wheel Arrangement: 2-2-Bo-2.   **Weight:** 87 tonnes.
Accommodation: 16/27 (11) 1TD + –/66 + –/66.

351		354	
352	Pater Karel	355	Connie Palmen
353 (S)	Ernst Daniel Smit	356	

GTW 2/6 & GTW2/8   3/4-SECTION EMUS

AB + B (DTCO–M–DTSO).

Built: 2008 for Maastricht–Kerkrade. Details as for DMUs (above) except engine replaced by electrical equipment. Numbers not yet known.
Weight: ?

GTW2/6. 3-section unit.

xxx	xxx
xxx	xxx
xxx	

GTW2/8. 4-section units.

xxx	xxx
xxx	

PLAN V8   2-CAR ELECTRIC UNITS

For details see NS section.

841	843	845	847	848	849
842	844				

4.5. EURO-EXPRESS-TREINCHARTER EETC

Euro-Express-Treincharter operates the *Ski Trein* during the winter from Utrecht to Zell am See, the *Alpen Express* (the winter ski train from Utrecht to Brig, Bischofshofen and Landeck) and the *AutoSlaap Trein* (summer motorail service from 's Hertogenbosch to Avignon, Bologna and Livorno).The coaches were mainly ex-NS Internationaal, which finished operating overnight services in 2002. Maintenance is carried out by NedTrain at Watergraafsmeer.

VANS FOR LUGGAGE/BIKES   Df
Ex Deutsche Post. Owned by NS Internationaal

Built: .   **Builder:**
Length over Buffers: 26.40 m.   **Weight:**   tonnes.
Maximum Speed: 200 km/h.

51 84 09-90 051-2	(51 84 92-70 051-4)	WG Df ex-NS
51 84 09-90 054-6		WG
51 84 09-90 056-1		WG
51 84 09-90 057-9		WG

COUCHETTES
Ex DB type Bcm. These coaches have six berths per compartment.

Built: 1963–68.   **Builder:**
Length over Buffers: 26.40 m.
Accommodation: 10 compartments with six berths in each.
Weight: 39 tonnes.   **Maximum Speed:** 160 km/h.

51 84 05-70 001-5	(51 80 50-30 012-9, 51 84 50-70 001-9)	WG
51 84 05-70 002-3	(51 80 50-30 017-8, 51 84 50-70 002-7)	WG
51 84 05-70 004-9	(51 80 50-30 023-6, 51 84 50-70 004-3)	WG
51 84 05-70 005-6	(51 80 50-30 025-1, 51 84 50-70 005-0)	WG
51 84 05-70 007-2	(51 80 50-30 031-9, 51 84 50-70 007-6)	WG
51 84 05-70 008-0	(51 80 50-30 035-0, 51 84 50-70 008-4)	WG
51 84 05-70 010-6	(51 80 50-30 038-4, 51 84 50-70 010-0)	WG
51 84 05-70 011-4	(51 80 50-30 048-3, 51 84 50-70 011-8)	WG
51 84 05-70 012-2	(51 80 50-30 049-1, 51 84 50-70 012-6)	WG
51 84 05-70 014-8	(51 80 50-30 054-1, 51 84 50-70 014-2)	WG
51 84 05-70 016-3	(51 80 50-30 065-7, 51 84 50-70 016-6)	WG (S)
51 84 05-70 017-1	(51 80 50-30 071-5, 51 84 50-70 017-4)	WG
51 84 05-70 018-9	(51 80 50-30 079-8, 51 84 50-70 018-2)	WG
51 84 05-70 021-3	(51 80 50-30 062-4, 51 84 50-70 021-7)	WG

COUCHETTES
Ex German Touristik Union International (TUI). These coaches have four berths per compartment.

Built: 1981.   **Builder:**
Length over Buffers: 26.40 m.
Accommodation: 11 compartments with four berths in each.
Weight: 53 tonnes.   **Maximum Speed:** 160 (200*) km/h.

61 84 05-90 103-3	(61 80 50-90 103-1, 61 84 50-90 103-7)	*	WG
61 84 05-90 104-1	(61 80 50-90 104-9, 61 84 50-90 104-5)	*	WG
61 84 05-90 107-4	(61 80 50-90 107-2, 61 84 50-90 107-8)	*	WG
61 84 05-90 108-2	(61 80 50-90 108-0, 61 84 50-90 108-6)	*	WG
61 84 05-90 109-0	(61 80 50-90 109-8, 61 84 50-90 109-4)	*	WG
61 84 05-90 110-8	(61 80 50-90 110-6, 61 84 50-90 110-2)	*	WG
61 84 05-70 111-0	(61 80 50-70 111-8, 61 84 50-70 111-4)		WG
61 84 05-70 115-1	(61 80 50-70 115-9, 61 84 50-70 115-5)		WG
61 84 05-70 117-7	(61 80 50-70 117-5, 61 84 50-70 117-1)		WG
61 84 05-70 118-5	(61 80 50-70 118-3, 61 84 50-70 118-9)		WG
61 84 05-70 120-1	(61 80 50-70 120-9, 61 84 50-70 120-5)		WG
61 84 05-70 121-9	(61 80 50-70 121-7, 61 84 50-70 121-3)		WG
61 84 05-70 122-7	(61 80 50-70 122-5, 61 84 50-70 122-1)		WG
61 84 05-70 123-5	(61 80 50-70 123-3, 61 84 50-70 123-9)		WG

```
61 84 05-70 124-3  (61 80 50-70 124-1, 61 84 50-70 124-7)    WG
61 84 05-70 125-0  (61 80 50-70 125-8, 61 84 50-70 125-4)    WG
61 84 05-70 126-8  (61 80 50-70 126-6, 61 84 50-70 126-2)    WG
61 84 05-70 127-6  (61 80 50-70 127-4, 61 84 50-70 127-0)    WG
61 84 05-70 129-2  (61 80 50-70 129-0, 61 84 50-70 129-6)    WG
```

SLEEPING CAR   TYPE AB30

Originally CIWLT Type P, these coaches have stainless steel bodies. They were rebuilt for 160 km/h in 1992 and refurbished. Note: 4-digit numbers in parentheses are CIWL numbers.

Built: 1955.   **Builder:**
Length over Buffers: 24.00 m.
Accommodation: 10 three-berth compartments.
Weight: 44 tonnes.   **Maximum Speed:** 160 km/h.

```
61 84 06-70 416-2  (4558, 61 84 70-70 016-1)    WG
61 84 06-70 417-0  (4552, 61 84 70-70 017-9)    WG
61 84 06-70 418-8  (4536, 61 84 70-70 018-7)    WG
61 84 06-70 419-6  (4529, 61 84 70-70 019-5)    WG
61 84 06-70 420-4  (4535, 61 84 70-70 020-3)    WG
```

SLEEPING CAR   TYPE MU

These coaches have been modernised and fitted with air conditioning by Wagons-Lits at Oostende. Note: 4-digit numbers in parentheses are CIWL numbers.

Built: 1973.   **Builder:** Fiat.
Length over Buffers: 28.40 m.   **Accommodation:** 12 three-berth compartments.
Weight: 55 tonnes.   **Maximum Speed:** 160 km/h.

```
61 84 06-70 615-9  (4792, 61 84 72-70 615-8)    WG
61 84 06-70 616-7  (4793, 61 84 72-70 616-6)    WG
61 84 06-70 617-5  (4794, 61 84 72-70 617-4)    WG
61 84 06-70 618-3  (4795, 61 84 72-70 618-2)    WG
61 84 06-70 619-1  (4796, 61 84 72-70 619-0)    WG
61 84 06-70 622-5  (4832, 61 84 72-70 622-4)    WG
```

RESTAURANT CAR

Built: 1971–72. Bought from DB in 1989.   **Builder:**
Length over Buffers: .   **Accommodation:** .
Weight: tonnes.   **Maximum Speed:** 140 km/h.

```
61 84 08-70 016-8  (61 84 88-70 016-1)    WG   ANDANTE
61 84 08-70 017-6  (61 84 88-70 017-9)    WG   ALLEGRO
61 84 08-70 018-4  (61 84 88-70 018-7)    WG   ALLEGRETTO
```

BUFFET/RESTAURANT CAR

Rebuilt from SNCF Gril-Express coaches.

Built: 1970–71.   **Builder:** CIMT or B&L.
Length over Buffers: 24.50 m.   **Accommodation:** 22 .
Weight: 54 tonnes.   **Maximum Speed:** 160 km/h.

```
61 84 08-70 020-0  (61 87 88 90 145-1, 61 84 88-70 020-3 )   WG
61 84 08-70 023-4  (61 84 88 70 131-5, 61 84 88-70 023-7 )   WG
61 84 08-70 025-9  (61 84 88 70 148-9, 61 84 88-70 025-2 )   WG
```

5. RAILION NEDERLAND

Railion was previously the NS's freight operation, NS Cargo, now owned by Deutsche Bahn. For livery and depot codes used in this section see Page 176. See also Pages 122 and 123 for leased Class 66 diesel locomotives.

5.1. ELECTRIC LOCOMOTIVES

CLASS 1600   B-B

For details see NS Class 1800. The locos work freight trains over all principal routes.

a On hire to ACTS.

1601	MT	AMSTERDAM	1612		MT	GOES
1602	MT	Schiphol	1613	a	MT	ROERMOND
1603	MT	ZUTPHEN	1614		MT	SCHIEDAM
1604	MT	DORDRECHT	1615		MT	ZANDVOORT
1605	MT(S)	BREDA	1616		MT	OLDENZAAL
1606	MT	HARDERWIJK	1617		MT(S)	ASSEN
1607	MT(S)	VLISSINGEN	1618		MT(S)	ALMELO
1608	MT(S)	'S-HERTOGENBOSCH	1619		MT	MAASTRICHT
1609	MT	HOOFDDORP	1620		MT(S)	ARNHEM
1610	MT(S)	HENGELO	1621		MT	DEVENTER
1611	MT	VENLO	1622		MT(S)	HAARLEM

CLASS 189   Bo-Bo

Electric locos for use on the Betuwe route. For details see page 119.

189 023-5 **R**	NN2	189 071-4 **R**	NN2	189 078-9 **R**	NN2	189 085-4 **R**	NN2
189 065-6 **R**	NN2	189 072-2 **R**	NN2	189 079-7 **R**	NN2	189 086-2 **R**	NN2
189 066-4 **R**	NN2	189 073-0 **R**	NN2	189 080-5 **R**	NN2	189 087-0 **R**	NN2
189 067-2 **R**	NN2	189 074-8 **R**	NN2	189 082-1 **R**	NN2	189 088-8 **R**	NN2
189 068-0 **R**	NN2	189 075-5 **R**	NN2	189 083-9 **R**	NN2	189 089-6 **R**	NN2
189 069-8 **R**	NN2	189 076-3 **R**	NN2	189 084-7 **R**	NN2	189 100-1 **R**	NN2
189 070-6 **R**	NN2	189 077-1 **R**	NN2				

5.2. DIESEL LOCOMOTIVES

CLASS 6400   Bo-Bo

Thyristor-controlled locomotives for freight and shunting use.

Built: 1988–94.
Builder: MaK.
Engine: MTU 12V396 TC 13 of 1180 kW at 1800 r.p.m.
Transmission: 4 x three phase BBC traction motors.
Train Heating: None (e Electric).   **Weight in Full Working Order:** 80 tonnes.
Maximum Tractive Effort: 290 kN.   **Length over Buffers:** 14.40 m.
Driving Wheel Diameter: 1000 mm.   **Maximum Speed:** 120 km/h.
Non-Standard Livery: N RailPro blue and grey.

b Fitted with Belgian ATP for working into Belgium.
e Being equipped with European Train Control System (ETCS).
d Fitted with German ATP (Indusi) for working into Germany.
h Fitted for hump shunting at Kijfhoek Yard.
i Can work into Germany as centre loco of a three loco set only.
n Fitted with ATP-NG ("New generation").
r Leased to RailPro.

Note 6461 and 6463 have been transferred to Railion Germany as 264 461-5 and 264 463-1. 6464 is working for DB subsidiary RAG.

6401	**N** r	FO	Mijndert		6404	**R** i	FO	Jo
6402	**N** r	FO	Marinus		6405	**R** i	FO	Jan
6403	**N** r	FO	Gijs		6406	i	FO	Tonnie

No.			Name		No.			Name
6407	i	FO	Henk		6464		SH	Jan
6408	R i	FO	Gerard		6465		SH	Lammert
6409	i	FO	Herman		6466		SH	
6410	i	FO	Toon		6467		SH	
6411	n	FO	Oliver		6468		SH	
6412	n	FO	Hans		6469		SH	
6413	n	FO	Foeke		6470		SH	
6414	n	FO	Sander		6471		SH	
6415	n	FO	Rens		6472		SH	Frank
6416	n	FO	Arie		6473	R	SH	
6417		FO	Bob		6474		SH	
6418		FO	John		6475		SH	Ed
6419		FO	Willem		6476	h	FO	
6420		FO	Horst		6477	h	FO	
6421	e	SH	Sebe		6478	h	FO	
6422	e	SH	Wim		6479	h	FO	
6423	e	SH	Chris		6480		SH	
6424	e	SH	Dirk		6481	i	SH	Lies
6425	e	SH	Chris		6482	i	SH	
6426	e	SH	Niko		6483	i	SH	
6427	e	SH	Hans		6484	i	SH	
6428	e	SH	Dirk		6485	d	FO	
6429	e	SH	Hans		6486	d	FO	
6430	R e	SH	Jan Adrianus		6487	d	FO	
6431	R e	SH	Antonius		6488	d	FO	Gerard
6432	e	SH	Hendrikus		6489	d	FO	
6433	e	SH	Han		6490	d	FO	
6434	e	SH	Henk		6491	R d	FO	
6435	e	SH	Joop		6492	d	FO	
6436	e	SH	Willem		6493	d	FO	Joke
6437	e	SH	Arie		6494	R d	FO	
6438	e	SH	Henk		6495	R d	FO	
6439	e	SH	Geert		6496	R d	FO	Herman
6440	e	SH	Jaap		6497	R d	FO	
6441		SH	Joyce		6498	R d	FO	
6442	R	SH			6499	d	FO	
6443		SH			6500	i	FO	
6444		SH	Eeltje		6501	i	FO	Edo
6445		SH	Wijbo		6502	i	FO	
6446		SH	Jo		6503	i	FO	
6447		SH	Maurits		6504	N	FO	
6448		SH	Rein		6505	b	FO	
6449		SH	John		6506	b	FO	
6450		SH	Hanja		6507	b	FO	
6451		SH	Daan		6508	R b	FO	Karla
6452		SH	Rein		6509	b	FO	
6453		SH	Frans		6510	b	FO	
6454	R	SH	Wim		6511	R	FO	
6455		SH	Klaas-Abel		6512	R b	FO	Peter
6456		SH	Hendrik		6513	R b	FO	
6457		SH			6514	R b	FO	Wim
6458		SH	Harry		6515	R b	FO	
6459		SH	Anton		6516	R b	FO	Wouter
6460		SH	Leo		6517	R	FO	
6461		SH			6518	R b	FO	
6462		SH	Olga		6519	R b	FO	
6463		SH	Theo		6520	R b	FO	

CLASS 204   B-B

Certain DB Class 204 (ex-DR Class 114) are now working in the Netherlands.

Built: 1964–78 for DR.
Builder: LEW.
Transmission: Hydraulic.

Engine: VBB-MWJ 12KVDZ1-AC4 of 1104 kW.
Driving Wheel Diameter: 1000 mm.

Maximum Tractive Effort: 222 kN.
Weight: 64 tonnes.

Length over Buffers: 14.24 m.
Maximum Speed: 100 km/h.

204 366-9 **R**	TN Johan Evertsen	
204 399-0 **R**	TN Michiel Adriaenszoom de Ruijter	
204 492-3 **R**	TN Jacob Roggeveen	
204 616-7 **R**	TN Frans Naerebout	
204 626-6 **R**	TN Cornelis Evertsen	

CLASS 232 Co-Co

Certain DB Class 232 (ex-DR Class 132) diesel locos are now operating in the Netherlands, having been fitted with ATB for that purpose.

Built: 1973–82 for DR.
Builder: October Revolution Locomotive Works, Voroshilovgrad, USSR.
Engine: Kolomna 16-cylinder 5D49.
Power: 2200 kW (2950 h.p.).
tonnes.
Transmission: Electric.
Train Heating: Electric.

Driving Wheel Diameter: 1050 mm. **Weight:** 123
Maximum Tractive Effort: 340 kN.
Length over Buffers: 20.62 m.
Maximum Speed: 140 km/h.

232 201-4	**R** DB	232 902-7 (232 161-0) **R**	DB	232 906-8 (232 504-1) **R**	DB
232 241-0	**R** DB	232 903-5 (232 170-1) **R**	DB	232 908-4 (232 699-9) **R**	DB
232 283-2	**R** DB	232 904-3 (232 320-2) **R**	DB	232 909-2 (232 657-7) **R**	DB
232 901-9 (232 072-9) **R**	DB	232 905-0 (232 423-4) **R**	DB		

CLASS 346 D

This DB Class 345 (ex-DR Class 105) shunter is now operating in the Netherlands.

Built: 1959–82 for DR.
Builder: LKM.
Maximum Tractive Effort: 175 kN.
Driving Wheel Diameter: 1100 mm.
Maximum Speed: 60 km/h.

Engine: 12KVD21SVW of 478 kW.
Transmission: Hydraulic.
Weight: 55 tonnes.
Length over Buffers: 10.88 m.

346 825-1 **Y** SH |

CLASS 363 C

The standard DB 0-6-0 shunter for use in areas where heavy trains are found. These locos are ballasted to give greater adhesion for shunting these heavy trains.

Built: 1955–64 for DB.
Builder: Krupp/MaK/Henschel/Krauss-Maffei/Esslingen.
Engine: Caterpillar 3412 E D1-TTA of 485 kW (650 h.p.).
Transmission: Hydraulic. Voith L27z Ub/L37z Ub/L217.
Maximum Tractive Effort: 138 kN.
Driving Wheel Diameter: 1250 mm.
Maximum Speed: 60 km/h.

Weight: 53 tonnes.
Length over Buffers: 10.45 m.

363 633-9 **R**	SH	363 716-2 **R**	SH	363 729-9 **R**	SH	363 833-5 **R**	SH
363 712-1 **R**	SH	363 723-5 **R**	SH	363 825-1 **R**	SH		

5.3. ELECTRIC POSTAL CARS

CLASS 3000 mP

These single units formerly used for postal traffic are now in service use.

Built: 1965–66.
Builder-Mechanical Parts: Werkspoor.
Builder-Electrical Parts: Smit.
Traction Motors: 4 x Heemaf 145 kW.

Weight: 54 tonnes.
Length over Couplers: 26.40 m.
Maximum Speed: 140 km/h.

3024 **R**	AF	3029 **R**	AF	3033 **R**	AF	3034 **R**	AF
3027 **R**	AF	3030 **R**	AF				

NOTES ON PRIVATE OPERATORS

The Netherlands has an increasing number of private freight operators. The Dutch freight market is open to any EU-approved train operator once the company has a safety certificate. There are cases of companies starting up using the safety certificate from another company and locomotives may also be borrowed or hired. Activity of all freight operators is concentrated around the port of Rotterdam which generates most freight in the Netherlands.

All of the companies here have very "light" operating methods – many do not have their own train maintenance depot and use the services of locomotive leasing companies or builders. Class 66 diesels go back to Nedtrain's Tilburg works for heavy maintenance and repairs. Vossloh diesel locos usually go to Moers in Germany for major attention.

The following railway undertakings have an operating licence, a safety certificate and a track access contract for operations in the Netherlands. Some of these are full open access freight operators while others are more concerned with track maintenance and, at the time of writing, do not operate "real trains". However, they may become active in the currency of this book and other companies may appear on the Dutch network either having gained the necessary licence and so on, or using the licence of another operator. The following railway undertakings had the necessary operating licence, safety certificate and access agreement on 1 October 2007.

Company	Activity	Note
ACTS Nederland	Freight	
BAM Rail	Track maintenance	
B-Cargo (SNCB/NMBS)	Freight	See section 5.5.
CTL	Freight	
ERS Railways	Freight	
Eurailscout	Track inspection	
HGK	Freight	See German Railways book 2.
ITL Benelux (now owned by Fret SNCF)	Freight	
Lloyd's Register Rail	Train testing	Owns no trains itself.
Railion Nederland	Freight	
Rail4Chem Benelux (now Veolia)	Freight	
Rotterdam Rail Feeding	Freight	
Spitzke Spoorbouw	Track maintenance	See German Railways book 2.
Strukton Railinfra Materieel	Track maintenance	
Veolia Cargo Nederland	Freight	
VolkerRail	Track maintenance	
Arriva (ex-Prignitzer Eisenbahn)	Passenger	See German Railways book 2.
Arriva Trains Nederland	Passenger	
Connexxion	Passenger	
DB Autozug	Passenger	See German Railways book 1.
DB Regio NRW	Passenger	See German Railways book 1.
Euro Express Trein Charter	Passenger	
NS Reizigers	Passenger	
Syntus	Passenger	
Veolia Transport Nederland	Passenger	
Zuid Limburgse Stoomtrein	Heritage passenger	See Preserved section.

The following companies operate in Belgium:

DLC (now Crossrail)	Freight	
Rurtalbahn	Freight	See German Railways book 2.

6. OPEN ACCESS FREIGHT OPERATORS & LEASING COMPANIES

6.1. ROLLING STOCK LEASING COMPANY LOCOMOTIVES

At the time of writing, a number of companies were leasing locomotives used the Benelux countries. All three have large and growing fleets but many of their locomotives are currently not equipped to operate in Belgium, Luxembourg or the Netherlands. We have decided to list the locomotives which are definitely equipped to operate in the Benelux countries. The leasing companies involved in main line operations are:

A ANGEL TRAINS CARGO

Although headquartered in Antwerpen many of Angel's locomotives, in particular the electric locos, are not equipped to operate in Belgium or other Benelux countries.

Livery: Pale grey body with blue (earlier) or green (later) cabs. Locos have white frontal panels specifically for operation in Netherlands.

C CB RAIL

CB Rail is a company owned by Australian company Babcock & Brown and the Bank of Scotland. CB Rail took over Porterbrook's continental European fleet, thus the first numbers starting in PB.
Liveries: Mainly pale grey with a yellow front end.

H HSBC RAIL

A British company, a subsidiary of the bank HSBC.

K KBC LEASE

A Belgian company involved in leasing almost anything, including cars.

M MRCE DISPOLOK (MITSUI RAIL CAPITAL EUROPE)

This company started operating as a leasing company in its own right then, in 2006 took over Siemens' subsidiary Dispolok. As with Angel Trains, by no means all locomotives are equipped to operate into Belgium and/or the Netherlands.

Livery: Black, plus white warning panel for Netherlands.

6.1.1. ELECTRIC LOCOMOTIVES

BOMBARDIER TRAXX (CLASS 186)   Bo-Bo

Bombardier produces its modular TRAXX electric locomotives in three basic versions – DC which is configured for 3000 V DC and is known as Class E.483 in Italy, AC for 15/25 kV AC, usually for Germany and Austria and numbered as Class 185 and MS (Multi System) which can operate off 1500 and 3000 V DC plus both 15 and 25 kV AC. The MS loco, known so far as Class 186, is only configured for whichever voltages the customer specifies and operating capability is conditioned by which signalling systems are installed. Class 186 has been ordered by Angel Trains Cargo and CB Rail. 186 111–125 are expected to be used to replace Class 11 on the Brussels–Amsterdam Benelux service, and then on the Hispeed Brussels–Amsterdam service until all V250 high speed trains are in service. During this period they will be finished in a red livery with white frontal panels. Based at Amsterdam Watergraafsmeer (WG). On freight, they will be used mainly on the Aachen–Antwerpen line in Belgium and the Betuweroute in the Netherlands.

Builder: Bombardier Transportation, Kassel.   **Weight:** 86 tonnes.
Continuous Rating: 5600 kW (4000 kW at 1500 V DC).
Length over Buffers: 18.90 m.   **Maximum Tractive Effort:** 300 kN.
Maximum Speed: 140 km/h (160 km/h 186 111–125).
Systems: 1500/3000 V DC, 15/25 kV AC.

118

Number	International Number	Works No.	Built	Leasco	Hired to	Number

Version DACHINL (Germany, Austria, Switzerland, Italy and the Netherlands.

Number	International Number	Works No.	Built	Leasco	Hired to	Number
E 186 101-2		34299	2006	A		
E 186 102-0	91 80 6186 102-0 D-BTK	34300	2006	A		
E 186 103-8		34317	2007	A		
E 186 104-6		34318	2007	A		
E 186 105-3		34319	2007	A		
E 186 106-1		34320	2007	A		
E 186 107-9		34327	2007	A		
E 186 108-7		34325	2007	A		
E 186 109-5		34328	2007	A		
E 186 110-3		34330	2007	A		

Version DABNL (Germany, Austria, Belgium and the Netherlands).

* sub-leased from NS Hispeed.

Number	International Number	Works No.	Built	Leasco	Hired to	Number
E 186 111-1		34303	2006	A		
E 186 112-9		34304	2006	A	NS Hispeed	
E 186 113-7		34302	2006	A	NS Hispeed	
E 186 114-5	91 80 6186 114-5 D-BTK	34310	2007	A	NS Hispeed	
E 186 115-2		34309	2007	A	NS Hispeed	
E 186 116-0		34311	2007	A	NS Hispeed	
E 186 117-8	91 80 6186 117-8 D-BTK	34321	2007	A	NS Hispeed	
E 186 118-6		34322	2007	A	NS Hispeed	
E 186 119-4		34323	2007	A	NS Hispeed	
E 186 120-2		34331	2007	A	NS Hispeed	
E 186 121-0		34339	2007	A	NS Hispeed	
E 186 122-8		34342	2007	A	NS Hispeed	
E 186 123-6		34312	2007	A	SNCB *	
E 186 124-4		34313	2007	A	SNCB *	
E 186 125-1		34316	2007	A	SNCB *	
E 186 141-8	-	34367	2008	C		
E 186 142-6	-	34373	2008	C		
E 186 143-4	-	34374	2008	C		
E 186 144-2	-	34376	2008	C		
E 186 145-9	-	34377	2008	C		
E 186 146-7	91 80 6186 146-7 D-BTK	34332	2007	C		
E 186 147-5	-	34336	2007	C		
E 186 148-3	-	34340	2007	C	ITL	148
E 186 149-1	91 80 6186 149-1 D-BTK	34344	2007	C	ITL	149
E 186 150-9	91 80 6186 150-9 D-BTK	34348	2007	C	ITL	150

Note: 186 126–140 are version DAPL (Germany, Austria, Poland) and are not the concern of this publication.

SIEMENS ES64F4 (CLASS189)   Bo-Bo

This loco is a four-voltage design which, like the TRAXX, can be equipped as required to operate in many countries. Railion Deutschland owns 90 of the type as Class 189 and 26 have been equipped to operate over the Betuweroute to Rotterdam. Dispolok (now part of Mitsui) owns another 60 of the type which are numbered both as Class 189 and ES64F4. 50 of these will be equipped with ETCS to operate to Rotterdam. 24 locos will be equipped for Netherlands, Germany and Austria, 15 for Netherlands, Germany and Belgium and 11 for Netherlands, Germany, Austria, Switzerland and Italy.

Builder: Siemens.
Weight: 86 tonnes.
Wheel Diameter: 1250 mm.
Maximum Tractive Effort: 300 kN.

Continuous rating: 6400 kW.
Length over Buffers: 19.58 m.
Maximum Speed: 140 km/h.

189 090 to 099 were purchased from Railion Deutschland.

Number	International Number	Works No.	Built	Hired to:
E 189 090	91 80 6189 090-4 D-DISPO	21076	2005	DB Autozug (MRCE Dispolok black)
E 189 091	91 80 6189 091-2 D-DISPO	21077	2005	
E 189 092	91 80 6189 092-0 D-DISPO	21078	2005	DB Autozug (MRCE Dispolok black)
E 189 093	91 80 6189 093-8 D-DISPO	21079	2005	Veolia (red/grey)
E 189 094		21080	2005	Veolia
E 189 095		21081	2005	Veolia (red/grey)
E 189 096		21082	2005	Railion
E 189 097		21083	2005	Railion
E 189 098		21084	2005	Railion
E 189 099		21085	2005	Railion

6.1.2. DIESEL LOCOMOTIVES

VOSSLOH TYPE G1206   B-B

Vossloh's most popular off-centre-cab type which can be found right across Europe. A small number of locos have MTU engines but none of these were used in the Benelux countries at the time of writing.

Builder: Vossloh
Engine: Caterpillar 3512 B DI-TA of 1500 kW.
Transmission: Hydraulic. Voith L5r4 zU2.   **Wheel Diameter:** 1000 mm
Maximum Tractive Effort: 254 kN.   **Length over Buffers:** 14.70 m.
Weight: 87.3 tonnes.   **Maximum Speed:** 100 km/h.

Works No.	Built	Leasco.	Hired to:	Number
1001138	2003	A	rail4chem	1206 138
1001374	2003	A	ERS	1201
1001375	2003	A	ERS	1202"Corina"
5001490	2004	Commerz Leasing	Rurtalbahn	V151
5001505	2004	A	ERS	1505
5001506	2004	A	ACTS	7104
5001507	2004	A	ACTS	7105
5001508	2004	M	rail4chem	1201
5001510	2006	M	ACTS	7106
5001511	2006	M	ACTS	7107
5001553	2004	M	ACTS	7101
5001554	2004	M	ACTS	7102
5001555	2005	M	ACTS	7103
5001571	2006	M	Veolia	500 1571
5001572	2005	M	rail4chem	1203
5001601	2005	M	rail4chem	1204
5001648	2006	M	Rurtalbahn	V152

VOSSLOH TYPE G2000   B-B

Vossloh's biggest diesel type which is used across Europe. Originally known as the G2000 BB now the MaK 2000 BB. Produced in five versions. The G2000-1 has unusual asymmetrical cabs but only 20 were built. The G2000-2 is a version for Italy with a cab for two drivers. Most locos seen in the Benelux countries are the G2000-3 version. The fourth and fifth versions, which have 2700 kW MTU 20V4000 engines, were only prototypes at the time of writing.

Builder: Vossloh
Engine: Caterpillar 3516 B-HD of 2240 kW.
Transmission: Hydraulic. Voith L620 re U2.   **Wheel Diameter:** 1000 mm.
Maximum Tractive Effort: 283 kN.   **Length over Buffers:** 17.40 m.
Weight: 87.3 tonnes.   **Maximum Speed:** 120 km/h.

These locos are all equipped to operated in the Netherlands and Germany and have been or are being equipped with ETCS. Those marked as such can also operate in Belgium.

Works No.	Built	Leasco.		Hired to:	Number
Type G2000-1 (asymmetrical cabs)					
1001029	2001	A		Kombiverkehr (D)	KV 1029
1001035	2001	A		HGK	DH 751
1001038	2002	A		HGK	DH 752
1001039	2002	A		–	–
1001042	2002	A		RBB (D) (Veolia)	1001042
1001043	2002	A		Kombiverkehr (D)	KV 1043
1001326	2002	A		Rail4Chem	1001326
1001384	2002	A		Rail4Chem	2001
Type G2000-3					
1001324	2003	A		Rail4Chem	2002
1001445	2004	A	*	Rail4Chem	2003
1001446	2004	A	*	Rail4Chem	2004
1001457	2004	M		Rail4Chem	2008
1001458	2004	M		Veolia	1458
5001604	2005	A	*	Rail4Chem	2005
5001605	2005	A	*	Rail4Chem	2006
5001606	2005	A	*	Rail4Chem	2007
5001607	2005	M	*	Rurtalbahn	V201 "Elena"
5001608	2005	M	*	Rurtalbahn	V202 "Victoria"
5001615	2006	A	*	Fret SNCF	
5001616	2006	A	*	Fret SNCF	
5001617	2006	A	*		
5001618	2006	A	*		
5001637	2007	A	*	Euro Cargo Rail	
5001640	2007	A	*	Euro Cargo Rail	
5001641	2007	A	*	Euro Cargo Rail	
5001669	2007	A	*	Euro Cargo Rail	
5001670	2007	A	*	Euro Cargo Rail	
5001756	2008	A	*		
5001757	2008	A	*		

Also equipped to operate in Belgium (also in France for locos from 5001615)

EMD TYPE JT42CWR (CLASS 66)   Co-Co

These locos are known in most countries as Class 66 after their British classification. This type is now used extensively in the Benelux countries and operated by ACTS, DLC, ERS, rail4chem, Rurtalbahn/TrainsporT and Veolia. From 2006, locos delivered have been Type JT42CWRM, M meaning Modified, the locos having improved cabs and engines.

Builder: EMD.
Engine: JT42CWR: General Motors Type 12N-710G3B-EC of 2238 kW.
       JT42CWRM: General Motors Type 12N-710G3B-T2 of 2238 kW.
Transmission: Electric. Six General Motors D43TR traction motors.
Wheel Diameter: 1120 mm.
Maximum Tractive Effort: 409 kN.   **Length over Buffers:** 21.35 m.
Weight: 126 tonnes.   **Maximum Speed:** 120 km/h.

Works No.	Built	Leasco.	Leasco No.	Hired to:	Number
20008254-1	2001	C	PB 01	rail4chem	
20008254-2	2001	C	PB 02	rail4chem	
20008254-5	2001	C	PB 03	DLC	
20008254-6	2001	C	PB 04	HGK	DE 63
20008254-7	2001	C	PB 05	rail4chem	
20008254-8	2001	C	PB 06	HGK	DE 64
20008254-9	2001	C	PB 07	ERS	6601 Blue Arrow
20008254-10	2001	C	PB 08	ERS	6602 Blue Bullet
20008254-11	2002	C	PB 09	ERS	6603 Blue Catapult
20008254-12	2002	C	PB 10	ERS	6604 Blue Dart
20018360-1	2002	C	PB 11	ERS	6605 Blue Excalibur
20018360-2	2002	C	PB 12	DLC	
20018360-3	2002	C	PB 13	DLC	
20018360-4	2002	C	PB 14	DLC	
20018360-5	2002	C	PB 15	DLC	
20018360-6	2002	C	PB 16	ERS	6613
20018360-7	2002	C	PB 17	rail4chem	
20018360-8	2002	C	PB 18	DLC	
20018360-9	2002	C	PB 19	DLC	
20018360-10	2003	C	PB 20	DLC	
20028453-1	2002	H		HGK	DE 668
20028453-2	2002	H		HGK	DE 669
20028453-3	2002	H		HGK	DE 670
20028453-4	2002	H		HGK	DE 671
20028453-5	2002	H		HGK	DE 672
20038513-1	2003	H	ER 1	ERS	6606
20038513-2	2003	H	ER 2	ERS	6607
20038513-3	2003	H	ER 3	ERS	6608
20038513-4	2003	H	ER 4	ERS	6609
20038513-5	2003	H	ER 5	ERS	6610
20038513-6	2003	K	ER 6	DLC	DE 6301
20038513-7	2003	K	ER 7	DLC	DE 6302
20038513-8	2004	M	ER 8	ERS	6612
20038513-9	2004	M	ER 9	ACTS	513-9
20038513-10	2004	M	ER 10	DLC	DE 6303
20038545-1	2004	C	EC 1	Rail4Chem	6602
20038545-2	2004	C	EC 2	Railion	266 452-2
20038545-3	2004	C	EC 3	Railion	266 453-0
20038561-01	2004	M		HGK	DE 673
20038561-02	2004	M		HGK	DE 674
20038561-03	2004	M		ERS	6611
20038561-04	2004	M		DLC	DE 6304
20038561-05	2004	M		DE (Veolia)	561-5

JT42CWRM sub type

20048653-01	2005	M		Veolia	8653-01
20048653-02	2005	M		ERS	6615 "Kayden"
20048653-03	2005	M		ERS	6614 "Lauryn"

20048653-04	2005	M		ACTS	653-4
20048653-05	2005	M		Rurtalbahn	653-05
20048653-06	2005	M		ERS	6616
20048653-07	2005	M		ERS	6617
20048653-08	2005	M		rail4chem	653-08 "Wessel"
20048653-09	2005	M		DLC	DE 6305
20048653-10	2005	M			–
20058725-06	2006	C		rail4chem	CB 1000 (92 80 1266 105-6 D-RCHEM)
20058725-07	2006	C		rail4chem	CB 1001 (92 80 1266 106-4 D-RCHEM)
20058725-01	2006	C	EU 01	Railion	266 107-2
20058725-08	2006	K		DLC	DE 6306 92 80 1266 101-5 D-DLC
20058725-09	2006	K		DLC	DE 6307 92 80 1266 102-3 D-DLC
20058725-10	2006	K		DLC	DE 6308 92 80 1266 103-1 D-DLC
20058725-11	2006	K		DLC	DE 6309 92 80 1266 104-9 D-DLC

6.1.3. SHUNTER BV

Shunter was founded in 2003 and is mainly a company supplying maintenance facilities to other operating companies. These include Railion Nederland. The company claims to maintain 110 diesel locos and almost 5000 wagons. Shunter now hires out shunting locomotives and in late 2007 bought two Class 203 (V100) main line diesels from Alstom and immediately hired them to ITL.

Depots: Geleen, Waalhaven.

CLASS 203 (V100) B-B

203 101 "Robert"	(ex DB 202 850)	(On hire to ITL)
203 102 "Arnold"	(ex DB 202 341)	(On hire to ITL)

SHUNTING LOCOMOTIVES

No.	Name	Axles	Builder	Works No.	Year	Type	Power	Notes
202	Nicky	B	O&K	26707	1971	MB125N	92 kW	ex ENKA, Ede.
203	Roos	B	O&K	26618	1967	MB5N	92 KW	ex Aluchemie, Botlek.
204	Faye	B	O&K	26795	1974	MB200N	147 KW	ex EBO, Bad Orb.
205	Sara	B	O&K	26811	1977	MB200N	147 KW	ex WRS, Duisburg.
206		B	O&K	26773	1972	MB170N	125 kW	ex Degussa, Frankfurt.
301	Monica	B	Vollert		1993	-	180 kW	ex ?
302		B	Moyse		1978	-	200 kW	ex ?
303	Andrea	B	O&K	26659	1968	MB9N	?	ex Combinatie Havenmond.
304	Myrthe	B	O&K	26656	1968	MB9N	?	ex Holcim, Untervaz.
305		B	O&K	26703	1971	MB9N	?	ex Pfleiderer, Neumarkt.
306		B	O&K	26667	1969	MB9N	?	ex Ford, Köln.
307		B	O&K	26684	1970	MB9N	?	ex Ford, Köln.
308		B	O&K	26702	1971	MB9N	?	ex Ford, Köln.
401	Kim	B	O&K	26555	1965	MB11N	250 kW	ex NBM Rail, Dordrecht.
481		B	Windhoff	?	?	?	-	
482		B	Windhoff	?	?	?	-	
501		B	O&K	26777	1973	MC500N	?	ex FTE, Emden.
502	key-leigh	B	O&K	26584	1967	MC14N	250 kW	ex Papierfabrik, Albbruck.
503	caithlin	B	O&K	26830	1967	MC14N	250 kW	ex Papierfabrik, Albbruck.
601		C	O&K	26954	1980	MEC502	510 kW	ex DE 761
602		C	O&K	26955	1980	MEC502	510 kW	ex DE 762
603		C	O&K	26957	1980	MEC502	510 kW	ex DE 764

6.2. DUTCH OPEN ACCESS OPERATORS

Many operators in the Benelux countries use ex-Deutsche Reichsbahn shunters and trip freight locomotives. Details of the main types are therefore shown here rather than repeated several times through the book.

LEW TYPE V60D   D

These are 0-8-0 diesel shunters used by Railion Deutschland as Classes 345 to 347 (former DR Classes 105 to 107) but also built in large numbers in East Germany for industry and other Eastern Bloc countries.

Builder: LEW.
Engine: 12KVD21VW of 478 kW.
Transmission: Hydraulic. Pirna.
Maximum Tractive Effort: 175 kN.
Weight: 55 tonnes.

Wheel Diameter: 1100 mm.
Length over Buffers: 10.88 m.
Maximum Speed: 60 km/h.

LEW TYPE V100   B-B

These shunting and trip freight locos were built for DR as Classes 108 and 110 to 114 then became DB Classes 201, 202, 204 and 298. Most locos are ex DB and have been re-engined and modernised by Alstom Locomotive Service at Stendal works. Some are hired out by ALS. Modernised locos are generally known as Class 203. At the end of 2007, there were 24 Type V100 in service in the Netherlands including five Class 204 with Railion Nederland, plus V100 093 preserved by VSM. This has been hired for main line work in the past.

Builder: LEW.
Engine (original): VEB-MWJ 12KVD 18/21 All of 736 kW (Classes 201 & 298); 12KVD 21AL-3 of 853 kW (Class 202); 12KVD 21AL-4 of 1104 kW (Class 204)
Engine (new): MTU 12V4000 R10 of 1380 kW or Caterpillar 3512B DI-TA of 1305 kW.
Transmission: Hydraulic. Pirna.
Maximum Tractive Effort: 206 kN.
Weight: 72 tonnes.

Wheel Diameter: 1000 mm.
Length over Buffers: 14.24 m.
Max. Speed: 100 km/h.

6.2.1. ACTS NEDERLAND   ACTS

ACTS was formed in 1989 and originally specialised in the transport of household waste in special containers (thus the name Afzet Container Transport Systeem) then started operating its own trains in March 1998. The company mainly runs trains within the Netherlands but also operates on international routes, together with partners in other countries. ACTS also hires out containers and carries out maintenance of railway rolling stock.

Livery Codes
All have black underframe and running gear.

A   Dark blue with a wide yellow stripe and yellow front end. Standard livery until 2006.
G   Dark green with a wide lime green stripe and white front end. New livery from 2007.
V   Vos Logistics. Black with wide orange stripe.

ELECTRIC LOCOMOTIVES
CLASS 1250   Co-Co

Former NS Class 1200. 1255 was purchased from Stichting Klassieke Locomotieven. Equipped to work in multiple with Class 67 diesels!! Class 1200 were constructed as "kit-form" locomotives with the bogies being supplied by Baldwin and electrical components by Westinghouse, the classic American styling clearly showing their design origin.

Built: 1951–53.
Builder–Mechanical Parts: Werkspoor.
Builder–Electrical Parts: Heemaf.
Traction Motors: 6 x Heemaf TM94 axle-hung.
One Hour Rating: 2360 kW.   **Weight:** 108 tonnes.
Maximum Tractive Effort: 194 kN.   **Length over Buffers:** 18.085 m.
Driving Wheel Dia.: 1100 mm.   **Max. Speed:** 130 km/h.

Multiple working fitted. Can be worked in multiple with Class 6700.

Number	Built	Works number	Hired from/notes
1251 A	1952	939	ex NS 1215
1252 A	1952	949	ex NS 1225
1254 A	1952	938	ex NS 1214
1255 A	1952	945	ex NS 1221

DIESEL LOCOMOTIVES
BR CLASS 58   Co-Co

These locos are on long-term hire from Axiom Rail, a subsidiary of British freight operator EWS. They are due to be returned in 2008.

Built: 1983–1987.
Builder: BREL at Doncaster Works.
Engine: Ruston Paxman 12RK3ACT of 2460 kW (3300 h.p.) at 1000 r.p.m.
Traction Motors: Brush TM73-62.
Continuous Tractive Effort: 240 kN (53950 lbf) at 17.4 m.p.h.
Maximum Tractive Effort: 275 kN (61800 lbf).   **Weight:** 130 tonnes.
Length over Buffers: 19.13 m.   **Wheel Diameter:** 1120 mm.
Maximum Speed: 80 m.p.h.

Number	Built	Works number	Hired from/notes
5811 A	1984	-	EWS 58039
5812 A	1984	-	EWS 58044
5814 V	1984	-	EWS 58038

CLASS 6000 (TYPE V60D)   D

Number	Built	Works No.	Notes
6003 A	1983	18105	ex Lokalbahnfreunde, SaZ Sázava
6004 A	1979	16539	ex Severokámen Koštálov
6005 A	1982	18001	ex Heizwerk Varnsdorf 716 511

CLASS 6700   Bo-Bo

Built: 1961–66.
Builder-Mechanical Parts: BN.
Builder-Electrical Parts: ACEC.
Engine: GM 12-567C of 1050 kW at 835 rpm.
Transmission: Electric. Four axle-hung traction motors.
Weight in Full Working Order: 78.6 tonnes.
Maximum Tractive Effort: 212 kN.   **Length over Buffers:** 16.79 m.
Driving Wheel Dia.: 1010 mm.   **Max. Speed:** 120 km/h.
Train Heating: Steam. Vapor OK4616 (except 6701).

Multiple working fitted. Can work in multiple with Class 1200.

6701 A	1966	-	for spares, ex SNCB 6321
6702 A	1966	-	ex SNCB 6325
6703 A	1966	-	ex SNCB 6391
6705 A	1966	-	ex SNCB 6393

ACTS also operates Vossloh G1206 and EMD Class 66 locomotives. See Section 6.1.

6.2.2. BAM RAIL   BAM

This is a small track maintenance firm with its headquarters in Breda and offices in Eindhoven, Rotterdam and Dordrecht. In 2007 the company had no locos of its own but was using a V100 hired from RRF and marked with the company's name.

6.2.3. ERS RAILWAYS   ERS

European Rail Shuttle, a joint venture involving shippers Maersk, Sealand, Nedlloyd and P&O, was set up in 1994 then started open access operations in 2002 after setting up subsidiary ERS Railways. The company is now wholly owned by Maersk. Until 2006, ERS only operated services from Rotterdam – to Belgium, Bulgaria, Czech Republic, Germany, Greece, Hungary, Italy, Poland and Slovakia. The company started to operate from Zeebrugge, Belgium in 2007. ERS currently does not have any electric locomotives and operates its Class 66 diesels through to Basel, Switzerland, subcontractiong traction beyond there. ERS carried 600 000 TEU in 2006. ERS is a 47% shareholder of BoxXpress, which operates container trains out of Hamburg and Bremerhaven.

ERS operates Vossloh G1206, G2000 and EMD Class 66 locomotives. See Section 6.1.

The company has no loco depot. Class 66 receive heavy maintenance from Nedtrain's Tilburg works and G1206 by Vossloh at Moers, Germany.

6.2.4. FRET SNCF

In 2007 Fret SNCF was expanding its operations to the ports of Antwerpen and Rotterdam using hired (unmarked) G2000 locos and staff from a private agency. the company also uses its own Class BB 67400 diesels and BB 36000 from Lille, Somain and Aulnoye to ports in Belgium, particularly Gent and Antwerpen.

6.2.5. LLOYD'S REGISTER RAIL

This company arrived in the Netherlands in October 2006 when it took over Nedtrain Consulting, the engineering consultancy division of Netherlands Railways. LRR is involved in approving new traction types and therefore requires an operating licence but does not have any traction of its own at the time of writing.

6.2.6. NEDTRAIN

This is the NS subsidiary dealing with train overhaul and maintenance. The company also has the contract to commission and maintain Class 66 locos for most of Europe. The company therefore has an operating licence but no main line traction of its own. The company's shunters are part of the NS fleet.

6.2.7. HÄFEN & GÜTERVERKEHR KÖLN   HGK

This company started as the river port rail network operator in Köln but expanded in recent years to become an open access operator. Full details of the fleet are given in the Platform 5 German Railways handbook Part 2. Only part of the fleet is equipped to operate in the Netherlands – all but one Class 66 loco (DE 61 , 63 and 64, DE 668 to 674 plus hired locos) plus three MaK Type DE 1002 locos DE 81 to DE 83. Other DE 1002 locos without Dutch ATB are sometimes used in multiple with an equipped loco. HGK expanded significantly in the Netherlands in late 2007.

HGK also operates leased Vossloh G2000 and EMD Class 66 locomotives. See Section 6.1.

DIESEL LOCOMOTIVES

EMD JT42CWR (CLASS 66)   Co-Co

HGK owns two Class 66 locos, DE 61/62. However DE 62 has no equipment to work into the Netherlands.

No.	Built	Works No.	Notes
DE 61	1999	998101-1	Originally to be EWS 66154.

MaK TYPE DE 1002   Bo-Bo

Basically very similar to NS Class 6400. Only DE 81 to DE 83 are equipped with Dutch ATB equipment but as leading loco, these can operate in multiple with non-equipped locos. Being equipped with new Cummins engines.

Built: 1987/1993
Engine: MWM TBD604BV12 of 1320 kW.
Transmission: Electric.
Weight: 90 tonnes.
Length over Buffers: 13.00 m.

Builder: MaK, Kiel.

Wheel Diameter: 1000 mm.
Maximum Tractive Effort:
Maximum Speed: 90 km/h.

DE 71	1987	1000833	ex KBE DE 81
DE 72	1987	1000834	ex KBE DE 82
DE 73	1987	1000840	ex KFBE DE 93
DE 74	1987	1000836	ex KBE DE 84
DE 75	1987	1000837	ex KBE DE 85
DE 76	1987	1000839	ex KFBE DE 92
DE 81	1993	1000882	
DE 82	1993	1000883	
DE 83	1993	1000884	
DE 84	1993	1000885	
DE 85	1993	1000886	
DE 86	1993	1000887	
DE 91	1987	1000838	ex KFBE DE 91
DE 92	1987	1000842	ex KFBE DE 95
DE 93	1987	1000835	ex KBE DE 83
DE 94	1987	1000841	ex KFBE DE 94

6.2.8. ITL BENELUX   ITL

ITL is a German company based in the Dresden area which started by carrying out track maintenance then expanded into open access freight operations. The company moved into the Netherlands during 2007. In April 2008 Fret SNCF bought 75% of ITL.

Livery: Green with white front ends.

ITL Benelux operates leased Class 186 electric locomotives. See Section 6.1.

DIESEL LOCOMOTIVES
TYPE V100   B-B

No.	Built	Works No.	Former number
101	1971	12877	Ex DB 202 368
102	1971	12878	Ex DB 202 369
103	1975	14658	Ex DB 202 777
104	1975	14476	Ex DB 202 775

6.2.9. NEUSSER EISENBAHN   NE

NE operates just over the border in Germany and has hired its one G2000 to Netherlands railways several times.

VOSSLOH TYPE G2000   B-B

No.	Built	Works No.	Notes
NE 9	2002	1001040	On hire to RRF in 10/07

6.2.10. RAIL4CHEM BENELUX

Rail4Chem was created in Germany by chemicals producer BASF plus partners Hoyer, VTG and Bertschi. The company came to the Netherlands through the takeover of the first Dutch open access operator Shortlines which went bankrupt in 2004. The company later entered the Belgian market. Rail4Chem has other locomotives, particularly electrics, which cannot be used in Benelux countries. Rail4Chem was a founder member and is the main driver behind European Bulls, an international alliance of private freight operators. The company was acquired by Veolia in early 2008. The fleets were not initially integrated.

Rail4Chem operates leased Vossloh G1206, G2000 and EMD Class 66 locomotives. See Section 6.1.

▲ Class 1800 No. 1846 "LEEUWARDEN" with a rake of ICK stock on IC 2539, the 10.50 Den Haag–Eindhoven at Dordrecht Zuid on 9 September 2006. **Brian Denton**

▼ Class 700 Vossloh shunters 701 and 702 are seen between duties at Brinckhorst near Den Haag Centraal in 2003. **Quintus Vosman**

▲ mDDM 7705 with set 7837 at Soest on train 5831, the 09.03 Uitgeest–Amersfoort Vathorst, on 18 August 2007.

▼ NS's only remaining DMU class is the DM'90. No. 57, on hire to Syntus from NS Financial Services, is seen at Zevenaar on 8 June 2005 with an early morning service from Arnhem to Doetinchem.

Quintus Vosman (2)

▲ Plan T 4-car EMU 516 with Plan V 886 at Tilburg-Reeman with a Breda–'s Hertogenbosch *Stoptrein* on 8 September 2006.   **Brian Denton**

▼ Refurbished 3-car Plan Y2 Sprinter No. 2937 at Nieuwekerk an der IJssel on 13 April 2007 Gouda–Rotterdam.   **Quintus Vosman**

▲ Three 4-car "Koploper" units Nos. 4223, 4238 and 4204 form the 10.06 Den Haag Centraal–
Enschede at Terschuur on 18 August 2007.   **Quintus Vosman**

▼ Thalys set 4539 near Dordrecht forming the 15.55 Paris Nord–Amsterdam Centraal on 8 September
2006.   **Brian Denton**

Facing page: NS-Hispeed has refurbished the ICR coaches to be used in the "HST - Priodienst" service
between Brussels and Amsterdam and painted them in different colours. These coaches are at present
being used on the conventional "Benelux" service between these cities. A rake of these coaches was
photographed on the 10.52 Amsterdam Centraal–Brussels Midi at Rotterdam Centraal on 19 March
2008. They are, in order:

Open firsts 485 (not shown – livery similar to 412) and 486, BD 974 and open seconds 418, 408 (not
shown – livery similar to 486) and 412. Note that the driving trailer, which will not be used on the new
service, has not been refurbished and remains in Benelux livery.   **Peter Fox (4)**

▲ Arriva Trains Nederland GTW2/6 DMU No. 239 "PIET OBERMAN" at Zuidbroek with train 30452 from Nieuweschans to Groningen on 17 February 2007.   **Quintus Vosman**

▼ Connexxion "Protos" 2-car EMU No. 5032 at Ede-Wageningen on 18 March 2008 having arrived with the 15.16 from Amersfoort.   **Peter Fox**

▲ A pair of Syntus LINT 41 2-car DMUs, No. 36 leading, at Zevenaar, Arnhem with the 07.04 Arnhem–
Winterswijk on 8 June 2005. **Quintus Vosman**

▼ Another GTW2/6 unit, Veolia No. 201 at Nijmegen with the 17.22 to Venray on 18 March 2008.
Peter Fox

▲ Railion Class 1600 No. 1614 "Schiedam" passes Tilburg with a westbound tank train in May 2004.
David Cable

▼ Former postal units (Type mP) 3024 + 3029 at Kijfhoek Yard on 16 June 2007.   **Quintus Vosman**

▲ Ex-DR 204 366-9 at Terneuzen on 6 November 2006.   **Keith Fender**

▼ Ex-DR 232-906-8 passes Tilburg with an eastbound intermodal train on 20 November 2006.
Colin J. Marsden

Railion coal trains from the Netherlands to Germany are hauled by three Class 6400 locos in multiple. The locos used are specially fitted with Indusi AWS for working into Germany. 6486, 6515 and 6485 pass Gilze Rijen with an eastbound service at 10.30 on 21 November 2006. The centre loco has been reliveried into Railion red whilst the outer locos are in NS livery with red cab sides.

Colin J. Marsden

▲ Railion Class 6400s 6401–3 are leased to Railpro. 6401 is seen here in Railpro livery at Roosendaal on 27 July 2007. **Keith Fender**

▼ ACTS electric 1251 (ex-NS 1215) with 6702 (ex-SNCB 6325) are seen at Amersfoort on an Intermodal working to Amsterdam in May 2004. **David Cable**

▲ ERS Class 66 No. 6612 passes through Dordrecht 6 June 2007.   **John P. Robinson**

▼ Rurtalbahn Type Vossloh G2000 No. V201 approaches Blauwe Toren Junction near Antwerpen with a train of container flats on 22 May 2008.   **Peter Fox**

▲ Rail4Chem operates leased Vossloh locos of two types. 1204 is a Type 1206 loco leased from MRCE (Mitsui) and is seen at Rotterdam Centraal on 8 July 2007. **Keith Fender**

▼ 2005 is a Type G2000 loco, leased from Angel Trains. It is seen ready to leave Amsterdam Westhaven Yard with container train 47135 on 6 August 2006. **Quintus Vosman**

▲ Strukton Railinfra operates three ex-NS locos of Class 600 (similar to BR Class 08). 300609 "Riek" (ex-NS 609) is seen as Roosendaal Yard pilot on 9 September 2006.　　**Brian Denton**

▼ Veolia Vossloh Type G1206 No. 1509 passes Gilze-Rijen with an empty car train on 17 April 2007.　　**Quintus Vosman**

▲ PFT-owned ex-PKP Kriegslok Ty2-3554, restored as SNCB 26101, with a demonstration freight between Ciney and Spontin on 9 September 2003. **Keith Fender**

▼ SNCB 29013 at Hasselt on 8 November 2003 with the "Return of the Consolidation" tour.
Keith Preston

▲ Ex-SJ 2-8-0 1040 at Schin Op Geul on the Zuid Limburgse Stoomtrein Maatschappij (ZLSM) line reversing onto the 11.20 service for Kerkrade on 17 August 2003.   **Phil Barnes**

▼ Preserved CFL centre-cab electrics 3611 and 3602 at Luxembourg depot on 26 July 2007.
Keith Fender

6.2.11. ROTTERDAM RAIL FEEDING   RRF

This company started operations in 2004 and both hauls its own trains and provides services to other train operators. Its V100 locos were some of the first to be equipped with ETCS Level 2 and the RRF was earning revenue from piloting non-equipped locos over the Betuweroute in 2007. The company was bought by US company Genesee & Wyoming in April 2008 and plans to start operations in Amsterdam and Antwerpen.

Depot: None. Maintenance carried out by Shunter.

NS CLASS 600   C

These ex-NS locomotives are similar to the British Class 08..

Built: 1950–57.
Engine: English Electric 6KT of 294 kW at 680 r.p.m.
Transmission: Electric. Two EE 506 4B axle-hung traction motors.
Train Heating: None.
Maximum Tractive Effort: 143 kN.
Driving Wheel Dia.: 1230 mm.

Builder: EE.

Weight in Full Working Order: 47 tonnes.
Length over Buffers: 9.07 m.
Max. Speed: 30 km/h.

No.	Built	Works No.	Notes
1	1956	2124	ex NS 684 (ex 626)
2	1956	2149	ex NS 689 (ex 652)
3	1955	2108	ex NS 676 (ex 611)
4	1955	2113	ex NS 679 (ex 616)
5	1956	2118	ex NS 683 (ex 621)
662	1956	2159	ex NS 662; spares bank; Nedtrain Tilburg.

TYPE V100   B-B

All equipped with ETCS Level 2 for the Betuweroute. They are leased from Sumitomo.

16	1971	12930	ex DB 202 421.
17	1974	14383	ex DB 202 682.
18	1975	15091	ex DB 202 819.
19	1971	12832	ex DB 202 323.
20	1974	14431	ex DB 202 730.

SNCB CLASS 73   C

See SNCB section for details.

101 (ex-SNCB 7382) | 102 (ex SNCB 7394)

6.2.12. VEOLIA CARGO NEDERLAND

The Dutch freight arm of French company Veolia which also operates in France and Germany. Locomotives belonging to the firm itself are in red and light grey livery.

TYPE G1206   B-B

See page xx for details.

1509	2006	5001509	-
1512	2006	5001512	-

Veolia also operates leased Vossloh G1206, G2000 and EMD Class 66 locomotives. See Section 6.1.

6.3. DUTCH TRACK MAINTENANCE COMPANIES

6.3.1. SPITZKE SPOORBOUW

Spitzke is a German track maintenance company based in Grossbeeren which has now started to work regularly in the Netherlands having taken over Dutch company GTI Infra in 2006. The Dutch headquarters is in Houten. Only three of the fleet (shown in bold) are actually with Spitzke's Dutch subsidiary but the other V100s and possibly the V60s and G1206s may be used in future. Spitzke also has ex DB Class 228 and 232 locos plus shunters but these are not shown. They can be found in Platform 5's German Railways Book 2. Livery is light blue with white line and front end.

TYPE V100   B-B

Number/name/UIC number	Built	Works No.	Notes
V100-SP-001	1976	15231	ex DB 202 846
V100-SP-003	1974	14378	ex DB 202 677
V100-SP-004 "Mariella"	**1974**	**14391**	**ex DB 202 690**
V100-SP-005 "Truus"	**1974**	**14445**	**ex DB 202 744**
V100-SP-006 "Mareike"	**1971**	**12849**	**ex DB 202 340**
V100-SP-007	1973	13575	ex DB 202 536
V100-SP-008 92 80 1203 128-4 D-SLG	1973	13568	ex DB 202 529
V100-SP-009 92 80 1203 129-2 D-SLG	1973	13567	ex DB 202 528

TYPE V60   D

Number/name/UIC number	Built	Works No.	Notes
V60-SP-011	1973	13746	ex ABC Coswig 319
V60-SP-012	1976	15202	ex ABC Coswig 318, ex BKK Bitterfeld Di 462-65-B4
V60-SP-013	1971	11258	ex Fels D01
V60-SP-014	1970	12686	ex Zementwerke Rüdersdorf 3
V60-SP-015	1979	16966	ex ABC GmbH Coswig 314

TYPE G1206   B-B

Number/name/UIC number	Built	Works No.
G1206-SP-021	2003	1001383
G1206-SP-022	2003	5001475

6.3.2. STRUKTON RAILINFRA MATERIEEL

Strukton's origins go back to the 1920s but the company only started to expand in its present form after the reorganisation of Dutch railways in 1997 and has now expanded outside the Netherlands – the company has a share in the Italian company CLF in Bologna. The Dutch head office is in Maarsen but depots are at Zutphen and Amersfoort. Locos can often be seen at the former NS depot in Roosendaal. It is still a subsidiary of NS Holdings.

It is a construction company, which has grown out of rail related construction projects in the NS company. Now its activities are wider than just railways. Among others, there are Strukton subsidiaries for construction of railway infrastructure and maintenance (Strukton Railinfrastructuur & Informatiesystemen). Strukton is not just involved in construction and maintenance in the Netherlands, but also in Sweden, Belgium and Germany.

For its logistics in rail construction and maintenance, Strukton has a subsidiary Strukton Materieel, which is a fully licensed railway undertaking. The company owns track maintenance machines, but also (shunting) diesel locomotives, among which a batch of modern Vossloh built G1206. Strukton Materieel has got a workshop, and offers services to third parties as well. In the reform process, NS privatised its construction acitivities, of which one became Strukton. The NS holding still owns the shares of Strukton. Strukton has a share in Eurailscout Inspection & Analyses, which operates track inspection vehicles.

Livery is all over yellow. Ex NS locos carry their old numbers preceded by 30 or 300.

NS CLASS 600   0-6-0

For details, see previous page.

These were being sold at the end of 2007, their work being taken over by the Deutz locos.

Number	Name	Built	Works No.		Notes
300609	Riek	1955	2106		ex NS 609
300640	Esther	1956	2137		ex NS 640
300650	Fransciene	1956	2147		ex NS 650

TYPE G1206   B-B

For details see page 120. 303001 was delivered to Angel Trains Cargo then bought by Strukton in 2003. Strukton is to acquire two more locos in 2008, one of them with ETCS.

303001	Carin	2002	1001147	–
303002	Willy	2003	1001173	–
303007	Danique	2008	5001681	
303008	Demi	2008	5001724	Owned by CB Rail.

OTHER LOCOMOTIVES

Number	Name	Axles	Builder	Year	Works No.	Type	Notes
300201	Tiny	B	O&K	1963	26256	MC14N	ex BPM, Pernis No. 1
300202	Herma	B	O&K	1967	26620	MB9N	ex H& B, Hoek van Holland
303005	Ankie	B-B	Deutz	1961	57187	DG1200BBM	ex HGK DH 31
303006	Irene	B-B	Deutz	1961	57188	DG1200BBM	ex HGK DH 32
1322320	Janine	B-B	Deutz	1963	57471	DG1200BBM	ex HGK DH 36
1322321	Monique	B-B	Deutz	1966	57983	DG1200BBM	ex HGK DH 38

6.3.3. EURAILSCOUT INSPECTION & ANALYSIS

Eurailscout, set up by Strukton and German company Knape, is engaged in track inspection. The company has inspection trains but no locomotives or rolling stock. Eurailscout hires Class 2200 locos from Strukton on a semipermanent basis.

NS CLASS 2200   Bo-Bo

These ex-NS locos are hired by Strukton to subsidiary Eurailscout. 2270 and 2328 are now equipped with lights and cameras to video the track. The other loco will also be equipped.

Built: 1955–58.
Builder: Allan (2201–2300), Schneider (2301–2350).
Engine: Stork Schneider Superior 40C-Lx-8 of 670 kW at 1100 rpm.
Transmission: Electric. 4 Heemaf TM98 traction motors.
Train Heating: None.   **Weight in Full Working Order:** 72 tonnes.
Maximum Tractive Effort: 181 kN.   **Length over Buffers:** 14.100 m.
Driving Wheel Dia.: 950 mm.   **Max. Speed:** 100 km/h.

302270	Berta	-	-	ex NS 2270
302282	Anneke	-	-	ex NS 2282
302328	José	-	-	ex NS 2328

ATB TEST CAR "JULES 2"   Bo-Bo

This is a test car for the Dutch form of ATP which is known as ATB. It was converted from a mP postal unit. It has been fitted with a diesel engine for operating on non-eletrified lines.

Converted: 1997
Builder:
Engine:
Traction Motors: 4 x Heemaf 145 kW.
Weight: 52 tonnes
Max. Speed: 140 km/h.

Length over couplings: 26.40 m.

80 84 978 1 003-2   (3032)   Amersfoort

6.3.4. VOLKER RAIL

Formerly Volker Stevin Rail & Traffic Materieel, this company is part of large Dutch construction group Volker-Wessels. The company has a safety certificate to operate in Germany as well as the Netherlands and is also active in Poland and Estonia.

Livery is a reverse of Angel Trains Cargo diesel livery – white cab and blue bonnets, but with a yellow front end.

TYPE V60D   D

No.	Name	Built	Works No.	Notes
106-1	Knabbel	1980	16144	ex SL 1001, MCHZ Ostrava
106-2	Babbel	1982	17699	ex SL 1002, ACTS 6002, Lokalbahnfreunde, ACHP Trebíc - Sedlec

TYPE V100   B-B

Number	Name	Built	Works No.	Notes
203-1	Tom	1973	13578	Ex DB 202 539
203-2	Spîke	1974	14392	Ex DB 202 691
203-3	Jerry	1975	14840	Ex DB 202 783
203-4		1971	12922	Ex DB 202 413
203-5		1973	13557	Ex DB 202 518.

OTHER LOCOS

No.	Name	Axles	Builder	Built	Works No.	Type	Power	Notes
208		B	MaK	1974	220099	G320B	390 kW	ex Railbouw, Leerdam.
209	Robin	C	Henschel	1961	30319	DH500Ca	-	ex Railbouw, Leerdam.

6.4. BELGIAN OPEN ACCESS OPERATORS

6.4.1. DILLEN & LEJEUNE CARGO (CROSSRAIL)
DLC

DLC was the first Belgian open access operator, set up in 2002 by Ronny Dillen and Jeroen Le Jeune. Most of DLC's operations are on the line to Aachen West, from Genk, Antwerpen and Zeebrugge. The company also operates into Germany, with an office in Mannheim, and uses the electric loco in that country. As well as the locos below, in early 2007, DLC also had three SBB Cargo Class Re 482 electric locos on hire. In September 2007, DLC announced that it would merge with Swiss company Crossrail. DLC's founders will be in charge of operations but the company will be renamed Crossrail.

HGK operates leased EMD Class 66 locomotives. See Section 6.1.

6.4.2. RURTALBAHN/TrainsporT

This company, based in Düren, Germany, is now operating into the Netherlands and into Belgium, in concert with Belgian operator TrainsporT. The company uses Class 66 and G2000 diesel locos, so far all hired from MRCE. Livery is black with yellow or white frontal panels. At the end of 2007, TrainsporT's two ex SNCB/NMBS Class 59 diesels were moved from Raeren to Düren, Germany. Apparently, TrainsporT would like to refurbish them for shunting duties in the port of Antwerpen.

Rurtalbahn operates leased Vossloh G1206 and EMD Class 66 locomotives. See Section 6.1.

SNCB CLASS 59   Bo-Bo

These vintage ex-SNCB locomotives are to be restored for use in the port of Antwerpen.

Built: 1954–55.
Builder–Mechanical Parts: Cockerill/BM/Niv.
Builder–Electrical Parts: ACEC.
Engine: Cockerill-Baldwin 680A of 1280 kW at 625 rpm.
Transmission: Electric. Four axle-hung traction motors.
Train Heating: None.   **Wheel Diameter:** 1118 mm.
Weight: 84 tonnes.   **Length over Buffers:** 16.18 m.
Maximum Tractive Effort: 196 kN.   **Maximum Speed:** 120 km/h.

5922 | 5930

7. INTERNATIONAL HIGH SPEED TRAINS

This section contains details of international high speed trains which may be seen in the Benelux countries. The following livery codes are used:

E Eurostar livery. White with dark blue window band roof and yellow lower bodysides.
I ICE livery. White with red stripe under windows.
T Thalys livery. Metallic grey with red front ends and roof.
V TGV livery. Metallic grey with blue window band.

Depot codes from outside the Benelux countries are:

LY Le Landy (Paris)
TI Temple Mills (London)

Note: Owner code EU denotes Eurostar (UK) Ltd.

7.1. TRAINS À GRAND VITESSE (Tgvs)

EUROSTAR   9-CAR "THREE CAPITALS" SETS

Eurostar sets work services through the Channel Tunnel between London and Paris and Brussels. The four-voltage sets also work London–Bourg St. Maurice ski trains in winter. 3203–04 and 3225–28 are not used on Channel Tunnel services. Eurostars are based on the French TGV design concept, and the individual cars are numbered like French TGVs. Each train consists of two 9-coach sets back-to-back with a power car at the outer end. All sets are articulated with an extra motor bogie on the coach next to the power car. Coaches are also referred to by their position in the set viz. R1–R9 (and in traffic R10–R18 in the second set). Coaches R18–R10 are identical to R1–R9. All units are now refurbished except 3101/2.

TGV + TGVZBD + 4 TGVRB + TGVRr + 2TGVRA + TGVRAD.

Systems: 25 kV AC 50 Hz/3000 V DC/(v also1500 V DC).
Built: 1992–93.
Builders: GEC-Alsthom/Brush/ANF/De Dietrich/BN Construction/ACEC.
Axle Arrangement: Bo-Bo + Bo-2-2-2-2-2-2-2-2.
Accommodation: 0 + –/48 1T + –/58 1T + –/58 2T + –/58 1T + –/58 2T + bar/kitchen + 39/– 1T + 39/– 1T + 25/– 1T.
Length: 22.15 + 21.845 + (7 x 18.70) + 21.845 m.
Max. Speed: 300 km/h.
Cab Signalling: TVM 430.
Non-standard Livery: O As E but Eurostar branding removed.

Trailer cars are numbered in the following sequence.
Set nnnn: 37nnnn1/37nnnn2/37nnnn3/37nnnn4/37nnnn5/37nnnn6/37nnnn7/37nnnn8/37nnnn9.

Set	Owner	Power Car			Set	Owner	Power Car		
3001	EU	3730010	E	TI	3020	EU	3730200	E	TI
3002	EU	3730020	E	TI	3021	EU	3730210	E	TI
3003	EU	3730030	E	TI	3022	EU	3730220	E	TI
3004	EU	3730040	E	TI	3101	SNCB	3731010	E	FF (S)
3005	EU	3730050	E	TI	3102	SNCB	3731020	E	FF (S)
3006	EU	3730060	E	TI	3103	SNCB	3731030	E	FF
3007	EU	3730070	E	TI	3104	SNCB	3731040	E	FF
3008	EU	3730080	E	TI	3105	SNCB	3731050	E	FF
3009	EU	3730090	E	TI	3106	SNCB	3731060	E	FF
3010	EU	3730100	E	TI	3107	SNCB	3731070	E	FF
3011	EU	3730110	E	TI	3108	SNCB	3731080	E	FF
3012	EU	3730120	E	TI	3201	SNCF	3732010	E	v	LY
3013	EU	3730130	E	TI	3202	SNCF	3732020	E	v	LY
3014	EU	3730140	E	TI	3205	SNCF	3732050	E	LY
3015	EU	3730150	E	TI	3210	SNCF	3732100	E	LY
3016	EU	3730160	E	TI	3211	SNCF	3732110	E	LY
3017	EU	3730170	E	TI	3212	SNCF	3732120	E	LY
3018	EU	3730180	E	TI	3213	SNCF	3732110	E	LY
3019	EU	3730190	E	TI	3214	SNCF	3732120	E	LY

3215	SNCF	3732150	E	v	LY		3222	SNCF	3732220	E	v	LY
3216	SNCF	3732160	E	v	LY		3223	SNCF	3732230	E	v	LY
3217	SNCF	3732170	E		LY		3224	SNCF	3732240	E	v	LY
3218	SNCF	3732180	E		LY		3229	SNCF	3732290	E	v	LY
3219	SNCF	3732190	E		LY		3230	SNCF	3732290	E		LY
3220	SNCF	3732200	E		LY		3231	SNCF	3732300	E		LY
3221	SNCF	3732210	E	v	LY		3232	SNCF	3732310	E		LY
3222	SNCF	3732220	E	v	LY		3999*	EU	3739990	E		TI

* Spare Power Car

Names:

3001	Tread Lightly	3012/3013	LONDON 2012
3002	Voyage Vert	3207/3208	MICHEL HOLLARD
3007/3008	Waterloo Sunset	3209/3210	THE DA VINCI CODE

THALYS PBKA   8-CAR FOUR-VOLTAGE SETS

This is basically a four-voltage version of TGV-Réseau but with the new generation of power car with a central driving position as first seen with TGV Duplex. Trailer cars are exactly the same as TGV Réseau PBA sets 4531–4540 (see below). The power car includes all equipment necessary for operation in France, Belgium, the Netherlands and Germany including German Indusi and LZB cab signalling. With all this extra equipment, it was necessary to design a lighter transformer in order to keep the power car weight to 68 tonnes because of the 17 tonne axle load limit on French high-speed lines. To be equipped with ETCS in 2008/9.

These sets operate Paris–Brussels–Köln/Amsterdam services. Sets can operate in multiple with TGV-Réseau sets. The sets belong to the four railways concerned but are based and maintained at Brussels Forest.

TGV + TGVRAD + 2TGVRA + TGVRr + 2TGVRB + TGVRBD + TGV.

Systems: 1500 V DC/ 25 kV AC 50 Hz/3000 V DC/15 kV AC 16.7 Hz.
Built : 1996–98.
Builder–Mechanical Parts: GEC-Alsthom/De Dietrich/Bombardier Eurorail.
Builder–Electrical Parts: GEC-Alsthom/ACEC/Holec
Continuous Rating: 25 kV AC 8800 kW; 3000 V DC 5120 kW; 1500 V DC and 15 kV AC 3680 kW.
Axle arrangement: Bo-Bo + 2-2-2-2-2-2-2-2-2 + Bo-Bo.
Accommodation:
0 + 42/– 1T + 39/– 1T + 39/– 1T + –/16 bar + –/56 2T + –/56 2T + –/56 1T + –/73 2T + 0.
Weight: 67 + 43 + 28 + 28 + 28 + 28 + 28 + 43 + 67 tonnes.
Length: 22.15 + 21.845 + 18.7 + 18.7 + 18.7 + 18.7 + 18.7 + 18.7 + 21.845 + 22.15 m.
Maximum Speed: 300 km/h.
Cab Signalling: TVM 430.

Trailer cars are numbered in the following sequence, prefixed TGVR:

Set nnnn: nnnn1 + nnnn2 + nnnn3 + nnnn4 + nnnn5 + nnnn6 + nnnn7 + nnnn8

Set	Owner	Power Car 1	Power Car 2	Liv	Depot
4301	SNCB	TGV 43010	TGV 43019	T	FF
4302	SNCB	TGV 43020	TGV 43029	T	FF
4303	SNCB	TGV 43030	TGV 43039	T	FF
4304	SNCB	TGV 43040	TGV 43049	T	FF
4305	SNCB	TGV 43050	TGV 43059	T	FF
4306	SNCB	TGV 43060	TGV 43069	T	FF
4307	SNCB	TGV 43070	TGV 43079	T	FF
4321	DB	TGV 43210	TGV 43219	T	FF
4322	DB	TGV 43220	TGV 43229	T	FF
4331	NS	TGV 43310	TGV 43319	T	FF
4332	NS	TGV 43320	TGV 43329	T	FF
4341	SNCF	TGV 43410	TGV 43419	T	FF
4342	SNCF	TGV 43420	TGV 43429	T	FF
4343	SNCF	TGV 43430	TGV 43439	T	FF
4344	SNCF	TGV 43440	TGV 43449	T	FF
4345	SNCF	TGV 43450	TGV 43459	T	FF
4346	SNCF	TGV 43460	TGV 43469	T	FF

TGV RESEAU (TGV-R) 8-CAR THREE-VOLTAGE SETS

Apart from three-voltage capabilities, these sets are otherwise identical to TGV-Réseau two-voltage sets and are designed to operate Belgium–south of France services.

TGV + TGVRAD + 2TGVRA + TGVRr + 2TGVRB + TGVRBD + TGV.

Systems: 1500 V DC/25 kV AC 50 Hz/3000 V DC
Built: 1994–96.
Builder–Mechanical Parts: GEC-Alsthom/De Dietrich.
Builder–Electrical Parts: Francorail-MTE.
Traction Motors: 8 x FM 47 synchronous of 1100 kW each.
Continuous Rating: 25 kV a.c. 8800 kW; 3000 V d.c. and 1500 V d.c. 3680 kW.
Axle Arrangement: Bo-Bo + 2-2-2-2-2-2-2-2-2 + Bo-Bo.
Accommodation:
0 + 42/– 1T + 39/– 1T + 39/– 1T + –/16 bar + –/56 2T + –/56 2T + –/56 1T + –/73 2T + 0.
Weight: 65 + 43 + 28 + 28 + 28 + 28 + 43 + 65 tonnes.
Length: 22.15 + 21.845 + 18.7 + 18.7 + 18.7 + 18.7 + 18.7 + 21.845 + 22.15 m.
Maximum Speed: 300 km/h.
Cab Signalling: TVM 430.

Trailers are numbered in the following sequence, prefixed TGVR:

Set nnnn: 38nnnn1 + 38nnnn2 + 38nnnn3 + 38nnnn4 + 38nnnn5 + 38nnnn6 + 38nnnn7 + 38nnnn8

Notes:

4501–4506 are equipped to work into Italy and do not work in the Benelux countries.
4507–4509 were split to become parts of TGV-POS and TGV-Reseau-Duplex sets.
4530 was converted to the Iris 320 test set which can cover all French LGVs plus Lille and Brussels.
4531 was transferred from thalys to SNCF and renumbered 4551.

4510	TGV 380019	TGV 380020	V	FF	
4511	TGV 380021	TGV 380022	V	FF	Villeneuve d'Ascq
4512	TGV 380022	TGV 380023	V	FF	
4513	TGV 380024	TGV 380025	V	FF	
4514	TGV 380027	TGV 380028	V	FF	
4515	TGV 380029	TGV 380030	V	FF	
4516	TGV 380031	TGV 380032	V	FF	
4517	TGV 380033	TGV 380034	V	FF	
4518	TGV 380035	TGV 380036	V	FF	
4519	TGV 380037	TGV 380038	V	FF	
4520	TGV 380039	TGV 380040	V	FF	
4521	TGV 380041	TGV 380042	V	FF	
4522	TGV 380043	TGV 380044	V	FF	
4523	TGV 380045	TGV 380046	V	FF	
4524	TGV 380047	TGV 380048	V	FF	
4525	TGV 380049	TGV 380050	V	FF	
4526	TGV 380051	TGV 380052	V	FF	
4527	TGV 380053	TGV 380054	V	FF	
4528	TGV 380055	TGV 380056	V	FF	
4529	TGV 380057	TGV 380058	V	FF	
4551	TGV 380061	TGV 380062	V	FF	

THALYS PBA 8-CAR FOUR-VOLTAGE SETS

The final 10 three-voltage sets have been equipped with a special pantograph and Dutch ATB automatic train protection in order to operate Paris–Brussels–Amsterdam services. Because of this they are known as PBA sets. These units also have a completely different "Thalys" livery and improved interiors with red moquette seats throughout. They will be equipped with ETCS in 2008/9.

4532	TGV 380063	TGV 380064	T	FF
4533	TGV 380065	TGV 380066	T	FF
4534	TGV 380067	TGV 380068	T	FF
4535	TGV 380069	TGV 380070	T	FF
4536	TGV 380071	TGV 380072	T	FF

4537	TGV 380073	TGV 380074	T	FF
4538	TGV 380075	TGV 380076	T	FF
4539	TGV 380077	TGV 380078	T	FF
4540	TGV 380079	TGV 380080	T	FF
Spare		TGV 380081	V	LY

7.2. INTERCITY EXPRESS (ICEs)

ICE-3M 8-CAR MULTI-VOLTAGE UNITS

These units have been under construction since 1998. They are expected to come into service from late 2000 on the Köln–Amsterdam route. Later some trains will start back from Basel. When the new high speed line between Frankfurt-am-Main and Köln is opened the units will work Frankfurt–Köln–Amsterdam and Frankfurt–Köln–Brussels–Paris.

DMFO–TFO–MFO–TRB–TSO–MSO–TSO–DMSO.

Systems: 1500 V DC/25 kV AC 50 Hz/3000 V DC/15 kV AC 16.7 Hz.
Built: 1998–
Builders: Siemens/Adtranz/Alstom/Bombardier.
Continuous Rating: 8000 kW (AC), 4300 kW (DC).
Axle arrangement: Bo-Bo + 2-2 + Bo-Bo +2-2 +2-2 + Bo-Bo +2-2 + Bo-Bo.
Accommodation:
46/– + 43/– 2T + 45/– 2T + 24 dining + –/44 1T 1TD + –/68 2T + –/66 2T + –/60.
Total Weight: 465 tonnes.
Length: 25.675 + (6 x 24.775) + 25.675 m.
Maximum Speed: 330 km/h (AC), 220 km/h (DC).

These units use the DB numbering system where each vehicle is separately numbered. Sets also carry NS set numbers 4601–4611, 4651–4654.

4601	406 001-8	406 101-6	406 201-4	406 301-2	406 801-1	406 701-3	406 601-5	406 501-7	DB	I	FGM
4602	406 002-6	406 102-4	406 202-2	406 302-0	406 802-9	406 702-1	406 602-3	406 502-5	DB	I	FGM
4603	406 003-4	406 103-2	406 203-0	406 303-8	406 803-7	406 703-9	406 603-1	406 503-3	DB	I	FGM
4604	406 004-2	406 104-0	406 204-8	406 304-6	406 804-5	406 704-7	406 604-9	406 504-1	DB	I	FGM
4607	406 007-5	406 107-3	406 207-1	406 307-9	406 807-8	406 707-0	406 607-2	406 507-4	DB	I	FGM
4610	406 010-9	406 110-7	406 210-5	406 310-3	406 810-2	406 710-4	406 610-6	406 510-8	DB	I	FGM
4611	406 011-7	406 111-5	406 211-3	406 311-1	406 811-0	406 711-2	406 611-4	406 511-6	DB	I	FGM
4651	406 051-3	406 151-1	406 251-9	406 351-7	406 851-6	406 751-8	406 651-0	406 551-2	NS	I	WG
4652	406 052-1	406 152-9	406 252-7	406 352-5	406 852-4	406 752-6	406 652-8	406 552-0	NS	I	WG
4655	406 053-9	406 153-7	406 253-5	406 353-3	406 853-2	406 753-4	406 653-6	406 553-8	NS	I	WG
4654	406 054-7	406 154-5	406 254-3	406 354-1	406 854-0	406 754-2	406 654-4	406 554-6	NS	I	WG

7.3. NS Hispeed

V250 "ALBATROSS" 8-CAR SETS

These new high speed trains are for use on the Brussels–Amsterdam "Hispeed" service operated by the High Speed Alliance. They will also work internal high speed services in the Netherlands (Amsterdam–Rotterdam–Breda). The first one of 19 sets was outshopped in Spring 2008, but no details or numbers are to hand at the time of writing.

Systems: 1500/3000 V DC, 25 kV 50 Hz AC.
Total Weight: 435 tonnes.
Maximum Speed: 250 km/h

8. PRESERVED LOCOMOTIVES & RAILCARS

STATUS CODES

A   Active (location could vary).
P   Plinthed.
K   Retained for special excursions.
M   Museum or Museum line loco.
R   Under restoration (perhaps at another place).
S   Stored or for spares..

For society and railway abbreviations see the "Museums and Museum Lines" section.

8.1. BELGIUM

8.1.1. Steam Locomotives

Number	Type	Built	Status	Location
1.002	4-6-2	1923	M	Treignes museum.
7.039	4-6-0	1921	MS	SNCB, FLV
10.018	4-6-2	1911	MS	FLV
12.004	4-4-2	1939	MS	SNCB, FLV
16.042	4-4-2T	1907	MS	FLV
18.051	4-4-0	1905	MS	SNCB, FLV
29.013	2-8-0	1945	MA	SNCB, FLV
41.195	0-6-0	1910	MS	Haine St. Pierre, SNCB
44.021	0-6-0	1906	MS	FLV (as A621.11)
44.225	0-6-0	1907	MS	FLV
53.320	0-8-0T	1906	MS	FLV (as 5620)
64.045	4-6-0	1918	MS	FLV
2	2-2-2ST	1842	M	Brussels Nord, SNCB
615	0-8-0T	1859	MS	FLV (as MF72)
1152	0-6-0PT	1879	MS	FLV
336A	0-4-0VB	1877	MP	Starucca House, Susquehanna, PA, USA

8.1.2. Diesel & Electric Locomotives

Number	Type	Built	Status	Location
1802	C-C e	1974	MA	NK
1805	C-C e	1974	MA	PFT, St. Ghislain
2801	Bo-Bo E	1949	M	PFT, St. Ghislain
2802	Bo-Bo E	1949	MS	Salzinnes
2912	Bo-Bo E	1949	MS	SNCB, NK (as 101.012)
2913	Bo-Bo E	1949	P	SNCB, FM
5117	Co-Co DE	1961	MS	PFT, St. Ghislain (for spares)
5120	Co-Co DE	1961	MA	CFV3V
5128	Co-Co DE	1962	MA	PFT, St. Ghislain
5149	Co-Co DE	1961	MS	PFT, St. Ghislain
5166	Co-Co DE	1963	MS	SNCB, FNND
5183	Co-Co DE	1963	MA	PFT, St. Ghislain
5204	Co-Co DE	1955	MS	CFM
5910	Bo-Bo DE	1955	MA	SNCB, FNND (as 201.010)
5917	Bo-Bo DE	1955	MS	Haine St. Pierre
5927	Bo-Bo DE	1955	MS	PFT, St. Ghislain
5941	Bo-Bo DE	1955	MA	PFT, St. Ghislain
6003	Bo-Bo DE	1960	MS	FEO (stored for PFT)
6010	Bo-Bo DE	1965	MS	PFT, St. Ghislain
6019	Bo-Bo DE	1965	MA	PFT, St. Ghislain

6041	Bo-Bo DE	1965	MA	SNCB, NK
6077	Bo-Bo DE	1965	MA	PFT, St. Ghislain (as 210.077)
6086	Bo-Bo DE	1965	MA	CFV3V
6106	Bo-Bo DE	1965	MA	PFT, St. Ghislain
6289	Bo-Bo DE	1966	MA	PFT, St. Ghislain
6406	B-B DH	1962	MS	FLV (as 211.006)
7001	Bo-Bo DE	1954	P	Flawinne
7005	Bo-Bo DE	1955	MA	PFT, St. Ghislain (as 270.005)
7103	D DH	1957	MS	FLV
7209	D DH	1956	MS	SNCB, FNND
7304	0-6-0 DH	1965	MA	CFV3V
7309	0-6-0 DH	1965	MA	Train 1900, Fond de Gras, Luxembourg
8040	0-6-0 DH	1961	MR	SCM, Maldegem
8061	0-6-0 DH	1963	MA	PFT
8062	0-6-0 DH	1963	MA	MKO, Germany
8309	C DH	1956	M	CFV3V
8319	C DH	1956	MA	SNCB, Haine St. Pierre
8320	C DH	1956	MA	PFT, St. Ghislain
8428	0-6-0 DH	1962	MA	PFT, St. Ghislain
8463	0-6-0 DH	1959	MR	BVS
8467	0-6-0 DH	1959	MA	BVS
8509	0-6-0 DH	1955	MA	BVS
8516	0-6-0 DH	1955	MS	BVS
8524	0-6-0 DH	1957	MA	PFT, St. Ghislain
9206	0-6-0 DH	1960	P	FAZ
9209	0-6-0 DH	1960	MA	PFT, St. Ghislain

8.1.3. Diesel & Electric Railcars

Number	Type	Built	Status	Location
4001	3-car DHMU	1957	MS	PFT, St. Ghislain
4006	3-car DHMU	1957	MS	SNCB, FLV
4302	2-B DHMU	1954	MA	Bertrix, private
4309	2-B DHMU	1954	MS	SDP, Basrode (as ES409 for spares)
4333	2-B DHMU	1955	MA	PFT, St. Ghislain
4403	B-2 DH	1954	MA	SCM, Maldegem
4405	B-2 DH	1954	MR	SCM, Maldegem
4406	B-2 DH	1954	MR	CFTSA, Attigny, France
4407	B-2 DH	1954	MR	CFV3V, Mariembourg
4505	A1-1A DH	1955	MS	CFV3V, Mariembourg (SNCB)
4506	A1-1A DH	1954	MA	PFT, St. Ghislain
4601	1A-A1 DHMU	1952	MR	NK
4602	1A-A1 DHMU	1952	MA	PFT, St. Ghislain
4603	1A-A1 DHMU	1952	P	Charleroi Sud
4604	1A-A1 DHMU	1952	P	ULM, Isières
4605	1A-A1 DHMU	1952	MA	PFT, Spontin
4608	1A-A1 DHMU	1952	M	CFV3V, Mariembourg
4609	1A-A1 DH	1952	MS	Montzen
4610	1A-A1 DHMU	1952	MS	CFV3V, Mariembourg
4611	1A-A1 DHMU	1952	MA	CFV3V, Mariembourg
4613	1A-A1 DHMU	1952	MA	PFT, St. Ghislain
4614	1A-A1 DHMU	1952	P	Maredsous station as restaurant/buffet
4616	1A-A1 DHMU	1952	MA	CFV3V, Mariembourg
4618	1A-A1 DHMU	1952	MA	PFT, St. Ghislain (as 554.18)
4620	1A-A1 DHMU	1952	MA	SCM, Maldegem
4903	1A-A1 DMMU	1942	MS	FNND
4905	A1-1A DM	1942	MS	FLV
4906	1A-A1 DMR	1942	MA	PFT, St. Ghislain (as 553.29)
551.26	A-A DMMU	1939	MS	PFT, FSR (ex ES 308)
551.34	A-A DMMU	1939	MS	FLV (ex-ES 301)
551.48	A-A DMMU	1939	MS	PFT, St. Ghislain
608.05	1A-A1 DMMU	1939	MS	SNCB, FKR
654.02	1/3 DEMU	1936	MS	FLV
ES 102	Single car	1949	MA	PFT, Ciney

ES 106	Single car	1949	MA	BVS
ES 202	Single car		MA	SCM Maldegem
ES 205	Single car	1974	MS	Private, Maldegem, Assoc. Modeliste Haute Meuse
ES 206	Departmental		MS	LSV, Winterslag
ES 208			MS	BVS
ES 301	B DM	1939	MS	FLV (551.34)
ES 303	B DM	1939	MR	SCM, Maldegem (551.15)
ES 409	2-B DH	1955	MS	BVS. Spares for 4302
002	2-car EMU	1939	MS	SNCB,Haine St. Pierre
002	2-car postal EMU	1935	MS	SNCB, Haine St. Pierre
027	A1-1A EMU	1950	MS	SNCB, Haine St. Pierre
039	A1-1A EMU	1953	MS	SNCB, Haine St. Pierre
082	2-car EMU	1954	MR	FSR, PFT
220 902	2-car EMU	1957	MR	FLV
7.312/7.724	4-car EMU	1935	MA	FSR

8.1.4. Foreign Locomotives & Railcars

Railway	Number	Type	Built	Status	Location
CFR	230 084	4-6-0		MA	PFT, St. Ghislain (as "SNCB 64.169")
DR	50 3696	2-10-0	1939	MA	CFV3V
ÖBB	52 3314	2-10-0	1944	MS	CFV3V, Treignes
DR	52 8200	2-10-0	1943	MA	CFV3V, Mariembourg (as 52 467)
PKP	Ty2-3554	2-10-0	1943	MA	FSR, PFT (as "26.101")
DB	64.250	2-6-2T	1930	MR	CFV3V, Mariembourg
DB	310 778	B dm	1939	P	Restaurant "Chez Tacky"
DB	323 149	B dh	1959	MA	Vennbahn, Raeren (as Köf 6436)
DB	795 662	A1 DMMU	1955	MA	CFV3V (as 551.662)
PKP	Ol49.12	2-6-2	1952	MA	SCM, Maldegem
PKP	TKt-48.87	2-8-2T	1952	MS	CFV3V, Treignes
SNCF	12120	Bo-Bo E	1959	M	CFV3V, Treignes
SNCF	63121	Bo-Bo DE	1955	MA	CFV3V, Treignes
SNCF	63123	Bo-Bo DE	1955	MA	CFV3V, Treignes (as "Em4/4 1123")
SNCF	63149	Bo-Bo DE	1954	MA	CFV3V, Treignes
SNCF	X 3998	B-2 DMMU	1957	MA	CFV3V
SNCF	X 4345	2-car DMMU	1965	MR	CFV3V, Mariembourg
SNCF	X 4367	2-car DMMU	1965	MR	CFV3V, Mariembourg
SNCF	Y 5130	B de	1961	M	CFV3V
SNCF	Y 6502	B de	1956	MA	CFV3V
SNCF	Y 6563	B de	1957	MA	CFV3V

8.2. NETHERLANDS

8.2.1. Steam Locomotives

Number	Type	Built	Status	Location
13	2-4-0	1865	M	NSM, Utrecht
89	2-4-0	1880	M	NSM, Utrecht
107	4-4-0	1889	M	NSM, Utrecht
326	2-4-0	1881	M	NSM, Utrecht
2104	4-4-0	1914	M	NSM, Utrecht
3737	4-6-0	1911	M	NSM, Utrecht
5085	2-10-0	1945	M	NSM, Utrecht (ex-WD 73755)
6317	4-8-4T	1931	M	NSM, Utrecht
7742	0-6-0T	1914	MA	SHM
8811	0-6-0ST	1943	M	SSN
8815	0-6-0ST	1943	MR	Ribble Steam Railway, Preston, UK
8826	0-6-0ST	1943	MR	ZLSM, Simpleveld
657	0-4-0T	1901	MA	MBS

8.2.2. Diesel & Electric Locomotives

No.	Type	Built	Status	Location
103	4w DM	1930	M	NSM, Utrecht
116	4w DM	1931	MR	VSM, Beekbergen
122	4w DM	1931	MR	SGB, Goes
125	4w DM	1931	M	MBS, Haaksbergen
137	4w DM	1932	MS	NSM, Blerick
162	0-4-0 DM	1941	MR	STIBANS, Watergraafsmeer (Ex WD 33, 70033)
204	Bo DE	1934	MA	STAR, Stadskanaal
210	Bo DE	1934	MS	SDL, Watergraafsmeer
211	Bo DE	1934	MA	SDL, Blerick
214	Bo DE	1935	MS	GSS, Nijmegen
217	Bo DE	1935	P	Uden
218	Bo DE	1935	MR	VSM, Beekbergen
222	Bo DE	1935	MA	HIJSM, Haarlem
225	Bo DE	1935	MA	VSM, Beekbergen
228	Bo DE	1935	MA	SSN, Rotterdeam Noord
230	Bo DE	1935	P	Onnen
231	Bo DE	1935	MR	GSS, Nijmegen
232	Bo DE	1935	MA	WIJS, Haarlem
234	Bo DE	1935	P	Nedtrain, Tilburg Works
238	Bo DE	1935	P	Uithoorn
242	Bo DE	1935	MA	MBS, Haaksbergen
243	Bo DE	1935	MA	SHD, Amersfoort
246	Bo DE	1935	MA	HIJSM, Haarlem
247	Bo DE	1935	MR	GSS, Nijmegen
248	Bo DE	1935	MA	ZLSM, Simpelveld
249	Bo DE	1935	MR	STAR, Stadskanaal
250	Bo DE	1935	MR	STAR, Stadskanaal
251	Bo DE	1935	P	SGB, Hoedekenskerke
252	Bo DE	1935	MA	SDL, Amersfoort
253	Bo DE	1935	P	Horn (Existance now doubted)
254	Bo DE	1936	MA	STIBANS, Watergraafsmeer
259	Bo DE	1936	MA	MBS, Haaksbergen
262	Bo DE	1936	MA	SGB, Goes
264	Bo DE	1936	MA	SGB, Goes
265	Bo DE	1936	MR	VSM, Beekbergen
270	Bo DE	1936	P	Winterswijk
271	Bo DE	1936	MA	Werkgroep 1501, Den Haag
274	Bo DE	1936	P	Nedtrain, Haarlem Works
276	Bo DE	1936	MA	SDL, Amersfoort
283	Bo DE	1938	P	Loon op Zand

285	Bo DE	1938	MA	SDL, Arhem, Nederlands Openluchtmuseum
286	Bo DE	1938	MS	STIBANS, Blerick
288	Bo DE	1938	MR	HIJSM, Beverwijk
289	Bo DE	1938	MA	VSM, Apeldoorn workshop
291	Bo DE	1938	P	Tijnaarlo
293	Bo DE	1938	MA	MBS, Haaksbergen
294	Bo DE	1938	MS	Blerick
297	Bo DE	1938	P	Deventer
301	Bo DE	1938	MA	VSM, Beekbergen
306	Bo DE	1938	MA	VSM, Beekbergen
307	Bo DE	1938	MS	VSM, Beekbergen
309	Bo DE	1940	MA	VSM, Beekbergen
311	Bo DE	1940	MA	NSM, Utrecht
314	Bo DE	1940	MR	GSS, Nijmegen
316	Bo DE	1940	MA	Stoom Club Corus, Ijmuiden
319	Bo DE	1940	P	Uden
320	Bo DE	1940	MS	Veendam
321	Bo DE	1940	MA	VSM, Beekbergen
323	Bo DE	1949	P	Sneek
326	Bo DE	1950	MA	HIJSM, Nieuwegein
327	Bo DE	1950	MS	GSS, Nijmegen
329	Bo DE	1950	P	Dordrecht
334	Bo DE	1950	MA	VSM, Beekbergen
335	Bo DE	1950	P	Ruinen
345	Bo DE	1950	M	NSM, Utrecht
346	Bo DE	1950	MR	STAR, Stadskanaal
347	Bo DE	1950	M	SDL, Rotterdam Havenmuseum
352	Bo DE	1950	P	Aalsmeer
353	Bo DE	1950	MA	STAR, Stadskanaal
354	Bo DE	1951	P	Waterhuizen
355	Bo DE	1951	P	Den Haag
357	Bo DE	1951	P	Enschede
358	Bo DE	1951	P	Best
359	Bo DE	1951	P	Hollandscheveld
361	Bo DE	1951	MS	Blerick
362	Bo DE	1951	M	NSM, Utrecht
363	Bo DE	1951	MR	HIJSM, Haarlem
366	Bo DE	1951	P	Valekenburg (ZH)
368	Bo DE	1951	MA	MBS, Haaksbergen
369	Bo DE	1951	P	Brock op Langedijk
451	C DE	1956	MA	MBS, Haaksbergen (MBS 11)
508	C DE	1944	MS	NSM, Blerick. (WD 70269)
512	C DE	1954	M	NSM, Utrecht
521	C DE	1953	MA	SGB, Goes
532	C DE	1954	MA	VSM, Beekbergen
604	C DE	1955	MS	VSM, Beekbergen
618	C DE	1956	MS	VSM, Beekbergen
629	C DE	1956	MA	NSM, Blerick
636	C DE	1956	MR	VSM, Beekbergen
639	C DE	1957	MR	ZLSM, Simpelveld (ZLSM 10)
641	C DE	1957	P	Kijfhoek
653	C DE	1956	MA	RMS Locotec, Wakefield, UK.
658	C DE	1957	MS	SSN, Rotterdam
661	C DE	1957	MA	VSM, Beekbergen
663	C DE	1957	M	NRM, Shildon, UK
671	C DE	1955	MR	Ribble Steam Railway, Preston, UK. (Originally 601)
685	C DE	1956	MA	PD Ports, Teesport, UK. (Originally 627) (Now H045)
687	C DE	1956	MA	RMS Locotec, Wakefield, UK. (Originally 632) (Now H046)
690	C DE	1956	MA	PD Ports, Teesport, UK. (Originally 625) (Now No.16)
692	C DE	1956	MA	PD Ports, Teesport, UK. (Originally 649) (Now No.13)
1010	1ABoA1 E	1949	M	STIBANS, NSM Utrecht
1107	Bo-Bo E	1951	MS	NSM, Blerick
1122	Bo-Bo E	1951	MA	SKLOK, Kijfhoek
1125	Bo-Bo E	1955	M	NSM, Utrecht. (Displayed as 1122)

```
1136   Bo-Bo E    1951  MS   SGB, Goes
1145   Bo-Bo E    1952  MS   SGB, Goes
1201   Co-Co E    1951  MR   SKLOK, Den Haag
1202   Co-Co E    1951  MA   NSM, Utrecht
1208   Co-Co E    1951  MS   SKLOK, Den Haag (Spares?)
1211   Co-Co E    1954  MS   NSM, Amsterdam
1302   Co-Co E    1952  MS   NSM, Blerick
1305   Co-Co E    1952  MS   SKLOK (Spares?)
1312   Co-Co E    1956  MA   NSM, Utrecht
1315   Co-Co E    1956  MS   SSN, Rotterdam
1501   Co-Co E    1954  MA   SKLOK, Rotterdam
1502   Co-Co E    1954  M    Midland Railway–Butterley, UK
1505   Co-Co E    1954  M    Greater Manchester Museum of Science & Technology, UK
2203   Bo-Bo DE   1955  MA   VSM, Beekbergen
2205   Bo-Bo DE   1955  MR   SHD, Amersfoort (Later 2226 then SNCB 7618)
2207   Bo-Bo DE   1955  MA   VSM, Beekbergen
2208   Bo-Bo DE   1955  MA   VSM, Beekbergen (Some doubt as to whether this is 2208 as "2233")
2215   Bo-Bo DE   1955  MA   NSM, Amsterdam
2225   Bo-Bo DE   1955  MR   SMMR
2264   Bo-Bo DE   1956  MR   NSM, Blerick
2275   Bo-Bo DE   1956  MS   SHM ?
2278   Bo-Bo DE   1957  MA   SMMR, Beverwijk
2299   Bo-Bo DE   1958  MA   VSM, Beekbergen
2368   Bo-Bo DE   1957  MA   SMMR, Beverwijk  (Originally 2296)
2459   Bo-Bo DE   1956  MA   VSM, Beekbergen
2498   Bo-Bo DE   1956  M    NSM, Utrecht
2530   Bo-Bo DE   1957  MA   VSM, Beekbergen
```

8.2.3. Diesel Multiple Units

No.	Type	Built	Status	Location
20	Bo-Bo DE	1954	MR	Nedtrain, Tilburg
27	3-Car DE	1934	M	NS Museum, Utrecht
113	3-Car DE	1960	MA	HIJSM, Haarlem
114	3-Car DE	1960	MS	NSM, Blerick
115	3-Car DE	1960	MA	HIJSM, Haarlem
121	3-Car DE	1961	MR	HIJSM, Zwolle
179	2-Car DE	1954	MR	ZLSM, Simpelveld
180	2-Car DE	1952	MS	HIJSM, Haarlem
186	2-Car DE	1954	MA	HSA, Winterswijk

8.2.4. Electric Multiple Units

No.	Type	Built	Status	Location
252	2-Car	1938	MS	STIBANS, Blerick
273	2-car	1952	MS	NSM, Arnhem
375	2-Car	1962	M	Verkeerspark, Assen
386	2-car	1962	M	NSM, Utrecht
419	2-car	1967	MS	Stichting Mat'64, Amsterdam
766	4-car	1960	MA	Stichting Mat'54, Amsterdam
3031	Single car	1966	MA	NSM Utrecht
9002	Single car	1924	MA	Werkgroep JAAP, Haarlem (also reported at Goes!)
9006	Single car	1926	MS	STIBANS, Blerick . (Also known as "JULES")
9107	Single car	1927	MA	NSM, Utrecht
9911	Single car	1908	M	NSM, Utrecht

8.2.5. Foreign Locomotives & Railcars

Railway	Number	Type	Built	Status	Location
DB	01 1075	4-6-2	1937	MA	SSN
DB	23 023	2-6-2	1952	MR	SSN
DB	23 071	2-6-2	1956	MA	VSM
DB	23 076	2-6-2	1956	MR	VSM
DB	41 105	2-8-2	1939	MR	SSN

DB	41 241	2-8-2	1939	MR	SSN, Rotterdam
DB	44 1085	2-10-0	1942	MR	VSM, Beekbergen
DR	44 1593	2-10-0	1943	MA	VSM
DB	50 1255	2-10-0	1941	MR	SSN
DR	50 3520	2-10-0	1943	MS	VSM
DR	50 3564	2-10-0	1940	MA	VSM
DR	50 3654	2-10-0	1942	MR	VSM
DR	50 3645	2-10-0	1961	MS	STAR, Stadskanaal
DR	50 3666	2-10-0	1961	MS	VSM, Beekbergen (as 50 0073)
DR	50 3681	2-10-0	1940	MS	VSM
ÖBB	52 3879	2-10-0	1944	MA	VSM, Beekbergen
DR	52 8010	2-10-0	1943	MS	VSM
DR	52 8053	2-10-0	1943	MA	VSM
DR	52 8060	2-10-0	1962	MS	STAR, Stadskanaal
DR	52 8082	2-10-0	1943	MA	STAR, Veendam
DR	52 8091	2-10-0	1943	MS	VSM, Beekbergen
DR	52 8139	2-10-0	1944	MA	VSM
DR	52 8160	2-10-0	1943	MA	VSM (as 52 532)
DB	64 415	2-6-2T	1936	MA	SSN
DB	65 018	2-8-4T	1956	MA	SSN
DB	80 036	0-6-0T	1929	MR	VSM
DB	94 1640	0-10-0T	1923	P	Gennep
DB	201 093	B-B dh	1968	MA	VSM (as V 100 093)
DB	323 036	B dh	1941	MA	STAR, Stadskanaal (as BE 010)
DB	332 187	B dh	1964	MA	ZLSM, Simpleveld
DB	798 647	AA DMU	1956	MA	ZLSM
DB	798 668	A-A DMR	1959	MA	ZLSM, Simpelveld
SJ	E2 1040	2-8-0	1910	MR	ZLSM
SJ	E 1090	0-8-0	1911	MA	ZLSM
SJ	B 1220	4-6-0	1914	MR	ZLSM
SJ	B 1289	4-6-0	1916	MA	ZLSM
SJ	S6 1611	2-6-2T	1918	MS	STAR, Stadskanaal
SZD	TE-5933	2-10-0	1943	MA	STAR, Stadskanaal

8.3. LUXEMBOURG

8.3.1 Locomotives & Railcars

Number	Type	Built	Status	Location
Z 105	1A-A1 DMMU	1949	MA	Luxembourg
Z 151	A-1 DMMU	1951	MA	Fond de Gras
201 + 211	2-car DMMU	1956	MA	CFV3V
206 + 216	2-car DMMU	1956	MA	Fond de Gras
208 + 218 *	2-car DMMU	1956	MA	Luxembourg (numbered 208A + 208B)
455	C dh	1955	MS	Luxembourg
804	Bo-Bo DE	1954	MS	Luxembourg
856	Bo-Bo DE	1956	MS	Luxembourg
1602	Co-Co de	1955	MA	PFT, St. Ghislain (B) (as "202.020")
1603	Co-Co de	1955	MA	PFT, St. Ghislain (B)
1604 *§	Co-Co de	1955	MA	Luxembourg. Named 'FOND-DE-GRAS'.
2001	B dh	1957	MA	Fond de Gras
3602	Bo-Bo E	1958	M	Bahnpark, Augsburg, Germany
3608	Bo-Bo E	1958	MS	Luxembourg
5519	2-10-0	1947	MA	Luxembourg

* Preserved by CFL as a "listed national monument".

8.3.2 Foreign Locomotives & Railcars

Railway	Number	Type	Built	Status	Location
ÖBB	52 3504	2-10-0	1943	MR	GAR, Luxembourg (as CFL 5621)
DB	795 669	A-1 DMMU	1955	MA	AMTF, Rodange (as "551 669")
SNCB	7309	0-6-0 DH	1965	MA	Train 1900, Fond de Gras

9. MUSEUMS & MUSEUM LINES

Museums, museum collections and museum lines continue to grow. The Netherlands has seen an amazing number of "siks" preserved and steam locomotives continue to be imported. The NS Museum in Utrecht has been refurbished and now calls itself the Spoorweg Museum. The withdrawal of first generation diesels and electrics has led to the formation of several new groups. In Belgium there is still no official railway museum more than forty years after the end of steam workings. The problem here is of course that there will probably have to be two of them! The enthusiast organisation PFT has gone from strength to strength and has now got its own museum in St. Ghislain. What the state cannot do gets done privately.

The only major loss has taken place in Belgium as the Vennbahn has closed. This may be political as parts of it may in fact be reopened as a normal railway linked to Aachen. Time will tell.

9.1. BELGIUM

Association pour le Musée du Tramway/Buurtspoorwegmuseum Schepdaal   AMUTRA/BS
Ninoofsesteenweg 955, B-1703 Schepdaal.

600, 1000, 1435 mm. Website: www.amutra.be or www.trammuseum.net,
A large collection of tramway equipment which includes 2 steam locos. Located 13 km from Brussels, access is by bus N Brussels–Ninove. The museum is normally open Sundays and holidays Easter–October and also Saturdays in July and August, 14.00–18.00 but is understood to be closed for refurbishment.

2 steam tram locomotives, 1 diesel tram, 25 trams and trailers.

Association pour la Sauvegarde du Vicinal   ASVi
Lobbes–Thuin. 5 km. 1000 mm. Website: www.asvi.be.

Operates Sunday and holiday afternoons April to October. Access: Trams 88 or 89 from Charleroi Sud to Anderlues Depot then Bus 91 to Thuin, or train to Thuin and walk. First departure is 11.30 from Thuin Museum. Depots are at Gosselies and Thuin.

1 steam tram loco, 1 diesel tram, 20 trams & trailers.

ATF Kinkempois
This is a regional railway museum located at the SNCB depot where the staff have restored and look after diesel 6041 and railcar 4601. There is also a small exhibits museum in an old station building.

Chemin de Fer de Sprimont   CFS
Rue du Mierdy 2b, B-4140 Sprimont. 600 mm. Website: www.users.skynet.be/cgs-sprimont.

This line is built on the trackbed of a former SNCV line and uses old mining diesel locos. Operates on the first and third Sundays of the month May–September from 14.00. There is usually a festival on the last weekend of August. Public transport access is believed to be by bus from Poulseur–Trooz. Nearest main towns are Liège and Spa.

20 diesels.

Chemin de Fer à Vapeur des Trois Vallées   CFV3V
Chaussée de Givet 49-51, B – 5660 Mariembourg. Website: http://cfv3v.in-site-out.com

Mariembourg–Treignes. 14 km.

The CFV3V has stopped operating between Dinant and Givet and has now concentrated activities from its main base at Mariembourg running to Treignes where there is a fine museum building complete with shop and refreshment facilities. Locos are kept at both ends of the line. Operations are at weekends mid-April to end of October but with daily operation in July and August but check the website for actual days of steam operations.

25 steam, 1 electric, 14 diesel, 12 diesel railcars.

De Bakkersmolen ("the Baker's Mill").

St. Jansstraat 194, B-2910 Essen-Wildert (about 1 km east of Wildert station).

Historic windmill and bakery with 600 mm railway circuit which operates Sundays May–September. 3 steam, 1 diesel.

De Mijlpaal

Regional railway museum located in part of the NMBS workshops at Mechelen.

1 electric, 1 EMU.

Haine St. Pierre Depot

The old SNCB depot here (adjacent to La Louvière Sud station) is now closed and being used to store and restore SNCB locomotives and rolling stock. Not normally open to the public.

1 steam, 4 diesel, 4 EMU.

Kolenspoor.

Stationsstraat zn, B – 3665 As.   Website: www.kolenspoor.be

As–Eisden and As–Waterschei.

This is the former Zolder and Limburgse Stoomvereniging operation. It is not clear what has become of the four steam locomotives. Operates on the first and third Sundays of May, June and September and all Sundays in July and August.

8 diesels.

Musée Nationale des Chemins de Fer/Museum van de Spoorwegen

The National Railway Museum is located in Brussels Nord station, the entrance being off the booking hall. Only one loco is present, the others in the collection being stored at Leuven and Haine St Pierre until suitable premises can be found. There are many models and photos etc. explaining the development of railways in Belgium. Open Monday–Friday and first Saturday of the month if it is not a holiday. 09.00–16.30.

Leuven Depot

Former NMBS depot and workshop. Most of the locomotives and rolling stock belonging to the national collection are housed here. The premises are classed as a workshop and are not open to the public. Restoration work is carried out here. However, recognising the public interest in the collection, there are usually open days several times a year especially in early September.

17 steam, 4 diesel, 2 EMUs, 8 DMUs.

Musée des Transports en Commun du Pays de Liège

Rue Richard Heintz, 9, B – 4020 Liège.   Website: www.tec-wl.be (follow initiatives, actualities).

An excellent collection of trams and buses in the former Natalis tram depot. The museum is on bus route 4. The layout is very spacious and excellent for photography. Open March – November weekdays 10.00 – 12.00 and 13.30 – 17.00 but at weekends 14.00 – 18.00.

1 steam, 11 trams.

Musée du Transport Urbain Bruxellois   MTUB

Avenue de Tervuren 364b, B-1150 Brussels.   Website: www.trammuseumbrussels.be

This tram and bus museum is located in the Brussels suburb of Woluwe St. Pierre at the old depot there. Open weekends and holidays April–mid October 13.30–19.00. Access is by lines 36, 39, 44 to Musée du Tram or line 42 to Woluwe. A preserved tram service is operated to Tervuren and Cinquantenaire-Jubelpark whilst on Sundays April to October there is a 35 km run around Brussels taking from 10.00 – 13.45.

More than 45 trams/trailers.

Patrimoine Ferroviaire Touristique   PFT

Musée du Rail. St. Ghislain.   Website: www.pfttsp.be

PFT have taken over the old wagon shop at St. Ghislain where most of their stock is now located. It is now an official museum. Some stock is still kept at Schaerbeek as many members live in the Brussels area and work on the stock there. The society continues to preserve many SNCB diesel locos and railcars and has recently imported a working P8 from Romania now renumbered "64.169".

The organisation also operates a museum service using DMUs on the Ciney–Spontin–Purnode line on Sundays July–October.

2 steam, 22 diesel, 1 EMU, 11 DMU.

Rail Rebecq–Rognon.   RRR

Rebecq–Rognon. 3 km. 600 mm.

Located near Tubize from where there is an infrequent bus service or a 45 minute walk. The line serves a pleasant area along the River Senne. Operates Sundays and holidays May–September.

3 steam, 2 diesel.

Stoom Centrum Maldegem   SCM

Stationsplein 8, B-9990 Maldegem. 600 mm and 1435 mm. Website: www.stoomcentrum.be

A museum has been established alongside the old station at Maldegem and a 2 km narrow gauge line constructed. The society also operates over the SNCB line to Eeklo (10 km). The museum is open daily July and August and Sundays and holidays 1st May–30th September, 10.00–17.00. Trains operate Sundays and holidays 1st May–30th September. Traction engines and agricultural equipment are also present.

6 steam, 3 diesel, 1 battery electric (600 mm); 8 steam, 6 diesels, 5 diesel railcars (1435 mm).

Stoomspoorlijn Dendermonde–Puurs   SDP

Fabriekstraat 118, B-9200 Baasrode (Dendermonde). Website: www.stoomtrein.be.

Dendermonde–Puurs. 14 km.

Operates over a closed NMBS line on Sundays in July and August with some extra operating days on certain Saturdays and holidays. Mixed steam and diesel operation. The stock is kept at Baasrode Noord.

6 steam, 11 diesel, 6 diesel railcar.

Tramway Touristique de l'Aisne   TTA

Rue du TTA, B-6997 Erzée. Website: www.tta.be.

Erezee–Dochamps. 12 km. 1000 mm.

An interesting preserved tramway deep in the Ardennes and rather inaccessible. Access by bus from Liège or Namur if by public transport. Operates Sundays and holidays mid-April–mid-October and also Tuesday, Thursday, Saturday in July and August.

1 steam, 4 diesel trams.

Vlaams Tram & Autobus Museum   VLATAM

Diksmuidenlaan 42-44 B-2600 Berchem.   Website: www.delijn.be (de lijn/museum)

This museum used to be at Edegem which was closed in 1999. The museum is now located in the old Groenenhoek tram depot which is quite close to Berchem station (500 metres) or accessed by trams 8 and 11 and bus route 14. The museum is open on Saturdays, Sundays and holidays mid-April to mid-October 14.00 – 17.30

1 steam tram loco, 1 diesel tram, 16 trams and trailers.

9.2. NETHERLANDS

Amsterdams Openbaar Vervoer Museum   AOM

Jan Rebelstraat 18B, 1069 CC, Amsterdam. Website: www.museumtram-amsterdam.nl.

This organisation operates museum trams on the GVB network in Amsterdam from 12.00 to16.00 mid-June–Mid-September from Amsterdam Centraal Station. The trams are based at museum depots at Tollenstraat and Oranje Vrijstaatkade.

Corus Excursietrein   CSY

Beverwijk. Website: www.csy.nl

This is a steam hauled excursion train around the vast steelworks covering 18 km return journey which takes around 1½ hours. Photo stops are made on the journey. Departure is from Velserwijk station at 10.45 and 13.00 on the last Sunday of the month May to September. Note: This station is near the steelworks – some 4 km from Beverwijk.

2 steam, 3 diesel.

Decauville Spoorweg Museum   DSM

Infanterie Schietcamp, Otterloseweg 5, Harscamp. Website: www.decauville.nl

This new organisation is located in a former military area and currently has a 1 km line. It can be accessed by bus 107 from Arnhem station or bus 100 from Putten station. It is open Monday–Friday 13.00–16.00 but with limited operations.

1 steam, 1 steam outline diesel, 16 diesel.

Eerste Drentse Vereniging van Stoomliefhebbers   EDS

Veenpark, Berkenrode 4, 7884 TR Barger Compascuum. Website: www.veenpark.nl

2.5 km. 700 mm.

This operation is in the National Veenpark and a short train journey is made through the old village. This Moorland Park is open every day from April to October. The train rides are included in the entrance fee. The nearest railway station is Emmen then by bus No. 45.

2 steam, 9 diesel.

Efteling Stoomtrein Maatschaappij

Kaatsheuvel. 1.5 km. 600 mm.

This is a steam operation in a vast amusement park close to Tilburg. The park is open and trains run each day April to October 10.00 – 18.00.

4 steam.

Electrische Museumtramlijn Amsterdam   EMA

Haarlemmermeerstation, Amstelveenseweg 264, 1075 XV Amsterdam. Website: www.museumtram.nl

Amsterdam Haarlemmermeer–Bovenkerk 7 km.

This organisation operates museum trams on Sundays and holidays April–October and also Wednesdays in July and August. Reached by tram lines 6/16. The EMA operates a large collection of museum trams and trailers, not only from the Netherlands but also from Berlin, Bonn, Lisboa, Praha and Wien. Most of the stock is at the Karperweg depot but some may also be found at Havenstraat depot.

60 trams, 20 trailers, 4 electric locomotives, 5 diesel locomotives and numerous other tramway type equipment.

Gelderse Smalspoor Stichting   GSS

Steenbakkerij Randwijk, Renhumse Veerweg 3, Heteren. Website: www.smalspoor.nl

This relatively new narrow gauge group has only a 1 km line with 600/700 mm gauge stock. There are limited opening days. The group also owns some standard gauge Siks which are stored at Nijmegen. Access by bus 6 from Arnhem for Heteren alighting at Sprokkelenburg.

40 narrow gauge diesels, 5 standard gauge diesels.

Stichting Haarlem IJmuidense Spoorweg Maatschaapij HIJSM

Website: www.hijsm.nl

This society started out with plans to preserve the old Ijmuiden line but has changed its ideas since then and has now preserved some old DMUs that used to work the line and uses them for excursions over NS routes.

4 diesels, 4 DMUs.

Haagse Openbaar Vervoer Museum   HOVM

Parallelweg 224, Den Haag. Website: www.hovm.nl

Museum trams operate on Sundays April–October (and other odd dates) around Den Haag from this museum and depot. Entrance to the museum is free but a charge is made for rides. Trams 9,11, 12 from Den Haag HS or 9 from Den Haag CS.

19 trams 1 electric locomotive and some trailers

Stichting Historisch Streekvervoer Achterhoek   HSA

Website: www.stichting-hsa.nl

The new group has preserved "Blue Angel" DMU 186 at Winterwijk station.

Industrieel Smalspoormuseum   ISM

Griendtsveenstraat 140 7887 TK Erica. 700 mm. Website: www.smalspoorcentrum.nl

This is a tourist line on a railway used for transporting turf. The nearest station is Emmen then take a 44 bus to Schoonbeek. The museum is open Thursdays and Saturdays 10.00–16.00, Sundays 12.00–17.00 May to mid-September

69 diesels, 1 electric.

Museum Buurt Spoorweg   MBS

Stationstraat 3, 7481 JA Haaksbergen.

Haaksbergen–Boekelo. 7 km. Website: www.museumbuurtspoorweg.nl

The depot is located at Haaksbergen which is 9 km from Enschede and can be accessed by bus 53 from Hengelo and buses 20, 73 from Enschede. Operates Sundays April–October and Wednesdays and Thursday in July and August plus other odd days. Three round trips normally operate departing Haaksbergen at 11.00, 13.15 and 15.30.

7 steam, 11 diesel, 1 DMU.

Musemstoomtram Hoorn–Medemblik   SHM

Van Dedemstraat 8, Horn. Website: www.museumstoomtram.nl

Hoorn–Medemblik. 20 km.

This line is well established and a visit is recommended. The depot is adjacent to Hoorn NS station. It is possible to do a train-boat-train circular journey. During July/August operation is daily whilst at other times between April and October there is a daily except Monday service.

9 steam, 3 diesel.

NZH Vervoer Museum

Leidsevaart 396. Haarlem. Website: www.nzh-vervoermuseum.nl

This small museum is dedicated to the former Den Haag "blue trams" (NZH) undertaking. Open Saturdays 11.00–16.00. Free. Reached by Connexxion bus 90 from Haarlem station.

4 trams.

Nederlands Openlucht Museum, Arnhem

This well-established museum has a tramway and has acquired stock from various cities.

1 steam, 7 trams, 1 diesel.

Nederlands Spoorweg Museum (Now referred to as Het Spoorwegmuseum) NSM

Maliebaanstation, Johan van Oldenbarneveldtlaan 6, 3581 XW Utrecht.
Website: www.spoorwegmuseum.nl

The NS museum has been completely rebuilt is recent years and new display areas opened but even so there is still not enough room to show everything and some stock is stored, mostly at Blerick. The museum is open Tuesday–Sunday 10.00–17.00 but also on Mondays during school holidays. There is a special hourly train service from Utrecht Centraal station to the museum. Otherwise use bus No. 3

10 steam, 6 electric, 12 diesel, 6 EMU, 4 DMU and trams.

Stichting RoMeO

Website: www.stichtingromeo.nl

This organisation is basically the Rotterdam Tramway Society which runs preserved trams over the network in Rotterdam

16 trams.

Stichting RTM Ouddorp RTM

De Punt West, G.C. Schellingerweg 2, Ouddorp (ZH). Website: www.rtm-ouddorp.nl

RTM De Punt Remise–Port Zélande te Ouddorp. 1067 mm. ca 8.5 km.

Steam and diesel trains run on this line in the dune area of Ouddorp in June and July with steam on Wednesdays and diesel on Saturdays. Trains also run on other odd days. There is a museum and depot at RTM De Punt-West. It can be reached by Connexxion bus 101 (Spijkenisse MetroCentrum–Hellevoetsluis) then change to Bus 104 (Renesse).

4 steam, 5 diesel trams.

Stichting De Locomoteur SDL

Website: www.locomotor.nl

A new society whose aim is to preserved the different forms of shunting tractors. They have no official museum but do work on restoring locomotives at the old wagon shops in Amersfoort. Some of their locomotives are on show at other centres.

7 diesels

Stoomtrein Goes–Borsele SGB

Albert Plesmanweg, Goes. Website: www.destoomtrein.nl
Goes–Hoedekenskerke 11km.

This line uses a former NS line. The depot is located at Goes station and is in fact the old NS depot. Trains run on Sundays and holidays April–October, Sunday–Friday July and August with some Saturday running in the peak holiday period.

5 steam, 6 diesel, 2 electric.

Stichting Historisch Dieselmaterieel   SHD
Website: www.dieselteeinen.nl
Another new organisation whose aim is to preserve a selection of diesel locomotives. Early days but progress is being made.

2 diesels

Stichting Klassieke Lokomotieven.   SKLOK
Website: www.werkgroep1501.nl
This is a new name for werkgroep1501 as the organisation now aims to preserve several types of NS main line electric locomotives.

4 electric, 1 diesel.

Stichting Mat'54
Website: www.mat54.nl
This group is behind the preservation of NS 4-car emu No. 766

Stichting Ryssens Leemspoor   SRL
Markeloseweg 78 B, 7461 EE Rijssen. Website: www.leemspoor.nl

600 mm, 1.2 km.

Operates every Saturday in July and August plus other odd days April–October. Nearest NS station is Wierden.

1 steam, 16 diesel, 3 electric

Stichting Stadskanaal Rail   STAR
Stationstraat 3, 9503 AD, Stadskanaal. Website: www.stadskanaalrail.nl
Veendam–Wildevank–Stadskanaal–Musselkanaal. 26 km.

A relative newcomer to the Dutch preservation scene, this line started up when stock was acquired from a closed line in Germany. Since then it has continued to gain stock which can be found at various locations on the line. Operating days are Sundays July, August, October plus some Wednesdays and Thursdays in July and August. Access is by bus from Assen, Emmen or Groningen stations

7 steam, 10 diesel.

Stichting tot Behoud van af te voeren Nederlands Spoorwegmaterieel   STIBANS
Website: www.stibans.nl
This society is active in preserving old Dutch locomotives and rolling stock. It has two centres where restoration work is done, Amsterdam and Blerick.

1 electric, 2 EMUs, 7 diesels.

Stoomtrein Valkenburgse Meer   SVM
Jan Pellenbargweg 1, 2235 SP Valkenburg (ZH). Website: www.smalspoormuseum.nl

3 km line.

This is the new location for the Nederlandse Smalspoorweg Stichting, previously at Katwijk. A completely new depot and workshop has been built to house their ever increasing fleet of stock. Operates each Saturday and Sunday mid-May to end September, also Thursdays in July and August. Access Bus route 43 Leiden–Wassenaar–Den Haag.

17 steam, 70 diesels, 1 electric (700, 900 mm gauges).

Stoom Stichting Nederland SSN

Bosdreef 75, 3062 CA, Rotterdam. Website: www.stoomstichting.nl

SSN is now well entrenched at its new depot depot near the NS yard of Rotterdam Noord Goederen. The depot also houses a museum. The SSN does not have a museum line but is able to run its locos several times each year on excursion trains over the NS. Most of the locos are former DB ones. The depot is open each Wednesday 10.00–15.00 and Saturday 10.00–17.00. Ten minutes walk from Bosdreef on bus routes 37 (Paradijsplein) and 38 (Kerkhoflaan)

8 steam, 2 diesel.

Tramweg Stichting (Rotterdamsch Trammuseum) TS

Nieuwe Binnenweg 362, 3023 ET Rotterdam. Website: www.tramwaystichting.nl

Tramweg Stichting has preserved several Rotterdam trams. Their museum is open on Saturdays May–September 11.00–16.00. Tram 4 from Rotterdam Centraal to Heemraadsplein, or Metro Calandlijn, station Delfshaven.

The organisation also has a depot in Den Haag at Harstenhoekplein Scheveningen which is open on Mondays 11.00–15.00 and Wednesday evenings 19.00–22.00.

trams.

Veluwsche Stoomtrein Maatschaappij VSM

Dorpstraat 140 7361 AZ Beekbergen. Website: www.stoomtrein.org

Apeldoorn–Dieren. 22 km.

Operates over a closed NS branch line on which the depot is located at Beekbergen. Main operating days are Mondays–Fridays in July and August. Uses mostly former DB locos.

19 steam, 24 diesel.

Zuid Limburgsche Stoomtrein Maatschaappi ZLSM

Stationstraat 20-22, 6369 ZH Simpelveld. Website: www.miljoenenlijn.nl

Valkenburg–Schin op Geul–Simpelveld–Kerkrade. 23 km; Simpelveld–Vetschau. 6km.

The ZLSM operates over a closed NS line using mostly Swedish steam locomotives, but also has an ex-DB railbus and trailer and in 1999 obtained NS railcar 179 which is very apt as these units used to work in this area at one time. Operates Wednesdays and Sundays May – September and also Thursdays in July and August. Good NS connections.

5 steam, 7 diesel, 3 DMU.

9.3. LUXEMBOURG

NB: The internet portal for Luxembourg is www.rail.lu. An excellent site with various links. Where no website is given below, use the portal and follow museums and monuments.

Association des Musée et Tourisme Ferroviaires   AMTF

Train 1900 Petange – Fond de Gras – Bois de Rodange 8 km. Website: www.train1900.lu

This line now runs through to Petange station where there is easy interchange with CFL trains. The depot for this line is at Fond de Gras. Operations are on Sundays and holidays May to September. There are a mixture of steam and dmu workings.

10 steam, 6 diesel, 2 DMU.

CFL Luxembourg Depot   CFL

Staff here have restored CFL 5519 (a DR Class 42 Kriegslok 2-10-0) and it is used on excursions from time to time. The CFL is building up a museum collection but for the time being the locos are kept at the running depot.

1 steam, 4 diesel, 1 electric.

Groupement des Amis du Rail   GAR

This society is also based at the CFL Depot and has a former ÖBB Class 52 2-10-0 and a CFL diesel railcar.

Minièresbunn Doihl au Fond du Gras.

Fond de Gras – Lasauvage – Saulnes. 700 mm

This narrow gauge mining railway starts from Fond de Grass close to the train 1900 station. The train journey is in three parts. A steam locomotive works from Fond de Gras to the mine entrance from where an electric locomotive goes through the mine to emerge in France from where another steam locomotive works to the end of the line. Well worth the effort of making a visit. Operates on Sundays and holidays May to September as Train 1900.

3 steam, 1 Compressed Air, 25 diesel, and 18 electric locomotives

Musée Nationale des Mines de fer Rumelange.

Website: www.mnm.lu

This mining museum has a collection of about 30 diesel and electric locomotives.

Musée des Tramways et de bus de la ville de Luxembourg

63, Rue de Bouillon, L-1248 Luxembourg. (Hollerich area). Access: Bus 17 from the city stops nearby.

This small museum is open Thursday, Saturday, Sunday and holidays 13.30 – 17.30.

2 trams, some trailers and buses.

APPENDIX I. BUILDERS

The following builder codes are used in this publication:

ABR	Ateliers Belges Réunis SA.
ABC	Anglo Belgian Corporation, Gent.
ACEC	SA Ateliers de Constructions Electriques de Charleroi.
AFB	Société Anglo-Franco-Belge des Ateliers de la Croyère.
Alsthom	Société Générale de Constructions Electriques et Mechaniques Alsthom.
Alstom	Alstom Transportation (various works).
ANF	Ateliers Construction du Nord de la France.
Ansaldo	Ansaldo Trasporti SA, Napoli, Italy.
B&L	Brissonneau & Lotz.
BLC	Usines de Braine le Comte. Belgium
BM	Baume et Marpent SA, Morlanwelz, Belgium
BN	La Brugeoise et Nivelles SA.
BND	La Brugeoise, Nicaise & Delcuve SA.
Bombardier	Bombardier Eurorail (various works).
BREL	British rail Engineering Ltd., Doncaster Works, England.
Breda	Società Italiana Ernesto Breda per Construzzione Meccaniche, Milano, Italy.
CFC	Établissements Carel Fouché & Cie., Le Mans, France.
CFCF	Constructions Ferroviaires du Centre (Familleureux).
Cockerill	SA Cockerill-Ougrée (Seraing).
CWFM	SNCB Central Workshops, Mechelen.
De Dietrich	De Dietrich et Cie, SA Reichshoffen, France.
Dessau	Fahrzeug Technik Dessau, Germany
Deutz	Klöckner, Humboldt, Deutz AG, Köln.
Donelli	Donelli SpA, Poviglio, Reggio, Emilia, Italy.
Duewag	Duewag Uerdingen.
EE	English Electric (Dick Kerr Works, Preston).
EMD	General Motors-Electro-Motive Division, later EMD, London, Ontario, Canada.
Esslingen	Maschinenfabrik Esslingen. Esslingen an Neckar.
Fiat	Fiat, Torino,Italy.
GM	General Motors, USA.
Geismar	Société des Anciens Établissements L. Geismar, Colmar, France.
Germain	Ateliers Germain, Monceau.
Hansa	Hansa Waggon, Bremen, Germany.
Heemaf	Heemaf NV., Hengelo .
Henschel	Henschel und Sohn GmbH, Kassel.
Holec	Holec-Riddekerk
Jenbach	Jenbacher Werke, Jenbach, Austria.
Jung	Arnold Jung Lokomotivfabrik GmbH, Kirchen an der Sieg, Germany.
Krauss-Maffei	Krauss Maffei, München Allach.
Krupp	Fried. Krupp, Essen, Germany
LEW	Lokomotivbau-Elektronische Werke "Hans Beimler", Hennigsdorf, East Germany.
LKM	VEB Lokomotivbau Karl Marx, Babelberg.
MaK	Maschinenbau Kïel GmbH, Kiel, Germany.
Maybach	Maybach Motorenbau, Friedrichshafen.
Moyse	Etablissements Gaston Moyse, La Courneuve.
MTE	Société de Matériel de Traction Électrique, France.
Niv.	Les Ateliers de Construction Metallurgiques S.A., Nivelles, Belgium.
	October Revolution Locomotive Works, Voroshilovgrad, USSR
Oerlikon	Oerlikon, Switzerland.
O&K	Orenstein & Koppel
Ragheno	SA Usines Ragheno, Malines, Mechelen, Belgium.
St. Eloi	Société Metallurgique d'Enghien-St Eloi, Enghien, Belgium.
SEM	Société d'Électricité et de Mécanique, Charleroi.
SEMG	Société d'Électricité et de Mécanique, Gent.
Siemens	Siemens Transportation (various works).
SIG	Schweizerische Industrie Gesellschaft, Neuhausen am Rheinfall.
Smit	Smit, Slikkerveer.
Stadler	Stadler Rail, Bussnang & Pankow.
Stork	Gebroeders Stork, Hengelo.
Talbot	Waggonfabrik Talbot, Aachen.

Voith   J. M. Voith, Heidenheim.
Vollert   Hermann Vollert, KG, Maschinenfabrik Weinsberg, Germany.
Vossloh   Vossloh Kiel, former Siemens Schienenfahrzeug Technik, GmbH, previously MaK.
Wegmann   Wegmann & Co., Kassel, Germany.
Werkspoor   Werkspoor NV, Utrecht.
Windhoff   Windhoff AG, Rheine, Germany.

APPENDIX II. VEHICLE TYPE CODES FOR MULTIPLE UNITS AND HAULED STOCK

These are given in the continental system with the British codes in parentheses.

Continental System:

f*   Bicycle Van (Dutch – bicycles=fietsen)
k*   Vehicle with with driving cab(s)
m*   Motor
s*   Driving Trailer
A   1st Class
B   2nd Class
D   Luggage, i.e., vehicle with luggage space and guard's compartment
R   Restaurant
K   Buffet Kitchen
P   Post, i.e., vehicle with compartment(s) for mail (and guard)

* NS only.

Examples:

BD   Second Class with luggage/guard's compartment
AB   Composite

Note-The continental system does not differentiate between open and compartment stock.

British System:

Coaching Stock codes are as used in our British Railways books e.g., F=first, S=second, C=composite, B=brake, O=open, K=side corridor with lavatory, so=semi-open. However note that the use of the word "brake" to denote a vehicle with a guard's compartment is a misnomer on the continent.

The number of seats, toilet compartments and wheelchair spaces are shown as nF/nS nT nTD nW, e.g.: 24/36 1T 1TD 1W has 24 first class seats, 36 second class seats, two toilet compartments (1 suitable for a disabled person) and 1 wheelchair space.

APPENDIX III. UIC HAULED STOCK NUMBERING SYSTEM

Loco-hauled coaches are numbered according to the UIC standard system as follows:

The number consists of four pairs of digits, which describe owner, speed, heating type etc., a three digit serial number and a check digit. The system is as follows:

(a) Digits 1 and 2. These indicate the exchange condition.

50	Passenger coach. Internal use only
51	Passenger coach. International use
60	Departmental passenger coach
61	Special service hauled stock
71	Sleeping cars. International use

(b) Digits 3 and 4. These give the railway of origin, e.g.

80	DB (German Railways)
82	CFL (Luxembourg Railways)
84	NS (Netherlands Railways)
87	SNCF (French Railways)
88	SNCB (Belgian Railways)

(c) Digit 5. The fifth digit gives the class or type of vehicle.

1	First class
2	Second class
3	Composite
4	Couchette-first class
5	Couchette-second class or composite
6	Sleeping car-first class
7	Sleeping car-second class or composite
8	Special purpose vehicle
9	Postal or luggage van

(d) Digit 6. The sixth digit gives the number of compartments (or windows/seating bays in the case of open stock).

0	10 compartments or bays
1	11 compartments or bays
2	12 compartments or bays
3	six-wheeled carriage
4	four-wheeled carriage
5	Reserved
6	6 compartments or bays or double decker
7	7 compartments or bays
8	8 compartments or bays
9	9 compartments or bays

(d) Digits 7 and 8. These give the maximum speed and type of operation.

Digit 7:

0	120 km/h, electric heating
1	120 km/h, dual heating
2	120 km/h, steam heating (except for 29 – no heating)
3	121–140 km/h, electric heating
4/5	121–140 km/h, dual heating
6	121–140 km/h, steam heating (except for 69 – no heating)
7	141–160 km/h, electric heating
8	141–160 km/h, dual heating (except for 84 – steam, 89 – no heating)
9	Above 160 km/h

Digit 8 sometimes depends on digit 7, but in general:

0	All voltages
6	All voltages except 3000 V DC
7	1500 V DC or 50 Hz AC

8   3000 V dc
9   If digit 7 is 0,1,7 – 3000 V d.c. If digit 7 is 3,4,5 – 3000 V d.c. + 1000 V 16²/₃ Hz a.c.

Digits 9, 10 and 11. These give the serial number of the individual vehicle.

Digit 12. This gives the check digit. Multiply as follows:

Digit	1	2	3	4	5	6	7	8	9	10	11
x	2	1	2	1	2	1	2	1	2	1	2

Add all resultant digits and subtract the last number of the result from 10. This gives the check digit, example:

	5	0	8	4	2	9	3	7	2	4	8
x	2	1	2	1	2	1	2	1	2	1	2

1+0   +0   +1+6   +4   +4   +9   +6   +7   +4   +4   +1+6 = 53

Subtract 3 from 10 – check digit is 7.

 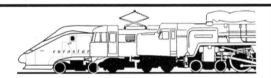

APPENDIX IV. COMMON TERMS IN ENGLISH, FRENCH & DUTCH

English	French	Dutch
railway	le chemin de fer	de spoorweg
train	le train	de trein
locomotive	la locomotive	de locomotief (de loc)
passenger coach	la voiture	het rijtuig
freight wagon	le wagon (de marchandises)	de goederenwagen
sleeping car	la voiture-lits	het slaaprijtuig
stock	le materiel	materieel
passenger	le voyageur	de reiziger
station	la gare	het station
platform	le quai	het perron
ticket	le billet	het kaartje
single	aller simple	de enkele reis
return	aller-retour	het dagretour (day return)
first class	la première classe	de eerste klas
second class	la deuxième classe	de tweede klas
to change (trains)	changer	overstappen
rail	le rail	de rail
track	la ligne/la voie	het spoor
steam	la vapeur	de stoom
wheel	la roue	het wiel
class (of vehicles)	la série	de serie
marshalling yard	(la gare de) triage	het rangeerterrein (NL)
late	en retard	de vertraging
driver	le conducteur	de machinist
guard, conductor	le chef de train/controleur	de conducteur

PLATFORM 5 MAIL ORDER

EK ASPEKTE 27: DB LOKS UND TRIEBWAGEN 2008 (AUG 2008)

Eisenbahn Kurier

This is the complete listing of locomotives and multiple units of Germany's mail rail operator Deutsche Bahn, with depot allocations as at 1st July 2008. Also includes a brief description of developments in the DB locomotive and multiple unit fleet in the past 12 months. Well illustrated with high quality colour photographs of many locomotive classes. German text. 74 pages. *£8.95 TR Subscriber Price £7.50*

MALY ATLAS LOKOMOTIV 2007

Gradis Bohemia

Fully revised and updated to 2007, this is a detailed guide to the locomotives and multiple units of Czech and Slovak railways. Includes a colour photograph, descriptions and tabulated data for every class, followed by a full fleet list of all powered vehicles in depot allocation order. Also includes a chronological history of railways and rail vehicles in Czechoslovakia, an explanation of the numbering and livery schemes, lists of railway companies, lists of preserved locomotives and maps of the rail network. Czech text. 352 pages. *£14.95 TR Subscriber Price £12.95*

Special Note: Also available is the 2004 edition of this book, Czech and Slovak Locomotives, in ENGLISH language. £13.50 *TR Subscriber Price £11.50*

ATLAS LOKOMOTYW 2007

Poznanski Klub

Fully revised and updated to 2007, this book contains full details of all Polish diesel and electric locomotives and multiple units. For each class, a photograph, technical details and a description are included along with details of fleet allocation at the time of publication. Also included are details of non-PKP owned locomotives and multiple units. Contains information for all classes that have been operated by PKP, including early classes where no examples survive today. Also includes a brief introduction to Polish railways. Polish text. 192 pages in colour. *£14.95 TR Subscriber Price £12.95*

TASCHENLEXIKON TRIEBFAHRZEUGE DER SCHWEIZ STAND 1. JANUAR 2006

Minirex

This is an encyclopaedia of locomotives and multiple units working in Switzerland. Listed by company, each page contains a high quality picture of the vehicle and also technical information such as gauge, construction dates, top speed and other details. Also included are museum locomotives which are in working condition and artist's impressions of new vehicles due to enter service during 2007/8. German text. 512 pages. *£29.50 TR Subscriber Price £26.50*

HOW TO ORDER

Telephone your order and credit/debit card details to our 24-hour sales hotline:
0114 255 8000 (UK) + 44 114-255-8000 (from overseas) or Fax: +44(0)114-255-2471.
An answerphone is attached for calls made outside of normal UK office hours.
Please state type of card, card number, issue no./date (maestro cards only), expiry date and full name & address of cardholder.
Or send your credit/debit card details, sterling cheque or British Postal order payable to Platform 5 Publishing Ltd. to:

Mail Order Department (EHB), Platform 5 Publishing Ltd.,
3 Wyvern House, Sark Road, SHEFFIELD, S2 4HG, ENGLAND
Please add postage & packing: 10% UK; 20% Europe; 30% Rest of World.

APPENDIX V. DEPOT & LIVERY CODES
DEPOT CODES
SNCB
The SNCB has official depot codes as follows:

FEO	Ronet	FSR	Schaarbeek Diesel
FHS	Hasselt	FSRE	Schaarbeek Electric
FKR	Merelbeke (Gent)	GCR	Charleroi Sud Quai
FNND	Antwerpen Noord	MKM	Stockem (Arlon)
FSD	Oostende	NK	Kinkempois (Liège)

NS & RAILION NEDERLAND
There are no official depot codes in the Netherlands, but the following unofficial depot codes are used:

AM	Amersfoort	ON	Onnen
AZ	Amsterdam Zaanstraat	SH	Maintained by Shunter (Rotterdam
LD	Leidschendam-Voorburg (Den Haag)		Waalhaven)
MT	Maastricht	TN	Terneuzen
NN2	Nürnberg Rangierbahnhof (DB)	WG	Watergraafsmeer (Amsterdam)

(S) after the code denotes the vehicle is stored.

LIVERY CODES
Note: Where two colours are shown, the first colour mentioned is the colour on the lower half of the body.
SNCB
Unless a code is shown, electric locos are blue with a yellow band, diesel locos are yellow with a green band and EMUs are Bordeaux red.

B Benelux push-pull livery (yellow & bordeaux red).
C SNCB/NMBS couchette livery (dark blue with pink stripe)
G Original green livery.
M "Memling" livery. Silver with red and blue. First applied to stock used on EC "Memling" service.
N New standard EMU/internal coaching stock livery (white with red and blue lower bodyside stripes and red doors).
R CityRail livery. Similar to livery N but with CityRail logos and black panels on yellow front ends.
S Class specific livery (refer to text).
Y Blue lower bodyside & yellow upper bodyside or departmental yellow.
W New standard international coach and DMU livery (white with dark grey lower bodyside stripe and window surround).

NS & RAILION NEDERLAND
Where no code is shown against the individual vehicle, it is assumed that locomotives are yellow and NS multiple units are yellow with three blue trapeziums on the side. Railion 6400 Class are grey with yellow ends and cabs and red cabside panels. Where two colours are shown, the first colour mentioned is the colour on the lower half of the body.

B Benelux push-pull livery (yellow & bordeaux red).
G Lime green with yellow ends.
H NS Highspeed livery (various styles of red, white and pink).
I NS Intercity livery (yellow & blue).
N Non-standard livery (refer to text).
R Red (NS Cargo or DB *Verkehrsrot*)
S New Sprinter livery (white/yellow/blue).
Y Plain yellow.